£15

A SAY IN THE END OF
THE WORLD

A SAY IN THE END OF THE WORLD

MORALS AND BRITISH NUCLEAR WEAPONS
POLICY, 1941–1987

ROGER RUSTON

CLARENDON PRESS · OXFORD
1989

Oxford University Press, Walton Street, Oxford OX2 6DP

Oxford New York Toronto
Delhi Bombay Calcutta Madras Karachi
Petaling Jaya Singapore Hong Kong Tokyo
Nairobi Dar es Salaam Cape Town
Melbourne Auckland

and associated companies in
Berlin Ibadan

Oxford is a trade mark of Oxford University Press

Published in the United States
by Oxford University Press, New York

British Library Cataloguing in Publication Data
Ruston, Roger
A say in the end of the world: morals and
British nuclear weapons policy, 1941–1987.
1. Great Britain. Nuclear weapons. Policies
of government. 1945–1983
I. Title
335′.0335′41
ISBN 0–19–827565–X

Library of Congress Cataloging in Publication Data
Ruston, Roger.
A say in the end of the world: morals and
British nuclear weapons policy, 1941–1987/Roger Ruston.
Bibliography   Includes index.
1. Great Britain–Military policy.   2. Nuclear weapons–Great
Britain.   3. Great Britain–Politics and government–1936–4. Just
war doctrine.   5. Nuclear Warfare–Moral and ethical aspects.
I. Title.
UA647.R89   989   335′.0335′41–dc19   88–29792
ISBN 0–19–827565–X

Printed in Great Britain
by Courier International
Tiptree, Essex

*For Sean
and his generation*

ACKNOWLEDGEMENTS

Intending to write a book on a subject I did not know enough about, I first applied to write a thesis and was lucky enough to have Professor Adam Roberts as my supervisor. Although I was a very late starter he managed to teach me something about writing history. He showed me how to leave things out as well as how to find things out. At a later stage, I was rescued by Dr Martin Ceadel from saying too much on the topics of appeasement and the Cold War. As a result of his gentle but firm criticism I rewrote Chapter 2 completely. My friends Clare Prangley and Christine Butler read early versions of the book and made it much easier for me to work out what I really wanted to say to people who do not work in university departments. Dr Anthony Kenny, who examined my thesis, sent me a page of comments which proved very valuable in revising what I had written. Serving on working parties with Dr John Finnis and reading his books have taught me a great deal about how to do ethics in the real world. Herbert McCabe read Chapter 1 on just war and made me understand what innocence in war means. Gilbert Márkus read the entire final script and told me where it did not make sense. To all these, and to the people I live with who have been waiting for me to finish this book for far too long, I owe much thanks.

R. R.

CONTENTS

ABBREVIATIONS

ABM	Anti-Ballistic Missile
ANF	Atlantic Nuclear Force
BAOR	British Army of the Rhine
CEP	Circular Error Probable
FR	Flexible Response
GLCM	Ground-Launched Cruise Missile
ICBM	Inter-Continental Ballistic Missile
IISS	International Institute of Strategic Studies
INF	Intermediate-Range Nuclear Force
IRBM	Intermediate-Range Ballistic Missile
Kt	Kilotons (of TNT)
LRTNF	Long-Range Theatre Nuclear Force
MAD	Mutual Assured Destruction
MIRV	Multiple Independently-targetable Re-entry Vehicle
MOD	Ministry of Defence
MR	Massive Retaliation
MRBM	Medium-Range Ballistic Missile
Mt	Megatons (of TNT)
NATO	North Atlantic Treaty Organization
NEC	National Executive Committee (of the Labour party)
NPG	Nuclear Planning Group
QRA	Quick Reaction Alert
RIIA	Royal Institute of International Affairs
SAC	Strategic Air Command
SALT	Strategic Arms Limitation Talks
SIPRI	Stockholm International Peace Research Institute
SLBM	Submarine-Launched Ballistic Missile
USAAF	United States Army Air Force
USAF	United States Air Force
WP	Warsaw Pact

INTRODUCTION

Since the early 1950s, when the first American atomic bombers arrived in this country, Britain has been defended with weapons which, if it ever came to their use, would violate what most people—including those in government—took for granted only ten years previously as the basic moral standards of civilized humanity. But such violations had become commonplace during World War II. The indiscriminate destruction of very large numbers of civilians came to be seen as the necessary means of fighting the enemy. So it came to be accepted after the war that future aggressors could only be deterred by threatening their populations with destruction by the most powerful weapons available. Moral arguments largely disappeared from public discourse until they were forcefully put back there by the anti-nuclear movement in the mid-1950s. In Britain, as in other countries which acquired nuclear weapons, each stage of commitment to them was rationalized in a number of ways. Sometimes these rationales sought to ignore the moral issue altogether, sometimes to outflank it with seemingly unanswerable arguments based on other considerations, notably security, international status and economy.

This book sets out to answer the following questions:

1. What rationales have been offered by successive British governments for making, possessing and using weapons of mass destruction, especially nuclear weapons?

2. How have they handled the moral problems involved?

3. Will such moral arguments as have been offered in official and semi-official sources stand up to scrutiny?

Too often morals and history have been divorced from one another in the nuclear debate: while the anti-nuclear case appropriates moral principle, the pro-nuclear case appropriates history. Those who have argued about nuclear weapons in moral terms have often conducted the debate in a manner that seems remote from practical policy and historical events, whilst those who have stuck to 'practical realism' have often appeared to be ignorant of the most basic requirements of justice. The result is two opposing arguments which seem to their proponents to be watertight in themselves, but which fail to engage with each other. However, morals and history are enmeshed with one another in a number of important ways. For instance, the history which is brought forward as evidence for the rightness of current defence policy is largely in the form of unexamined 'myths': over-simplified stories about the recent past, elevated to the status of self-evident truths. The 'official history' may even be said to be a collection of such myths, the function of which is to make current policies morally supportable. Thus, in so far as the post-war defence stance of Britain violates earlier standards of morality in obvious ways (e.g. by threatening the total destruction of Russian cities), it has been necessary to adhere to some very powerful myths about the past in order to make it acceptable. Such are the myths of appeasement, of Germany's defeat by bombing, of the Cold War, of the Soviet threat, and the stability of deterrence. In calling these things myths I am not claiming that they are nothing but a parcel of lies. It so happens that each of the myths just mentioned has been the subject of fierce controversy, of revisionism and counter-revisionism. However, it is their *function* rather than their truth content which allows them to be called myths. There is undoubtedly a core of real historical events behind them, but their function is to show that the current direction of national life and policy are justified, even inevitable, and that to break with them would be flying in the face of reality. They have a powerful shaming function in political life which makes a questioning of assumptions and the presentation of alternative policies almost impossible. Having this function, the myths are necessarily highly selective and abstract accounts of the recent past which tend to ignore evidence which would support alternative stories.

On the other hand, the moral criteria which are used by radical critics of defence policy sometimes appear to their opponents as non-historical absolutes having nothing whatever to do with the actual experience of the human race. This should not be so. The just-war doctrine, for instance—the basis of the moral arguments presented in this book—has been shown to be a historical product: the result of centuries of reflection on corrective force and its limitation in order that it may respect the real, and developing, interests of human life on this planet (see Chapter 1).

If this work has an overall goal, it is to try to loosen the deadlock between the historical and moral arguments. It is hoped that an historical account of the official rationales for British defence policy since World War II will help in this task. It is a limited goal, and a number of important related topics fall mostly outside the scope of the book: for instance, the origins of the Cold War, the exact state of the East–West military balance, Soviet intentions, and the arms control process.

The book deals mostly with official rationales: with the reasons offered in public, and sometimes in private, for certain key policy decisions. It is an obvious thought that they might not necessarily express the real motives present in the minds of the decision-makers. The latter are not easy to get at, although a glimpse of them is occasionally to be had in reminiscences of public servants long out of office. And some behind-the-scenes information is now available with respect to the making of the British bomb. However, we need to consider the possibility that rationales offered for particular nuclear decisions are *rationalizations* of programmes which have become unstoppable for political reasons. As we shall see, this seems to have been the case with the Chevaline programme in its later stages. It may also have been true of the 1964 Labour government's decision to continue with Polaris, and, in an international context, it has been true of the cruise missile decision of 1979. In each of the purely British cases, intense lobbying by MOD bureaucrats, service chiefs, nuclear technicians, laboratory team leaders, and weapons manufacturers may be fairly suspected.[1] There is also the 'bureaucratic momentum' factor to take into account: whereas ministers usually spend less than four years in office, the time necessary for a major weapons system to go from drawing-board to deployment is now fifteen to twenty years.[2] Someone has to try to make sure it survives successive ministers and defence reviews. The government of the day, perhaps newly arrived in office, with its short-lived ministries, will find itself to be only a part of a very large and complex system of interests and decision-making bodies, which have all kinds of opportunities for pre-emption and pressurizing. Being up against some very long-term interests and expensive programmes—on which many a career

---

[1] Cf. Scilla McLean (ed.), *How Nuclear Weapons Decisions Are Made*, (London; Macmillan, 1986) 85–153. This work makes the important observation that there is much interchange of personnel between the MOD and the defence contractors (p. 126 f.).

[2] Ibid. 99. See also S. Zuckerman, *The Times*, 21 Jan. 1981, on the role played by nuclear technicians in initiating the lobbying for weapons programmes.

depends—ministers would tend to reach for ready-made rationalizations in the areas of security (e.g. the Soviet threat, American unreliability), status, and economy (e.g. 'too costly to stop now'). If such pressures are brought to bear for the sake of particular programmes, we may suppose that the pressure will be immensely greater if nuclear deterrence itself is seen to be threatened by political changes. However, not too much should be made of the possible hidden motives behind the decisions. The official rationales, meant to establish public agreement and neutralize dissent, are the proper subjects of moral critique, as are the weapons programmes and strategies themselves.

The sources of historical narrative in Chapters 4 to 8 are largely secondary works, since too great a span of history is covered in a short space for primary sources to be of much help. However, the annual defence statements and parliamentary debates on defence since about 1947 have been used as the primary sources of rationales of defence policy. Also, I have consulted the documents released for study at the Public Records Office, especially Cabinet committee memoranda and minutes of discussions relating to the decisions to make the atomic and hydrogen bombs. Unfortunately, many important documents have been retained or even withdrawn, but those which have escaped the net are sufficient to illuminate some of the thinking behind the public statements. Other sources of official arguments are a number of Defence Ministry publications, especially those relating to the Trident and cruise missile decisions. Some reports of Parliamentary Committees on defence and expenditure have been very useful, especially where the Ministry of Defence has given evidence. Some prime-ministerial memoirs have also thrown light on certain decisions, especially those of Harold Macmillan and Harold Wilson.

The existing literature which is closest to the subject of this book is of two kinds: historical works on Britain's post-war defence policies, including the development of nuclear weapons; and works belonging to the moral debate on deterrence. Of the former category, the two works of Margaret Gowing, *Britain and Atomic Energy 1939–45* (1964) and *Independence and Deterrence* (1974), are indispensable and provide most of the known facts about the early history of the British nuclear project up to the first test explosion in 1952. For the following period, to 1970, *Nuclear Politics* (1972) by Andrew Pierre is of great value, being a very full account of the political events behind the development of British nuclear policy. For the events of the next ten years, to 1980, Lawrence Freedman's *Britain and Nuclear Weapons* (1980) provides a useful summary and some interesting insights into government thinking. *The Independent Nuclear State* (1986) by John Simpson and *The British Nuclear Deterrent* (1984) by Peter Malone have also provided some helpful information. Freedman's comprehensive larger work, *The Evolution of Nuclear Strategy* (1981), is essential for an understanding of the otherwise baffling changes in nuclear doctrines which have taken place in the last forty years. On NATO policy, a number of works belonging to an enormous volume of strategic literature have been consulted, but *NATO's Nuclear Dilemmas* (1983), by David N. Schwartz, may be singled out as especially helpful. On the special nuclear relationship, *Anglo-American Defence Relations 1939–1984* (1984) by John Baylis, and Simon Duke's *US Defence Bases in the United Kingdom* (1987) are very useful sources of facts and official texts. Apart from a few interesting asides, there is no discussion of the moral issues in any of these works.

The existing ethical literature is of a very different kind. The output has been enormous at certain periods. But so far as is known, there has been no work which sets out to analyse the course of the debate throughout the whole period under discussion, or to relate it to policy developments. John Groom's book, *British Thinking About Nuclear Weapons* (1974) comes nearest to it, but it does not offer any moral analysis of its own. Otherwise there have been a very large number of works—books, pamphlets, articles in specialist journals (particularly theological) and in the press—produced over a forty-year period. A chronological listing of these works shows that the moral debate has taken place in two well-defined periods, from 1955 to 1968, and from 1979 to the present, so far with no sign of falling off. For reference purposes we can call these periods the First Nuclear Debate and the Second Nuclear Debate (or the New Nuclear Debate) respectively. Since the chief matter of this book is the arguments of government rather than those of independent moralists and critics, I do not attempt to give a full account of these debates. I mention specific episodes in the moral debate where I think them to be an important part of the story being told. Nevertheless, I have learned a great deal from previous critics, especially Walter Stein, who has been tirelessly engaged in the debate for forty years.

Part I prepares the ground. The purpose of these three chapters is to put the British nuclear deterrent in the historical and moral contexts to which it belongs. Part II, the central part of this book, is a history of the British bomb and of official attempts to justify it. Part III is an analysis of the present predicament. Readers may be disconcerted by a change of tone in Chapter 6 where, after several chapters devoted to the history of British nuclear policies, I appear to cast aside the historian's detachment and to plunge into the dispute about the morality of deterrence. This is not such a break as it may seem, since I am there taking on a moral argument developed by Ministry of Defence civil servants, the gist of which has appeared in official publications. But even in the historical chapters I do not pretend to present a morally neutral exposition of the 'facts'. It would be impossible to approach such a contentious topic with a perfectly open and uncommitted mind, expecting to weigh up the evidence and arrive at conclusions which are entirely in the nature of morally neutral end results. There are several reasons for this. First, government statements are not morally neutral, and simply to restate them—with necessary selection and added emphasis—is to enter into an historical controversy about values and their embodiment in policy. Second, my involvement in eight years of controversy on this issue makes it too late for total openness of mind, even though the purpose of writing the book was to learn from history. Third, I do not accept the view of history which sees it as a sequence of objective happenings which just have to be told in the right order to reveal the truth. There are always 'myths' involved in telling history, because telling it always has a contemporary purpose: to justify policies, to overturn them, to confirm accepted values, to replace them with others. So it is impossible to tell history without implying, assuming, or denying certain moral values. But this does not necessarily make it hopelessly subjective. That would only be the case if moral values themselves were purely subjective, originating from individual preferences alone. And that position is not accepted either, although this is not the place to enter into one of the basic questions of moral philosophy. The chapters should be considered as belonging to a single argument. I have tried to remain open to the upsetting influence of historical truth and, in the course of writing, have found my views about the past overturned on a number of issues.

PART I

FOUNDATIONS

JUST WAR AND ITS ENEMIES

Just-war categories are frequently referred to in the following chapters. In order not to take too much for granted, this chapter explains what they mean and justifies their use in the nuclear era when many deny their relevance.

Should War be Humanized?

The suggestion that war might be justified or, if not justified then at least humanized, has always made some people marvel at the power of human self-deception and our capacity for rationalizing folly under respectable headings. Just war might have been an option when knights rode on horseback and there was no one else to see that justice was done across political borders, but how can it be an option in the twentieth century, when millions may perish as a result of a regional conflict drawing in the Great Powers, and when everyone is fighting for 'justice'? The term 'just war' rightly sets so many alarm bells ringing that it ought to be used only with caution and with as much precision as possible, with the limits of its usage clearly exposed.

There are three limits on its usage in these chapters. First, the term will be used to refer to a moral and legal doctrine and not to any particular practice of war. It is a mental construct which helps us to understand the rights and wrongs of human conduct in the midst of war. Second, the use of the term does not imply that the user believes that any of the wars that have been fought in the contemporary world have been just ones. But it does imply that practical steps ought to be taken to make sure that any future war that is forced upon a country should have a good chance of being fought with just means. Just-war theory is a practical theory, even though there may be near-insuperable political obstacles when it comes to applying it. Third, the primacy is given to the *jus in bello* aspect of just-war tradition, i.e. to the justice of conduct *in* war, rather than to the justice of going *to* war in the first place (*jus ad bellum*). Just causes are not the main issue, but just conduct in war is. This is in keeping with the development of just-war tradition since the sixteenth century: the idea of war as an instrument of justice faded into the background as it was assumed that some measure of justice would exist on both sides—or would at least be claimed by both sides—and the emphasis came to be placed on the conduct of the combatants. It is the principal strength of modern just-war theory that it obliges us to apply the same rules of restraint to all sides in a conflict, whatever the justice of their cause. It is not the case that the more justice is on one's side (e.g. that one's country is fighting a defensive rather than an aggressive war), the more right one has to break the rules, by, for instance, killing prisoners of war, making terrorist attacks, taking civilian hostages, etc. Both sides can commit war crimes. Both sides may claim to be defending essential human values against aggression. Whether or not this is true, the task is to get them to observe as much of the essential values as can be preserved in the process.

Justifying war and humanizing it are two different issues. People who think that no war is justifiable may nevertheless believe that it is possible and necessary to make war less destructive and less inhumane when it occurs. However, they will be met with objections from both pacifist and militarist directions. Militarists are likely to object that efforts to humanize war can only prolong the agony and increase the number of casualties. As a recent writer on limited war puts it: 'a little humanity in the short run, to the extent that it thwarts war's business, may entail a lot of inhumanity in the long run'.[1] According to this view, it would be better to fight all out, without restraints of any kind, to make war more, rather than less, destructive and insufferable, in order to get the enemy to capitulate as quickly as possible. Over and over again it has been claimed that new and more powerful weapons, by killing more people at one go, will shorten wars and so make them less destructive in the long run.[2] All efforts to make war more humane can only foster the false belief that it can somehow be, if not exactly

---

[1] Ian Clark, *Limited Nuclear War* (Oxford: Martin Robertson, 1982), 15.

[2] Thus John Donne praised the invention of artillery in 1621: 'So by the benefit of this light of reason, they have found out Artillery, by which warres come to quicker ends than heretofore, and the great expence of bloud is avoyded; for the numbers of men slain now, since the invention of Artillery, are much lesse than before, when the sword was the executioner' (cited by Bernard and Fawn M. Brodie, *From Crossbow to H-Bomb* (Bloomington and London: Indiana University Press, 1973), 70).

gentlemanly and civilized, then at least a cost-effective instrument of policy. It is better to make war as horrible as possible so as to discourage all illusions about it. In the twentieth century, weapons of mass destruction added a new dimension to this argument. Thus, theorists of air power between the World Wars argued that making war as dreadful as possible for civilians—on the assumption that they would have less powers of resistance than soldiers—would be a quick way of undermining a country's will to continue with a war (see Chapter 3). On the other hand, some pacifists are likely to object that the 'humanization' of war only serves to legitimize a fundamentally inhumane practice. It fatally distracts effort away from the real task, which is not to control it but to abolish it. Both positions believe that restraint in war is somehow a compromise with evil. The closeness of the absolute pacifist and total-war positions has often been remarked.[3]

One must distinguish two different issues here: first, the argument that *once a war has begun* there is no sense in restraints which will only prolong it, and second, the argument that *prior declarations of restraint* will make resort to war more likely. The first argument is a weak one. It is more an unconfirmed hypothesis than a fact that the more brutal a war is the shorter it will be. On the contrary, it can be argued with more justification that the abandonment of restraints on weapons and targets will embitter the enemy, stiffen the resistance and invite retaliation of an equally inhumane kind. The strategic bombing campaigns of World War II appear to confirm this. That war, by making war more dreadful for civilians, managed to kill some thirty million of them. By eroding the only barriers to murderous behaviour it will in any case leave a deposit of brutalization behind it on which interest will have to be paid for a very long time. There is no sound evidence from recent wars that barbarous actions saved lives or came anywhere near making war obsolete. But even if there were some truth in these arguments from consequences, considerations of justice and human rights would raise insuperable objections to such behaviour as, say, reprisals against prisoners of war, deliberate attacks on civilians, or the use of weapons causing widespread and indiscriminate death.

---

[3] See e.g. G. E. M. Anscombe, 'War and Murder', in W. Stein (ed.), *Nuclear Weapons and Christian Conscience* (London: Merlin Press, 1961; 2nd edn. 1981), 45–62, repr. in G. E. M. Anscombe, *Collected Philosophical Papers*, iii. *Ethics, Religion and Politics* (Oxford: Basil Blackwell, 1981), 51–61.

The second argument now plays an important part in the case for deterrence, especially as it appears in British and NATO defence doctrine: that is, any agreement about restraint on weapons which left the way open for a so-called conventional war would be a total disaster, given the vast increase in destructive power that conventional weapons have acquired since World War II. Some advocates of this viewpoint go the whole way in claiming that even restraints on nuclear targets, such as counter-force rather than counter-city, would be a dangerous weakening of the obstacles to war. This takes us to the heart of the apparent moral dilemma of deterrence, which it is not the purpose of this chapter to resolve. However, as a first determination, as it were, we can say that, from a just-war viewpoint, it is always wrong to threaten and prepare to fight an entirely unrestrained war. Just war is necessarily war that is limited. What are the rules of limitation?

Just-war theory[4] has come to us through two intellectual traditions with common roots in the sixteenth and seventeenth centuries: international law and moral theology. Both have played an important part in the post-war debates on nuclear weapons.

Weapons, Targets, and the Law

Since the mid-nineteenth century, when, for the first time, the achievements of the industrial revolution were used on a large scale in war, it has been a common view that winning wars depends more on access to new weapons than on new methods of manœuvring forces in the field. As Hilaire Belloc put it,

> Whatever happens, we have got
> The Maxim Gun, and they have not.[5]

---

[4] Just war may confusingly be referred to as a theory, a doctrine, or a tradition. It can be any of these three in different contexts. Calling it a *theory* may seem to be giving up any serious claim to practicality. However, a true moral theory is not merely a theory about morals. It is intended to be prescriptive, consensual, and effective, and to have an influence on legislation and judgement in international society. Just war is a *doctrine* in the sense that at any given time it may be set out in a coherent body of criteria which can be taught. It is a *tradition*, not in the sense of a single, fixed doctrine which has been handed down from authorities in the past, but in the sense of a more or less continuous debate in European culture going back to classical times, in which fresh responses to new developments in warfare have been made by moralists, building on what has been written before them. See James Turner Johnson, *Ideology, Reason and the Limitation of War* and *Just War Tradition and the Restraint of War* (Princeton, N.J: Princeton University Press, 1975, 1981).

[5] *The Modern Traveller*, vi (London, Edward Arnold, 1898).

World War I appeared to prove this, although it was not so much science as practical ingenuity which altered things. The machine-gun, after causing immense and indecisive slaughter, forced armies below ground to the trenches. The use of poison gas by both sides was also inconclusive. It was the invention of the tank by a British colonel, and its subsequent use by the British army, that broke the resulting stalemate.[6] But other new weapons developments in World War I—especially submarine and aerial warfare—not only greatly increased the intensity of war for combatants, but also offered ways of fighting it by direct attacks on non-combatant civilians.

Parallel with these developments there has been steady activity by international lawyers and the International Committee of the Red Cross to exercise humanitarian, legal control over the innovations of the weapons laboratories. The work began as a codification of customary international law (the unwritten law of nations) prohibiting the use of poison and materials causing unnecessary suffering. Military men had an obvious interest in this. The result was the Law of The Hague, which is largely concerned with restraining belligerents in the actual conduct of military hostilities, making war less brutal to those who fight it.[7] Thus the Hague Rules of 1899 forbade the use of asphyxiating gases and expanding bullets. The Hague Convention of 1907 established the funda-mental principle, in Article 22, that 'The right of belligerents to adopt means of injuring the enemy is not unlimited.'[8] The following article specifies this by, among other things, putting a ban on the use of poison, on killing the surrendered, and on refusal to give quarter, besides repeating the weapons ban of 1899. After about 1900, it became more a question of seeking prohibitions against indiscriminate weapons, those which could hardly be used without causing the mass slaughter of non-combatants.[9] In the 1925 Geneva Protocol—actually part of the Hague Law—there was an international agreement to prohibit the use of gas and bacteriological weapons. However, there are a number of serious

---

[6] See Brodie and Brodie, *From Crossbow to H-Bomb*, pp. 190–9.

[7] Cf. Sydney Bailey, *Prohibitions and Restraints in War* (OUP, 1972), 68. The Law of Geneva, on the other hand, is largely concerned with the rights of those *hors de combat*, now including civilians.

[8] Adam Roberts and Richard Guelff, *Documents on the Laws of War* (OUP, 1982), 52.

[9] Cf. Geoffrey Best, *Humanity in Warfare* (London: Methuen, 1980), 159.

flaws in the Chemical and Bacteriological Weapons Protocol: there is considerable ambiguity about what is forbidden by way of chemical agents, and most states have treated it as being only a prohibition on *first-use* of the weapons—i.e. they will refrain only so long as others do. But biological weapons have since been the subject of a convention prohibiting their development, production and stockpiling, which entered into force in 1975. Despite all efforts, there has been a total failure to prohibit weapons of aerial bombardment since the collapse of the International Disarmament Conference at Geneva in 1930–3. But it is these weapons which have been most responsible for drawing civilians into international conflict—not as active participants but as victims. And from the military point of view there is not such an obvious interest in prohibiting them, because they seem to hold the promise of making a quick end to a war by sudden overwhelming attacks.

The alternative approach to restraint—prohibiting certain targets instead of weapons—made some advance in the 1923 Hague Rules of Aerial Warfare, which, among other things, sought to prohibit the bombardment of civilians. But these were never ratified by governments and, although they were observed for the first nine months of World War II, they were completely abandoned thereafter. Subsequent humanitarian legislation, since 1945, has been largely an effort to extend to civilians the protection afforded to combatants who were injured, sick, or taken prisoner.[10] The object has been to add them to the list of those who must not be targeted in war or made the object of reprisals. Whereas the Geneva Conventions—concerned more with targets than with weapons— have since progressed so far as to prohibit direct and indiscriminate attacks on civilians (the 1977 Protocol), the Hague Law has lagged far behind in measures to prohibit the development and stockpiling of the weapons which are most likely to be used in such attacks. Although many lawyers hold that existing laws—such as those which prohibit the use of poisons—are sufficient to cover the use of nuclear weapons, there is so far no law which explicitly prohibits them. The 1977 Geneva Protocol clearly prohibits the use of weapons which are indiscriminate in their effects. However, in reservations which appear to contradict the law itself, Britain and

---

[10] Cf. Bailey, *Prohibition*, p. 70.

the United States specifically exclude its application to nuclear weapons.[11]

New Uses for an Old Theory

The laws of war are rooted in the just-war theory of earlier centuries, but it was not until the eve of World War II that there were notable signs of a revival of just-war thinking among theological moralists. The stimulus for this was undoubtedly the appearance of aerial bombardment, and the threat it embodied for the traditional immunity of non-combatants. Before the war began, there was a widespread agreement in Britain that it was immoral and against international law to bomb civilians. (The pre-war moral consensus and its collapse will be discussed in Chapter 3.) In 1939, for instance, the Catholic moralist Gerald Vann clearly identified the two areas in which modern war was most likely to conflict with just-war rules: the mass destruction of civilians and the disproportionate damage to the world community that it was likely to cause.

A nation, then, which takes up arms today cannot legitimately argue that the evils which the war will bring will be confined to its enemy, who has deserved them, and itself, who is willing to suffer them. To cause dislocation and distress, unless they are unavoidable, to the greater part of the world is a moral evil.[12]

When military men were forecasting the mass extermination of the civilian population, the Christian believer in just war was in a tragic dilemma:

We may be impelled to fight because the issue is wholly just and wholly vital to the existence and the preservation of Christian principles in our world; but at the same time confronted by the fact that we are powerless to choose our weapons: if we are to fight, it must be in a war arranged not by ourselves but by others who do not share our views in this respect, a war, therefore, in which the methods we regard as criminal will be used, not incidentally, by this or that individual, but consistently, as part of the general plan of campaign. What are we to do?

[11] See Roberts and Guelff, *Documents on the Laws of War*, p. 462.
[12] Gerald Vann, OP, *Morality and War* (London: Burns, Oates & Washbourne, 1939), 36.

Vann's answer was that, in the absence of a unified stand among Christians, the individual had to refuse co-operation in a war fought by unjust means. These considerations led him and others to a position that was close to practical pacifism, despite their just-war starting point.

In the event, the majority of Christian moralists accepted World War II as a just one, especially as its opening stages did not prove to be as apocalyptic as predicted. With a few significant exceptions, such as George Bell, bishop of Chichester, just-war scruples about the methods of fighting were largely silenced during the war, even though the bombing of civilians soon became routine. However, when, after the war was over, passions cooled and there was time to reflect on what had been done, just-war thinking began to widen its appeal. It provided a way of making moral judgements about the methods and weapons that had been used. It also provided a much-needed intellectual framework for judging the new weapons which emerged from the war. In particular it enabled those who were not against war as such to express their severe reservations about—or outright rejection of—the use of nuclear weapons. Just-war theory is now common intellectual currency among a wide circle of Christians and non-Christians who realize the need to bring moral distinctions to bear on methods of warfare *before* they are used. There is now a general recognition that it must be applied as much to preparations for war, as to the conduct of war itself. Just-war writers now have far more accurate knowledge of weapons and their effects than did their predecessors in 1939.

Recognizing these facts, a vigorous school of just-war writers in the United States has been concerned since the 1950s to make just-war theory once again a force in practical politics instead of merely a source of ineffectual criticism from the sidelines. Their main objective has been to influence American policy in the direction of producing nuclear weapons which, with limited yield and greater accuracy, could be used in just and limited war. They have campaigned on two fronts: on the one hand, against doctrines such as Massive Retaliation and Mutual Assured Destruction (MAD), which are based on the threat to destroy cities and even annihilate the enemy, in total disregard of the prohibition against killing the innocent; on the other hand, against nuclear pacifism, the belief that all nuclear weapons are bound to be so destructive and indiscriminate in their effects that no war in which they are used could be just. The concern then is to make just-war theory *serviceable* once more in the conditions of contemporary combat, so that their country is able to avoid the extremes of committing gross crimes against the human race or of capitulating to a nuclear-armed enemy.[13] According to this outlook, if nuclear weapons are not at present suitable to just and limited war, then morality and prudence demand that they be made so. Recognizing that the point of application of just-war theory is now in weapons development before it is anywhere else, these just-war theorists have periodically demanded that United States policy should move away from city-busting weapons and strategies of total destruction, towards the development of controllable, counter-force or counter-combatant weapons. It is an important instance of just-war theory in action. Whether, in the thirty years since these ideas were first put forward in public, there has been any of the desired progress, and if not, why not, are major questions. Despite the efforts of the just-war writers, United States deterrence policy continues to rest on a threat to attack 'value' targets, i.e. civilian populations. Whether it need be so is a question which lies outside the scope of this book, the focus of which is British policy and British moral debate, which has followed somewhat different pathways. Although there has not been such a vocal, reforming just-war school in Britain it is still true that much of the moral argument about defence policy since 1945—particularly of nuclear weapons policy—has taken place on the terrain of just-war tradition. Some of the stages in the British debate will be referred to in the appropriate places in the narrative of the following chapters. In order to prepare for this, the just-war rules can now be briefly explained.

The Rules of Just War

In keeping with the attitude adopted above—i.e. that primacy must be given to *jus in bello* restraints in planning weapons and strategy

[13] Authors and works in this tradition are: Thomas E. Murray, *Nuclear Policy for War and Peace* (Cleveland and New York: World Publishing Co., 1960); John Courtney Murray, 'Remarks on the Moral Problem of War', *Theological Studies* (Mar. 1959), 40–61; Paul Ramsey, *War and the Christian Conscience* (Durham, NC: Duke University Press, 1961); William O'Brien, *Nuclear War, Deterrence and Morality* (New York: Newman Press, 1967), and *The Conduct of Just and Limited War* (New York: Newman Press, 1981); James Turner Johnson, *Can Modern War be Just?* (New Haven, Conn.: Yale, 1984).

before there is any question of doing justice through an actual war—the usual order of the rules will be reversed.

Whether just or unjust in its beginnings, fighting must observe the two following criteria:

(a) *Discrimination*. This is generally interpreted as the immunity of non-combatant civilians from direct or indiscriminate attack. But it also includes all those who are *hors de combat* for other reasons, e.g. being sick or wounded, or prisoners of war. The correct interpretation of the discrimination rule is one of the most important things in just-war theory, and it will be discussed below.

(b) *Proportionality*. This must be considered in two respects: first, with regard to the war as a whole (*ad bellum* proportionality) and second, with regard to military actions taken in fighting the war (*in bello* proportionality). If it is likely to result in destruction and harm to the human race out of all proportion to the evil being fought against, or the good being aimed at, then the war is an unjust one (see Gerald Vann's misgivings about a second world war, above). It is easier to state this than to say how proportionality could be measured in any particular case. A judgement of proportionality will obviously look very different from the point of view of a people who believe their existence or freedom to be threatened—which is normally the case in contemporary wars—than from the point of view of some detached observer. All kinds of emotional calls for the ultimate sacrifice will be brought in to obscure the issue. Nevertheless, it is vital that somebody should think of the more objective considerations: whether the country would survive at all, how a war would effect the world environment or destroy the economic system on which many peoples depend, or cause immense suffering and death beyond the field of battle. It needs to be recalled that certain kinds of war in the modern world can never be won, even by superpowers. What also needs to be thought through is whether hostilities are likely to escalate quickly into all-out war against civilian populations.

However, it is not sufficient to determine that the overall evil consequences of a war will be proportionate to the evil being fought against. If this were the only thing to consider, then it might be thought that anything is permissible to achieve the desired result. Proportionality covers individual acts of war as well as the war itself. Of course, each and every act of war must be discriminate.

But besides being discriminate, it must also observe a principle of minimum force. Commanders and men in the field must not take actions which cause unnecessary destruction in particular places.

Since the time of the Spanish theologian Vitoria (1480–1546) it has been normal to recognize that legitimate military operations will inevitably cause innocent people to suffer. Subsequently, at least in the Catholic tradition, the situation has been dealt with by the principle of *double effect*. This recognizes that, in certain situations where an urgent remedy is required, it will be foreseen that a bad effect will result from the remedial action as well as the good one which is desired. The principle of double effect allows the action on certain conditions: first, the good effect must not be achieved *by means of* the bad effect, which must be only a consequence of the action; second, the bad effect must not be intended but, on the contrary, *regretted*, i.e. if the good effect could be obtained in any other way not involving the bad effect, it would be; third, the bad effect must not be *disproportionate* to the good effect. The double effect principle cannot be used to justify *any* actions which have both good and bad consequences. It is not a generalized utilitarian principle, but can only legitimately be used within a context of knowledge about what is to be aimed at in human life and what is to be avoided at all cost. So the double effect principle cannot, for instance, be invoked in order to justify the direct destruction of a city because killing civilians is a short way to win a war and 'save lives', since this would conflict with the principle of discrimination (and the first condition above). Nor can it be used to justify such an act on the grounds that it is a 'bonus' effect of destroying the military bases it contains (second condition); or because it is, for instance, the easiest way of cutting lines of communication (third condition).

Besides the requirement that the evil of a war shall not be out of all proportion to the good which may come of it, modern just-war theory usually recognizes the following other necessary conditions for going to war (*jus ad bellum*). Again the usual order is reversed so as better to express the primacy of weapons over causes in contemporary thought about the morality of war.

(c) *Last Resort*. Only after all other means of ending an offence have been exhausted can even a war of defence be considered a just one. If possible, economic sanctions, as well as legal and diplomatic efforts must be made while there is still time.

(d) *Just Intention*. This could include an intention to bring an end to aggression, to restore peace, but not to annihilate the enemy society, to enslave its people, or to make civilized life impossible. The dismantling of the enemy state might be a legitimate intention, but not the destruction of the people, the society, or the culture. World War II practice of demanding unconditional surrender cannot be a just intention since it implicitly threatens the destruction of the enemy nation if it is not accepted.[14] Further, retaliatory vengeance is not a just intention.

(e) *Right Authority*. In the medieval just-war tradition, this criterion was of supreme importance, as efforts were made to prohibit lesser princes making war in their own interests. It was a question of giving the monopoly of judicial force to the supreme authority, in so far as there was one. When Europe disintegrated as a political entity, it played an important part in the emergence of sovereign states from the feudal system. Most just-war writers would now agree that in situations of great oppression, right authority need not be legally constituted, but may come from popular support in case of just rebellion. But the advent of weapons of mass destruction has raised a fresh problem of authority. Authority is needed not simply to begin a war, but to conduct it in a just manner. Just war is essentially an act of controlled force, intended to restore a state of law-abiding peace. It is analogous to the judicial process in peace time, and bears the same relation to uncontrolled violence as does the judicial process to lynch-law. It could be said that once a war degenerates into a sequence of escalating retaliatory attacks ordered by military commanders using weapons with indiscriminate characteristics, then it ceases to be controlled, ceases to be under proper authority, and ceases to be just for that reason, if for no other. Chapter 9 will discuss this matter in relation to nuclear war in Europe.

(f) *Just Cause*. Where industrialized powers are concerned, this is usually now restricted to defence against aggression, although some recent wars of humanitarian intervention have been included, and the numerous wars of national liberation since 1945 have fostered a revival of the theory of just cause.

---

[14] Cf. Elizabeth Anscombe, 'Mr Truman's Degree', *Collected Philosophical Papers*, iii *Ethics, Religion and Politics* (Oxford: Basil Blackwell, 1981), 62–71.

Non-combatant Immunity and its Critics

In recent times, attacks on the principles of non-combatant immunity have been made on the grounds that it no longer makes sense in an age of total wars to declare some people absolutely immune from attack when whole nations are engaged in life and death struggle and everyone is implicated. The rule appears to some to be relative to a period of history in which armies fought battles for dynastic purposes and innocent civilians continued life as best they could. But nowadays, when nations fight for their very existence, this rule should not be allowed to inhibit the use of the only weapons—i.e. nuclear weapons—which could guarantee an adequate defence.[15] But this type of argument ignores the fact that there are two historical sources of the non-combatant immunity rule, and that while one of them—military necessity—results in a flexible rule which aims at reducing the overall destruction of war, the other—justice—results in an absolute rule which is not relative to the changing conditions of warfare.

Attempts to restrain the conduct of war at any given time can be shown to be a synthesis of 'military reason' and other, more transcendent moral principles. In the classical just-war theory of the medieval and sixteenth-century periods, the fundamental principle balancing military reason was justice, which meant that questions of guilt and innocence were prominent, and war was understood as a legal act in a world community governed by the 'law of nations'. Justice was viewed as a category of natural law, which meant that any human beings, Christian or not, who were not actually involved in unjust aggression could claim immunity from attack and rightly defend themselves if attacked. This idea promoted the transition of the just-war tradition from the sacral society of medieval Europe to the secular or multi-faith international society which succeeded it. Justice continues to be central for those who accept some kind of natural-law theory, even if it now often appears under the guise of human rights.

However, the progressive legislation of the humanitarian laws of war has, since the mid-nineteenth century, tended to avoid the

[15] See e.g. R. S. Hartigan in a series of papers, including 'Non-combatant Immunity: Reflections on its Origins and Present Status', *Review of Politics*, 29, (Apr. 1967), 204. Also O'Brien, *The Conduct of Just and Limited War*, p. 43.

entanglements of the theory of justice, and adopted the principle of 'humanity' to counteract the claims of military necessity.[16] This may seem a rather vague category, but it has been serviceable in obtaining a wide consensus against some of the more inhumane developments in weapons technology. But, as we noted above, the relentless ingenuity of the weapons scientists has far outstripped the legislative process. What we cosily call 'conventional war' became a system of mass-slaughter by any means available in 1914, and with the invention of such abominations as napalm and fragmentation bombs, conventional war between major powers or their clients has got quite beyond the stage where most of its operations can in any sense respect the humanity of the combatants. But at least in the humanitarian laws of war the foundations have been laid in law for a more comprehensive set of agreements if the political climate ever becomes more favourable.

I use the term 'military reason' to refer to the belief that military activity is a rational activity, bound by its own finality, with its own discipline and with limits imposed by other, transcendent human values such as justice, protection of the weak, and the establishment of peace. That is, it has its own professional ethics. Like other professional ethics, military ethics is largely a matter of using power with restraint, i.e. for social, rather than for self-serving ends or as an end in itself. Michael Howard has described war as a highly social activity which demands a unique intensity of organization and control.[17] It is far from being a condition of indiscriminate and purposeless violence, which is just as repugnant to the military profession as it is to everyone else. However there is no guarantee that what the military does in pursuit of its proper goals will coincide with the transcendent human values. There may be a convenient coincidence for a time, but more often there is tension and conflict. The problem that war presents is not introducing

---

[16] See the Preamble of the Hague Conventions (the 'Martens Clause'): 'Until a more complete code of the laws of war has been issued, the high contracting Parties deem it expedient to declare that, in cases not included in the Regulations adopted by them, the inhabitants and the belligerent remain under the protection and rule of the principles of the law of nations, as they result from the usages established among civilized peoples, from the laws of humanity, and the dictates of the public conscience.'

[17] Michael Howard, 'Temperamenta Belli: Can War Be Controlled?' in id. (ed.), *Restraints on War* (OUP, 1979), 1.

control as such but introducing the kind of control that is necessary if justice and humanity are not to be entirely cast aside.

The fundamental principle of military reason is that of *necessity*, i.e. that, subject to limits imposed by other fundamental principles such as justice, a belligerent is justified in applying the amount and kind of force necessary to achieve the complete submission of the enemy at the earliest possible moment and with the least expenditure of time, life, and resources.[18] This can be cast in the more negative form of a principle of *minimum force*: in the pursuit of military objectives it is wrong to apply force which is excessive, or which causes unnecessary suffering. It leads directly to a purely military form of *in bello* proportionality, an expression of the basic interest the military has in keeping war within limits.

A version of non-combatant immunity also has been derived from military reason. By the sixteenth century there was a general consensus about a comprehensive list of classes of people who were held to be immune from attack in war. This was a synthesis of military reason and the theory of justice. On the military side there was the code of chivalry, by which the fighting class of knights had given itself the privilege of protecting the weak and inferior, provided they did not take up arms. This was not a matter of right, but a gift from the superior protector to the inferior protected.[19] In later centuries, when wars came to be fought by armies of foot soldiers, it became a matter of military discipline not to attack unarmed civilians. It would reduce the efficiency of the fighting, and it might devastate the land from which the armies needed to find their food, besides needlessly increasing the destruction caused by war which was essentially limited in its objectives. So non-combatant immunity of a sort entered the code of professional ethics in the form of customary law. In this form it is not an absolute, since its central purpose is to restrict the scope of war's destruction, not to forbid altogether the direct killing of non-combatants. It is derived from the military principle of minimum force.[20] It is consequently relative and unstable, since it may be overridden by necessity, in the interests of fighting the war in a way

[18] This is a modified version of the definition in Roberts and Guelff, *Documents on the Laws of War*, p. 5.
[19] See Johnson, *Just War Tradition and the Restraint of War*, pp. 133–6.
[20] Ibid. 210, 219–22.

that the military regard as efficient. This is a reminder that limited war is not necessarily just war, although just war is necessarily limited.

Justice on the other hand—at least in the natural-law tradition, as opposed to the positivist tradition—is a moral category in the first place. When it comes to the execution of justice in any sphere of life, it becomes clear that *discrimination* is central to it. Doing justice often means precisely discriminating between the guilty and innocent. At the root of the European just-war tradition lies a fundamental Jewish–Christian moral rule which prohibits killing human beings unless they have, by their actions, shown themselves such violent enemies of the common good that they need to be killed to protect it. Even in societies with widely differing views about capital punishment and war, the fundamental prohibition is always the same. It forbids deliberately killing the innocent for any reason at all, even when it appears necessary for the sake of the community itself.[21] Consequently, no fighting could be just that did not discriminate between those who are a direct and violent threat to the common good and those who are innocent of this.

However, the principle of discrimination does not automatically lead to the non-combatant immunity rule as it has been developed in the just-war tradition. There need to be reliable ways of defining guilt and innocence in war. The basic criteria originated in medieval canon law, which claimed that those who do not have the social function of making war—clerics in the first place—should not have war made against them. In the form of the Peace of God this was extended to other classes in the interests of reducing the scope of wars: to pilgrims, traders, and peasants cultivating the soil. It was interpreted as a matter of *right*—not in the modern sense of individual human rights, but in the Roman law sense of *jus*—that which is strictly owed in justice. Where there was still the assumption that, in any given war, one side will be just and the other unjust, it was not too difficult to decide in a practical way between the innocent and the guilty: the guilty are those who take

---

[21] In all societies there has been a constant tendency to question this in times of stress: see Caiaphas' question in the Gospel of John, 11: 50 and 18: 14: 'Is it not better that one innocent person should be put to death than that the whole people perish?' According to the French literary critic and philosopher René Girard, the urge to resort to and justify scapegoating is central to the development of myths, religion, and the judicial system in all human societies. See *Things Hidden since the Foundation of the World* (London: Athlone Press, 1987).

up arms in an unjust cause. The innocent are not only those fighting in a just cause but also anyone who is not actually fighting, whoever they belong to.[22] So *function* was a fairly reliable indication of guilt and innocence in the context of war. By the end of the medieval period there was a generally accepted synthesis between the concept of immunity derived from justice and that deriving from the military code. The lists of those who must not have war made against them was virtually the same in both cases. However, there remained a tension between them which was always liable to become outright contradiction when new methods of making war put civilians at risk—as in the bombardment of fortified towns, for instance.[23]

As the modern just-war doctrine took shape in later centuries, the principle of limiting the violence to certain categories of people was maintained with remarkable consistency. It received added momentum from the rejection of war on grounds of religion by the founders of the international law tradition, Vitoria and Grotius. This represented a decisive shift away from any notion of collective guilt. It was not just to attack individuals because they held certain beliefs or denied others, which meant in effect that they could not be justly attacked because they belonged to a particular state. Thinking along such lines in our own day would lead to the conclusion that patriotism is not sufficient grounds for loss of immunity. It is, after all, something which the individual member of a modern state can hardly avoid, just as the ruler's religion was something which an earlier citizen could hardly avoid. The development of the *jus in bello* tradition meant a denial of collective guilt and a shift to purely functional criteria for judgement of who may be attacked and who not. In Vitoria, Grotius, and Vattel it is

[22] Cf. Vitoria, *De Jure Belli*, 36: 'Hence it follows that even in war with the Turks [still regarded as the implacable enemies of Christianity in Vitoria's time] it is not allowable to kill children. This is clear, because they are innocent. Aye, and the same holds with regard to the women of unbelievers . . . And this same pronouncement must be made among Christians with regard to harmless agricultural folk, and also with regard to the rest of the peaceable civilian population, for all these are presumed innocent until the contrary is shown [i.e. by actual fighting].'

[23] Thus Vitoria, who is quite clear on the categorical nature of the prohibition of killing the innocent, nevertheless allows that non-combatants may be knowingly killed during the bombardment of towns with cannon (being then extensively used for the first time in siege warfare), for otherwise it would be impossible to make just war at all. See *De Jure Belli*, 37. This judgement, from one of the most influential of all just-war writers, now seems like the thin end of the wedge of modern war waged against civilian populations.

social function alone which determines liability rather than the fact of being an enemy citizen.[24] Moreover, once the assumption that all justice is on one side was given up, there remained the functional criterion of innocence: it may not have been necessary or possible to assume that soldiers on the other side were guilty in a moral sense, but it certainly was morally impossible to assume that unarmed civilians were. This raises awkward questions about the status of conscripts but at least we can say that the tradition holds that genuine non-combatants have done nothing to forfeit their right not to be killed. Given that there always will be many individuals who are wholly innocent of the injustice of a war and that it is inherently unjust to kill them, even in a just cause, the just way to proceed is to attack only those who give evidence of their harmful role by bearing arms. Thus, 'innocent' in war came to be primarily not a moral category, opposite to 'guilty', but a functional category, the opposite of 'harmful'. Although it retains its roots in the morality of justice, it now relates not to the justification for punishment, but to the prevention of further harm. A soldier may be morally quite innocent, but nevertheless engaged in some violent harm to the common good, which needs to be prevented. Conversely, the non-combatant may be guilty of hatred, but nevertheless not actively engaged in doing harm, and therefore may not be directly attacked.[25]

There has been a continuous practical alliance and mutual influence between military reason and justice in the just-war tradition to the extent that the principles of proportionality and non-combatant immunity, at least before the twentieth century, have derived from both interests. However the alliance was never an easy one, and under certain conditions easily comes apart. The purpose of sparing non-combatants in the military, limited-war

[24] See Johnson, *Ideology, Reason and the Limitation of War*, pp. 196 ff.

[25] I owe the analysis in the last four sentences to Herbert McCabe. But the distinction between innocent as 'not-guilty' and as 'harmless' has not always been made. It belongs to the development of just-war doctrine in the 17th and 18th cent. Earlier writers did not make the distinction. Thus, for Vitoria *innocens* always has a strong moral reference and is opposed to *nocens*, which means both harmful and guilty of harm to the common good. This goes with the fact that war is envisaged as punishment as well as prevention. It was, for him, always a moral matter. Unjust killing was murder. However, sharpening the distinction between moral and functional definitions of innocence enabled a clearer distinction to be made between those guilty of war crimes and those merely guilty of fighting on the wrong side. Both civilian non-combatants and prisoners of war should have benefited from this.

tradition is to reduce total destruction, whereas the non-combatant immunity which is part of justice is to protect non-combatants as such. At its most extreme, the difference may be as Johnson describes:

There is, of course, some overlap in the implications of these two ideas in practice, but their fundamental distinctiveness can be grasped readily by conceiving of a hypothetical war in which a sudden and terrible slaughter of non-combatants brought an abrupt end to the fighting, as opposed to a war in which successful efforts to protect non-combatants prolonged the destruction of a country's economic and social base.[26]

It is important to note that this remains a hypothesis and is liable to the objections mentioned above (p. 9). However, it does bring out the characteristic weakness of military reason on its own—its inherent relativity. Under pressure for victory, for instance, anything can become a military target.

An important factor tending to separate military reason with its principle of minimum force from justice with its principle of discrimination is the immense increase in the destructive power of weapons used in modern war. This means that it is increasingly easy for actions done from military necessity to be indiscriminate. From the justice viewpoint, the drawback to the idea of minimum force is that this minimum must get greater and greater as the weapons used get more and more powerful. The minimum force needed to put an army division out of action in the 1980s is a great deal more—and needs to be applied with much greater speed—than it was in 1914.

It is certainly true that the category of those who may be targeted as combatants may be expanded in time of war to include those who manufacture, operate, support, and maintain weapons systems of great complexity. This includes a lot more people than those in active service in the forces. But there is no rational way of extending it to include all the citizens of a nation engaged in war, let alone all the citizens of a nation which *might be* engaged in war. In any modern city there will always be a very large number of individuals who are wholly innocent, whichever definition of innocence is used: the unborn, children under 14 say, the mentally retarded, the old and infirm, and most people going about their normal business of living and providing for the life of the community.

[26] Johnson, *Just War Tradition and the Restraint of War*, p. 208.

Furthermore, the assumption that entire nations are involved in modern warfare is not so much a fact as a construct of state ideology. Modern nation states have usually gained their identity and organization through war, often wars of revolution or liberation, and membership of the nation has usually been identified with readiness to fight for it. This has been carried to an extreme degree in the ideology of national security which has developed on a global scale since World War II. The tendency is to replace society by the state, and to weaken or abolish intermediate non-state organizations so that the individual is faced only by the state and its claims. Many things, normally impermissible, can then be done, or planned, by the state in the name of national security, over which it has sovereign control, answerable to no one. All loyalties that are independent of it or are transnational in character—and which would be good grounds for questioning the ideology of total war—are antagonistic to it or liable to be seen as treasonous, especially when war threatens, which it is said to do perpetually. Nevertheless, these loyalties include those which continue to give individuals their sense of identity, morality, and destiny: religion, class, or simply common humanity.[27] But an ideology of total threat is necessary in order to suppress these loyalties in face of the necessity of total war. It is no accident that the ideology of national security has flourished in the post-war world dominated by nuclear weapons and divided by two incompatible systems.

Moreover, when one examines the literature questioning the non-combatant immunity rule one finds that, in place of the rigorous proof that ordinary citizens are engaged in hostilities, which one has a right to expect, there is merely an assumption that the power of modern weapons makes it inevitable that they will be attacked. In other words, the conclusion that the non-combatant immunity rule is no longer valid is illegitimately derived from the observation that states no longer intend to respect it. However, it is not the case that total war *means* that all the citizens of a country are implicated in hostilities, but rather that they are liable to have unrestrained war made against them. It begins to look like nothing

---

[27] This is not to ignore the fact that religion and, to a lesser extent, class are still potent sources of total-war ideas. Nevertheless, they nearly always get their power to move masses of people through being harnessed to the survival of a particular national identity, which is said to be under threat from outside.

more than a rationalization: 'capable of being attacked' implies 'deserving to be attacked'. It would not be the first time in human affairs that guilt is imputed to particularly vulnerable groups of people in order to prepare the ground for attacks against them which may be necessary for other reasons. Total war *is* war in which military necessity and the employment of all weapons available are put before the considerations of justice and humanity which are at the centre of just-war traditions and the laws of war.[28]

In sum, thirty years of debate about the validity of the non-combatant immunity rule has resulted in a broad agreement among just-war moralists on both sides of the deterrence debate that direct or indiscriminate attacks on centres of population with the intention of destroying them is categorically forbidden. However, this theoretical agreement is more superficial than it might appear at first sight. It leaves large areas of disagreement about what constitutes legitimate weapons and legitimate intentions when using those weapons. These disagreements as they have occurred in the British debate will be touched upon in the following chapters and discussed more fully in Chapter 9.

[28] Cf. the judgement of John C. Ford on the obliteration bombing of the Second World War: 'Is it not evident that the most radical and significant change of all in modern warfare is not the increased co-operation of civilians behind the lines with the armed forces, but the enormously increased power of the armed forces, to reach behind the lines and attack civilians indiscriminately, whether they are thus co-operating or not?' ('The Morality of Obliteration Bombing', *Theological Studies*, 5 (1944), 281.)

2

LESSONS OF THE PAST: APPEASEMENT

British defence policy after World War II is a product of certain 'lessons' learned in the crucible of humiliation and near-defeat in the years 1938 to 1941, from Munich to the bombing war with Germany. Given that the men who conducted defence policy after the war were the same men who had led Britain into and through the war, it is difficult to see how they could have diverged radically from the course on which they were already set by the events which they had lived through, and their interpretation of them. Their range of choices was severely restricted by the very processes which brought them to power: they were the people who had purged the mistakes of the 1930s and who had won the war against the Nazis.

The 'lessons' were:

- the failure of appeasement to prevent aggression by a totalitarian state;
- the dangers of strategic isolation, especially from the United States
- the apparent efficacy of strategic bombing.

The Lesson and its Teachers

A major factor in justifying and rationalizing British nuclear policy has been the myth of appeasement. This is a simplified account of how the Western democracies failed to rearm against Hitler before it was too late, hoping to deal with his ruthless expansionism by diplomacy and concessions, sacrificing weak allies and failing to prevent another catastrophic European war. The Munich agreement is believed in hindsight to have been the outcome of an appeasement ethos shared by the British government and people throughout the 1930s. Consequently, that ethos and everything connected with it has been tarred with the brush of the Munich disaster. The entire policy, as a method of conducting international relations has, without distinction or nuance, been judged through the spectrum of the war it failed to prevent.

Moreover, the disastrous failure of 1938 has profoundly shaken the connection in people's minds between moral principles and good politics, between pacific behaviour and actual peace. Appeasement at its beginning was self-evidently noble as well as rational. It was a course of action motivated at its best by a genuine desire to give Germany its rightful place among European states, to rectify the worst results of the Treaty of Versailles, to conduct international relations without resort to armed force, and so to prevent anything like a repeat of World War I. But it appeared to end with an immoral retreat before totalitarian threats, a sacrifice of small countries, and then a further catastrophic war which might have been prevented if decisive action had been undertaken at an earlier stage. At best, it looks like 'well-meaning folly, the weakness of the virtuous', as Churchill called it in his memoirs.[1]

Largely as a consequence of this failure, the lesson that everyone thought they had learned from World War I—that arms races and the fear they engender lead to war—has been unlearned, and another, equally simplistic, has taken its place. This latter may be summed up under the notion of *deterrence*, interpreted in the narrow sense of superiority—or, at least sufficiency—of offensive armaments in permanent readiness for retaliatory attack against an aggressor. Like appeasement, it is presented as a panacea for the prevention of war. Mrs Thatcher, for instance, was applying the lesson when, addressing the US Congress in February 1985, she said, 'Wars are not caused by the buildup of weapons. They are caused when an aggressor believes he can achieve his objective at an acceptable price.'[2]

The fate of appeasement has, since the Cold War period, played a major part in the rhetoric of Britain's defence policy. It has become a powerful instrument with which to justify expensive force modernizations, to shame political opponents, and to frighten the populace in the cause of deterrence. It continues to be produced like the ace of trumps whenever serious questions are asked about certain key aspects of defence policy. But very few questions are asked about the meaning of the word or whether the lesson applies

---

[1] Winston S. Churchill, *The Second World War*, i. *The Gathering Storm* (London: Cassell, 1948), 15. The theme of the volume is 'how the English-speaking peoples through their unwisdom, carelessness and good nature allowed the wicked to rearm'.

[2] See *Observer*, 17 Feb. 1985.

any longer in a world utterly changed by the presence of nuclear weapons.

The myth is much more easy for politicians to handle than the reality. Its power lies in the simplifications of hindsight. The account of appeasement which has prevailed is, of course, that of the victors in the political struggles of the 1930s, since it was they who provided most of the political continuity. From the Attlee government of 1945 to the Douglas-Home government of 1964 some of the highest offices were occupied by men who had either played a leading part in politics during the appeasement period or who had lived through their formative early careers then. Many of them had been leading anti-appeasers, including Churchill, Eden, Bevin, Macmillan, and Sandys. Only Butler and Douglas-Home (as Chamberlain's Parliamentary Private Secretary at Munich) had been strongly associated with appeasement: a position which the latter afterwards attempted to justify by emphasizing its anti-communist rationale. But the myth of appeasement has powerfully affected everyone in both Conservative and Labour post-war governments, including those too young to have had much experience of the 1930s.

The myth was an essential ingredient in the Cold War policy of containment. Although the latter was basically a development in American foreign policy, it was much promoted by the attitude of Churchill and Bevin towards the Soviet Union and it became an integral part of Britain's foreign policy in the Western Alliance. Application of the appeasement lesson to the post-war world was given a decisive push by Churchill in his speech at Fulton, Missouri on 5 March 1946, and again in his memoirs of World War II.[3] The Fulton speech articulated for everyone the central ideas which were to govern public consciousness of the relationship between the Western nations and the Soviet Union for the post-war epoch. Among them were:

- The belief that, even if the Soviet leaders did not want war, they did want 'the fruits of war and the indefinite expansion of their power and doctrines'.
- The conviction that Russian ambitions, potentially unlimited,

[3] Churchill, *History of the Second World War*, i. *The Gathering Storm*. For a recent historical account and interpretation of the Fulton speech, see Fraser J. Harbutt, *The Iron Curtain, Churchill, America, and the Origins of the Cold War* (New York: OUP, 1987).

would not be allayed with a policy of appeasement: 'Last time I saw it coming and cried aloud to my fellow-countrymen and to the world, but no one paid any attention.' Just as Hitler might have been stopped by a united action of the democracies in 1933, or even 1936, so now Stalin must be stopped by a united Anglo-American front under the legitimizing authority of the United Nations.

- A judgement of Russian political character, which Churchill says he gained by experience during the war, that 'there is nothing they admire so much as strength, and there is nothing for which they have less respect than for weakness, especially military weakness'.

- A rejection of the old doctrine of 'a quivering, precarious balance of power' which offers 'temptations to ambition or adventure' and its replacement with a global English-speaking hegemony which would have unassailable superiority in science, industry, moral force—and military power.

- The necessity for a common, world-wide sharing of military bases between the United Kingdom and the United States.

- The maintenance of a permanent atomic superiority, even when the period of monopoly inevitably comes to an end.[4]

Application of the appeasement lesson was made much easier by evidence of Soviet government brutality to its own people and to those of subject nations. The purges and terror of the 1930s had already made a deep and lasting impression in the West. And after the war, the ruthless destruction of democratic governments in Soviet-occupied Europe and the imposition of regimes subservient to Stalin, accompanied by show-trials and mass deportations, led many to believe that the Soviet Union was an expansionist state which would seize every opportunity to spread its tyrannical system beyond its borders. However, in many ways the Soviet leaders showed caution in their foreign policies and a willingness to accommodate to Western interests, as in Greece, Finland, and Austria. And they relinquished interference in Iran and Turkey after pressure from the West.

From the beginning of the Cold War, there was a strong tendency towards simplification of the historical complexities of appeasement.

---

[4] For the text of the speech, see Randolph S. Churchill (ed.), *The Sinews of Peace, Post-war Speeches by Winston S. Churchill* (London: Cassell, 1948), 93–105.

It was said that the fundamental mistake of the Western democracies in the 1930s had been a failure to take notice of German
rearmament, so leaving themselves in an inferior position in which
they could neither protect their allies nor avoid a war. Thus the
essence of appeasement came to be identified with a failure to
acquire and demonstrate military power. And by 1945 the core of
Western power was already understood to be atomic weapons.

As a consequence, other aspects of appeasement which must play
a part in any normal peace-time relations between states were
forgotten or fell under suspicion: for instance, the acknowledgement of the vital interests and understandable fears of potential
enemies, a willingness to take their historical experiences into
account—especially their defeats and invasions—and the traumas
of nation-building they have endured. The narrowing of the idea of
appeasement was accompanied by a corresponding narrowing in
the concept of deterrence. From being thought of as a whole array
of security measures designed to discourage aggression, including
conventional forces, social and economic strength, the word came
to be applied in popular discussion primarily, and by 1955
exclusively, to the H-bomb, the 'Great Deterrent'.[5]

Arms and Security

Both appeasement and the post-war reaction to it are reflections of
the highly ambiguous relationship that exists between armaments
and security. There are two basic dilemmas, which interact with
each other. First, there is the so-called power–security dilemma.
This is a dilemma about how to interpret the behaviour—especially
the military behaviour—of potential enemy states. Does a buildup
of armaments, for instance, signify a bid for power, perhaps to be
achieved through the threat of armed aggression when the time is
ripe? Or does it signify anxieties about security only?[6] Let us

[5] Often, nuclear weapons are simply 'deterrents', as in Mrs Thatcher's speech at
the Berlin Wall on 27 Sept. 1987 when she said that 'our independent deterrent must
remain. It is also important that the Americans have some deterrents in Europe.'
Guardian, 26 Sept. 1987.

[6] See Barry Buzan, *Peoples, States and Fear* (Brighton: Wheatsheaf Books,
1983), 173: 'At its most extreme, the choice is between two views of international
relations: on the one hand, as a ceaseless struggle for survival and dominance among
states motivated by the pursuit of power; and on the other hand, as a tragic struggle
for security by states trapped in a system which distorts their legitimate efforts at
self-protection into a seamless web of insecurity and conflict.'

suppose—as most people do—that the policy of our own country is basically motivated by the desire for security, then the best responses to these two cases would obviously not be the same. If the potential enemy is also motivated by the desire for security, the right reaction would be reassurance, and attempts to overtake him in numbers and quality of armaments are likely to be counter-productive. Appeasement (or *détente*) of some kind is indicated, in the form of redressing grievances, pursuing common goals, improving peaceful commerce and, in general, reducing the level of threat. Arms races should be avoided and arms-control agreements may be a necessity. In this case there is an inverse correlation between the size of one's military arsenal and security, since increases would make the other country's security problem worse and the situation more dangerous. However, if the potential enemy is engaged in a bid to change or overturn the international system, such accommodating moves could lead to disaster. Deterrent policies of some kind would then be a priority, preferably through alliances with other countries which have a similar interest in maintaining the status quo.

Unfortunately, there are a number of intractable difficulties in the way of making the right response, which become more acute in situations of international tension. Strong defence armaments may play a part in either a power struggle or a security struggle. But armaments are very seldom unambiguously defensive, especially in an era of long-distance aerial warfare when there is a need to react with speed to neutralize an enemy's attack forces. Indeed, many of the weapons have a decidedly offensive aspect, since their purpose is to destroy the war-making capacity of an enemy at an early stage of a war, before they themselves are eliminated. Hence the familiar dilemma of capabilities and intentions. What are the other country's weapons for? Do they have defensive or offensive intentions? The dilemma is made more acute by an internal arms-dynamic, which demands continual modernizations and up-dating. Is this routine and independent or does it signify a push for supremacy? It may well be impossible to tell the difference between an arms race driven by technological advance and security concerns, and one driven by a wish for superiority and power.[7] But even the much sought-after goal of stable deterrence depends on an ability to distinguish these.

[7] Cf. Buzan, *Peoples, States and Fear*, pp. 187–92.

Thus, to outside and threatened observers, a bid for power may resemble a bid for security and vice versa. On the one hand, a country that is really motivated by aspirations to power and a desire to change the map of international society, might also suffer acute security problems as others build up their forces in response, and may precipitate war. On the other hand a country that is basically motivated by security anxieties might find itself making pre-emptive moves that can only be interpreted by others as naked aggression. International life can rarely be described in terms of either a pure security struggle or a pure power struggle, even though so much hangs on making the most accurate interpretation of events, as the problem of Hitler's rise demonstrated so clearly.

It is often said that the Western democracies made the mistake in the 1930s of taking the German problem for a security struggle instead of the power struggle that it actually was. So they got involved in the hopeless task of trying to curb the rise to power of what turned out to be a predatory state by the method of appeasement, which only made the problem worse by encouraging Hitler to think he could get away with anything. It has also frequently been suggested that, in the post-war world, reaction to the earlier mistake has gone so far as to produce the opposite mistake: to suppose that what were really the Soviet Union's attempts to deal with its chronic security problems, made so much worse by the West's atomic encirclement after 1945, were signs of a relentless drive to power and territorial gain on the German model. If this is so, the problem of living with the Soviet Union is made infinitely more dangerous than it might otherwise be, since the misinterpretation of a security struggle can become the self-fulfilling prophecy of a power struggle. The threat becomes only too real. And the situation begins to look like the prelude to World War I rather than the prelude to World War II. The danger then is not another Munich, but another Sarajevo, in which some local incident occurs which everyone thinks totally trivial but in which little by little the two sides keep raising the stakes until one or other cannot back off.

Supposing the common analysis of the pre-World War II situation, at least, to be more or less accurate, the source of the trouble at that time was that the Western Powers, particularly Britain, were, after World War I, heavily predisposed to deal with international problems in terms of security struggles rather than of power struggles. One reason for this was that the interpretation of international relations as a power struggle had already led to catastrophe for everyone. Henceforward, the object of foreign policy must be to make sure that the search for security by a nation like Germany did not again get out of hand, become a power struggle, and lead to unnecessary war. This was made the more necessary by the fact that British diplomats were working in an international environment from which all the old certainties had been removed. The disappearance of the old empires which had given structure to Eastern Europe had destroyed the balance of power on which Britain's security was traditionally thought to depend, leaving a reborn Germany as the most powerful nation on the continent. There was no scope for power politics of the traditional kind. Therefore, trying to restore Germany as a law-abiding member of the European system by setting right the injustices of the Versailles settlement was an obvious goal of British foreign policy. This meant sympathy for German unity and allowing a measure of rearmament without stimulating an arms race. To believe in such a programme, there had to be a belief that the wants of the German leaders were limited and ultimately reasonable.

Appeasement or Armageddon?

But there was an even more potent cause of the predisposition to see international relations as a matter of mutual security rather than as a power-struggle. This was a second kind of dilemma—the *defence dilemma*—in which the British government found itself after World War I.[8] The core of this dilemma was the belief, shared by public and government alike, that modern weapons had made war too destructive for Britain to fight, and that a repeat performance would destroy the civilization it was supposed to be defending. It no longer seemed possible for a single country to defend itself, even with superior arms, without unacceptable risks to its own survival. It was for this reason that British politicians, of both the left and the right, embraced the idea of collective security, embodied in the League of Nations. As it happened, the belief that

[8] Ibid. 156 ff.

modern war had become materially and socially too destructive to fight was mistaken, but only just. Only the timing was wrong, for these fears came to fulfilment in the bombing which brought the next war to a close. Nevertheless, the defence dilemma was so acute between the wars that it made it extremely difficult to take an objective view of the real purposes of German rearmament.

The new factor in international relations was aerial bombing, and the principal fear was of a knockout blow which, it was believed, would cause such sudden carnage and disorder that the power of a nation would be destroyed, whatever its forces managed to do in the field. Britain, with its high concentrations of population and industries—especially London, so close to the continent—was thought to be peculiarly vulnerable to this form of warfare. In May and June 1917, German Gotha bombers made raids on Folkestone and London in which, respectively, 95 and 162 people were killed and 195 and 432 people were injured. This sudden slaughter of civilians caused a great deal of panic. It was a terrible shock to the British people and transformed their understanding of their vulnerability in war. Until that time, Britain's war casualties had always been of servicemen in foreign lands or at sea. But now came the disturbing revelation that the British homeland could be directly attacked from the air, no matter how strong the army or navy. These events misled politicians in later years into thinking that truly vast numbers of people would be slaughtered in the opening days of any future war and that disorder and panic would make the country impossible to govern. These beliefs were greatly supported by propaganda from two disparate sources: on the one hand, from those who emphasized the horrors to come because they wanted a complete abolition of aerial bombing. This they hoped to achieve by means of the Geneva Disarmament Conference of 1932–4. On the other hand, there were plenty of dire warnings from the RAF and Air Ministry, which vigorously propagated a theory of airpower as a weapon for winning wars through the destruction of a nation's will to fight. They wanted Britain to maintain a deterrent bomber force superior to that of Germany.

The complete vulnerability of the civilian population appeared to have been demonstrated by the way World War I ended—not by real defeat of Germany on the field of battle, but by revolution at home and consequent collapse of the war effort, leaving its armed forces without the necessary support to continue the fight. It was widely believed that, in modern total war, it was the home front that was the more vulnerable, and therefore the more important as a target. If the bombers could attack it directly, without engaging with other forces, then a way was open to bring an enemy country quickly to its knees. Under bombing, and without the discipline of the armed forces, the civilian population would threaten revolt and the government would be forced to sue for peace. These ideas were much encouraged by the social instability of all European nations following World War I. In Britain especially, the General Strike of 1926 and the great Depression had left a chronic fear among the governing classes of civil strife and the unleashing of revolutionary forces which they believed were held in check only with difficulty even in normal times. There was consequently little faith that civilized society would survive a massive bombing attack. [9] Hence the vulnerability of London to sudden air attack became one of the main factors in the appeasement of Germany throughout the 1930s.

The doomsday quality of any future bombing war was harped upon continually during the inter-war period. As a generally-accepted truth it created a climate in which governments had to be seen to be doing all in their power to avoid war. It would have been politically suicidal to advocate massive rearmament. This was a view shared by many of those in government, including Stanley Baldwin who was expressing a sincere conviction when he said, in a carefully prepared speech on 10 November 1932, 'I think it is as well for the man in the street to realize that no power on earth can protect him from being bombed. Whatever people may tell him, the bomber will always get through.'[10] This view survived the collapse of the Geneva Conference: a large majority of those who answered the 1934–5 Peace Ballot favoured the abolition of military aircraft by international agreement.[11] Baldwin's catch-phrase about the invincibility of the bomber was widely repeated over and over again until the eve of World War II.

Understanding these fears is half-way to understanding appeasement, though it does not amount to justifying it, and there are many other factors to take into account in any satisfactory history of the period. It does not, for instance explain why Hitler's intentions were not recognized at a far earlier stage, when there was already

[9] See Malcolm Smith, *British Air Strategy Between the Wars* (OUP, 1984), 47.
[10] House of Commons Debates, vol. 270, 10 Nov. 1932, col. 632.
[11] Smith, *British Air Strategy*, p. 49.

plenty of evidence for them, and why the available non-military sanctions were not applied before it was too late. It does not explain why the Nazis' murderous conduct towards the Jews did not stop many people in Britain from continuing to think that, for Germany at least, Hitler's rule was beneficial. However, the central place occupied in people's minds by the fear of war was brought out by the immense relief, among people of all classes and most politicians, which greeted Chamberlain's return from Munich. They were profoundly grateful for a statesman who had taken such risks to snatch peace from the jaws of a war which they all believed would begin with a massacre of civilians and probably bring about the end of civilization as they understood it. Such fears were in the forefront of Chamberlain's justification as he wound up the Commons debate on Munich. He spoke of 'people burrowing underground, trying to escape from poison gas, knowing that at any hour of the day or night death or mutilation was ready to come upon them'.[12] It was only after Hitler's invasion of Czechoslovakia and the abandonment by Britain and France of all commitment to that fragile country that the illusion of limited German aims was shattered. And it was only then that appeasement began to acquire in the minds of the majority the wholly negative meaning that it has ever since retained: that of craven retreat before threats and the purchase of peace at others' expense.

There was also a strong moral component to many people's acceptance of the Munich Agreement. Thus, in 1939, the Catholic just-war moralist, Gerald Vann wrote of the predicament in which many Christians found themselves sixteen months after the bombing of Guernica had demonstrated how the next war would be fought:

It may be necessary to judge whether one's country's cause is right or wrong; whether a given war is not bound to produce more evil than that which it seeks to remedy; and therefore whether one can be justified in taking part in it. Those problems are difficult and tragic enough. But they are nothing in comparison with the final tragedy of believing it to be, not only the right, but the duty, of one's country to resort to force, and yet to feel unable to take part in that resort to force because of the methods adopted. That was the problem, that was the only problem, which many felt to be confronting them in September 1938.[13]

   [12] Smith, *British Air Strategy*, p. 215.
   [13] Gerald Vann, *Morality and War* (London: Burns, Oates & Washbourne, 1939), 58.

But there were alternatives to appeasement. Malcolm Smith has argued that there were three ways of dealing with Britain's vulnerability to attack: to develop a bomber strike-force powerful enough to amount to a credible deterrent; to abolish the bomber through international agreement, along with a diplomacy of appeasement; to challenge the theory of the supremacy of offensive air-power directly and to develop instead what is nowadays called strategic defence, using new fighting aircraft and radar.[14] By the mid-1930s, each of them carried great risks in the uncertain environment which was characterized by a great deal of misinformation about the relative armed strength of Britain and Germany, some of it deliberately put out by the Nazis. The situation was made much worse by the fact that Germany's new rulers, although they gave some appearance of playing the traditional diplomatic game, were adept at seizing every concession before it was offered, and were always able to hold the initiative.

For a variety of reasons the first alternative—although it was continually pushed by the Air Staff throughout the 1930s—was ruled out. It was simply not a practical option for Britain to develop a credible deterrent strike force in the 1930s. Besides a public opinion deeply opposed to a renewed arms race, other factors against it were: severe economic constraints which lasted throughout the 1930s owing to the need to recover from the great Depression; the fact that Britain almost certainly did not have the industrial base for such a huge project, which was potentially limitless; and the fact that it would have been perceived as destabilizing at a time when there was a great need for international stability. As Smith points out, 'only massive rearmament, far outstripping that of any European rival, could have offset Britain's relative vulnerability and given her a credible deterrent'.[15] On the political left there was a fear that Britain would become Fascist itself if it was to compete with Fascist countries in that way.

With the collapse of the Geneva Conference in 1934, the ideal of abolition was not obtainable. Hitler's withdrawal of the German delegation on 14 October 1933 had been the end of that hope. However, the failure of the Conference to reach an agreement on bombing is partly the responsibility of the British government, which persistently blocked it because of the economic advantages

[14] Smith, *British Air Strategy*, p. 311.
[15] Ibid. 109.

of using bombers to 'police' outlying parts of the Empire. After the breakdown the next best thing was to build a counterpoise to the German air-force without getting involved in an arms race. The government hoped to persuade the Germans that redress of their grievances would best be pursued by a return to the conference table, on the basis of military equality.[16] For these reasons, instead of trying to outdo them in threats, the British government used air-power as a bargaining counter for the purposes of getting the German leaders to accept parity. But it was not at all clear how such a strategy would be put into operation if the search for agreement should fail. The object of acquiring a limited air-power was still to get rid of it rather than to use it.

So it was a modified version of the second alternative that was practised until at least 1937, when its failure became apparent. It was then realized that parity was an undefinable and unachievable mirage and that Germany had held the initiative all along and had surged ahead of Britain in rearmament, especially in 'front-line' aircraft.

Early in 1938, conscious of the failure of appeasement to prevent German superiority in bombers, and against the deepest wishes of the Air Ministry, the Cabinet made a dramatic switch to the third option. It decided on fighter defence capable of resisting a knock-out blow, accompanied by the threat of a prolonged war of attrition which Germany would have great difficulty winning. It was deterrence of a kind, but a very different kind from that persistently advocated by the Air Ministry and the RAF. There were great risks involved—it was not at all certain at that time that fighter aircraft would be able to stop a knock-out blow. But it did not have the enormous financial and technical difficulties of trying to build a fully effective deterrent bomber force. Nor did the policy carry with it the implications of immorality that were inseparable from the threat to conduct war against civilians by massive bombing. And this was something that counted for a great deal at a time when such moral factors were in the forefront of public debate.

The fact that deterrence by massive retaliation appeared feasible to governments immediately *after* the war, in a way that it had not done before, was largely a result of two new factors which made the

---

[16] Smith, *British Air Strategy*, p. 110.

post-war world a very different place. The first was the demon-strated power of nuclear weapons, which made the acquisition of knock-out power relatively cheap, within the capacity of less-than-superpowers, and unlikely to destroy the economic and social aspects of security in the process of getting it. The second was the division of the world between the military superpowers, rendering Britain's defence parasitic on the United States in several respects. The way was then open to solve the economic problem of building massive deterrent power. The fact that such deterrence appeared openly *permissible* is a direct result of the breakup of the moral consensus that accompanied the bombing campaigns of World War II, as will be discussed in the next chapter. It has not solved, only intensified, the basic dilemmas of defence, and it continues to raise acute questions of a strategic and moral nature, as it did in the 1930s.

The Anti-Soviet Element

Emphasis so far in this account has been on the discontinuity between the pre-war and post-war periods. A more satisfactory account would also take note of some continuities, the most important of which is probably the enduring hostility to the Soviet Union among British politicians of the right, which soon reasserted itself when the forced alliance of the war was over. In the late 1930s Conservative politicians needed to be convinced that Nazi Germany was as brutal as Communist Russia and as much a threat to the *status quo* in Europe. To many, this judgement did not come until the very eve of war. As Alec Douglas-Home (by then the Earl of Home) put it in 1962,

I think the main thing to grasp is that Chamberlain, like many others, saw Communism as the major long-term danger. He hated Hitler and German Fascism, but he felt that Europe in general and Britain in particular were in even greater danger from Communism. Hitler was an evil man but in the short term one should—and one possibly could—do a deal with him, and after that he could be controlled. He didn't realize till too late, you see, that the man was mad and his policy *aimed* at war.[17]

[17] Cited by Margaret George, *The Hollow Men, An Examination of British Foreign Policy Between the Years 1933 and 1939* (London: Leslie Frewin, 1967), 238.

The role that hostility to Communism played in appeasement was probably not—unlike the fear of a bombing war—fundamental to it. It was more like a rationalization of something that was embarrassingly at variance with traditional British policy on the Continent: allowing a single dominant power to arise without challenge. German hegemony was a lesser evil than another war, and was acceptable so long as it could be seen as a 'bulwark against Communism', and so long as it had a natural limit—the unity of Germans in one Reich. As Martin Gilbert points out, anti-Communism came to play an increasingly important part as the dangers and embarrassments of the policy became more apparent:

Nazism added one more argument for appeasement: the need to check Communism. This made a strong impact in Britain. It was the basis of a new lease of life for appeasement, temporarily discredited by Nazi tyranny.

Hitler himself claimed to be acting as the principal guardian of Europe against the spread of Communism. Although the danger of a Communist crusade against capitalist Europe had been averted by the Polish defeat of the Bolshevik armies in 1920, Hitler claimed that the danger was still a serious one. Many Englishmen believed him; and in answer to those who asked how we could possibly side with one tyranny against another, they answered that the evils of Communism were eternal, but that the evils of Nazism would be killed by kindness. Fear of Communism, and the belief in Nazism's ultimate reformation, were powerful new assets to the appeasement argument.[18]

Lord Halifax, who was to become Foreign Secretary in 1938, visited Hitler in November 1937 and told him that:

Although there was much in the Nazi system that offended British opinion (treatment of the church; to perhaps a less extent, the treatment of Jews; treatment of Trade Unions), I was not blind to what he had done for Germany and to the achievement from his point of view in keeping communism out of his country and, as he would feel, of blocking its passage West.[19]

Although anti-Communism was not the main rationale of appeasement, it certainly made it more acceptable in right-wing quarters of British political life. Moreover, Halifax's various diplomatic roles bridge the two periods of British hostility to the

---

[18] Martin Gilbert, *The Roots of Appeasement* (London: Weidenfeld and Nicolson, 1966), 143.
[19] Ibid. 162.

Soviet Union and may indicate a strand of continuity between them. From 1941 until May 1946 he served as British ambassador to Washington. This was just sufficient to cover the period of Churchill's 1946 visit to the USA and his delivery of the 'Iron Curtain' speech at Fulton, in the preparation and reception of which Halifax played an influential part. He attempted, for instance, to pressure Bevin into accepting the main themes of the Churchill speech before they were delivered, in particular the abandonment of all attempts to achieve international control of atomic energy in favour of an exclusive Anglo-American relationship.[20]

Churchill did not differ from other Conservatives in the strength of his anti-Communist convictions, but in his political flexibility and his awareness of mortal danger masquerading as help. He had, in fact, a profound and long-lasting hatred for revolutionary Communism dating from the time of the Russian Revolution itself. In 1919, while Secretary of State for War, and directly responsible for British policy in Russia, he had vigorously campaigned for armed intervention to defeat the Bolsheviks.[21] But at some point between 1933 and 1936, Churchill came to recognize that the immediate threat to British security was not the Soviet Union but Hitler's Germany. Thereafter he and Eden pushed for an anti-Nazi pact with Stalin which was rejected by Chamberlain and the Tory establishment until August 1939, when it was too late, as Stalin had made his own appeasement of Hitler in the German-Soviet Non-Aggression Pact. In 1937, in order to express his deepening gloom about Nazism, Churchill likened it to Communism as 'similar in all essentials'.[22] So the comparison of Soviet Communism with German Nazism, which was later so important in the West as a justification during the Cold War, began life in the reverse order. In a broadcast made in 1941, Churchill began his explanation for his change of attitude to the Soviet Union, then being invaded by Hitler, by declaring that the Nazi regime was indistinguishable from the worst features of Communism.[23] But his flexibility showed itself in his capacity to separate his ideological animosity

[20] See Fraser J. Harbutt, *The Iron Curtain* (New York: OUP, 1987), 171.

[21] Ibid. 10.

[22] Ibid. 32.

[23] Churchill, *The Second World War*, iii. *The Grand Alliance* (London: Cassell, 1950) pp. 331–3.

from his strategic judgements: he realized that Russia's danger, fighting for hearth and home against the invader, was also Britain's, and that a military alliance was at that moment essential. It was at this time that he made his celebrated remark to his secretary that, 'If Hitler invaded Hell, I would at least contrive to make a favourable reference to the Devil in the House of Commons.'

While anti-Soviet attitudes made appeasement of Hitler a more attractive policy in ruling Conservative circles in Britain during the 1930s, the path from there to the Cold War was obviously not a straight one. It was, after all, largely the anti-appeasers who constructed post-war policy towards the Soviet Union. It is not suggested that exactly the same anti-Communist motive lay behind both appeasement and the Cold War—only that long-term hostilities towards the Soviet Union made the appeasement lesson easy to apply in an over-simplified fashion. In the final stages of the war, British politicians—including Churchill—were prepared to deal with the Soviet Union as with any other major power, by diplomacy and concessions, and there was much popular goodwill towards Russia. However, it was not long before the deepest suspicions about Communist intentions in Europe were reactivated. The causes of this reactivation fortunately lie outside the scope of this book. But for those who saw Soviet Communism as a long-term threat to the existence of free democratic states in Europe, there had to be something else erected as a bulwark, now that the main central European power had been destroyed.

One of the paradoxes of the situation is that Stalin too had his 'lesson of appeasement' to learn and apply. The Nazi-Soviet Pact had been an even greater catastrophe than the Munich Agreement. Henceforward it was axiomatic that the Soviet Union should be prepared to fight and win any war forced upon it by Western powers—but never again on its own territory. Soon after the war, both sides were ready, although with very different constellations of forces, to carry an offensive deep into the territory of the other side if another war should come. Where the Soviet Union ended the war with immense ground forces far to the west of its borders, the Western Allies ended it with large, operational bomber forces, soon able to deliver more atomic weapons. The initial openness to the Soviet Union displayed by the new Labour government in Britain gave way reluctantly before the deepening military confrontation. By the time of the Berlin crisis of 1948 Ernest Bevin was seeking a permanent military alliance with the United States and there was a widespread public fear of a new war to come. As the Cold War deepened, there was systematic discouragement of any dissenting views that might have survived the war—though not the outright suppression which occurred, in different ways, in the United States and the Soviet Union. So the lesson, well-learned at bitter cost on both sides, was duly applied in order to construct the bipolar world with its Manichaean division between the forces of light and the forces of darkness. Official propaganda made sure that the dualistic world view eventually penetrated the deepest consciousness of the populace, so as to prepare them for the necessary military measures which were dictated by it, including the deployment of nuclear weapons. The national security state had arrived.

Appeasement then was a much more complex reality than the myth allows, from the point of view of both politics and morals. On the positive side, it recognized the necessity of exploring all means of living together in Europe so as to avoid using weapons of mass destruction on innocent people. On the negative side it was the result not only of military weakness, but also of political weakness in the presence of a state which had given abundant evidence of its willingness to realize its bizarre ambitions by murdering large numbers of unwanted Europeans. The decisive opposition could have been made long before Munich, but hostility towards Communism was a pretext which helped to ensure it was not. The failure of appeasement perhaps shows the dangers of panaceas for preventing war: when people think they have discovered such a thing they tend to ignore the compromises with basic values which have to be made in order to keep it up.

As for the second lesson mentioned at the beginning of this chapter—the perils of isolation—this was learned in the days when Britain was the only Western democracy left fighting Germany and when it came nearer to invasion and defeat than at any time for over a century. The failure of the League of Nations, and with it all hopes of collective security, meant that Britain had to face the dangers of national defence on its own when the awful moment came. Then the emergence of the Soviet Union as the dominating power in Central Europe after 1945, together with the early failure of the hopes invested in the United Nations as a source of collective security, indicated to British politicians—especially Churchill and Bevin—that United States help was a permanent necessity for

Western democracies rather than a temporary stand-by to be called upon only in time of war. To secure it became one of Britain's main security goals as its economic and military weakness became clear. Churchill's ambitions from the outset involved an amalgamation of American power, now to be invested in the atomic bomb, and the world-wide network of British military bases, as the means of ensuring that the West would continue to dominate the post-war world.

The third lesson—the efficacy of strategic bombing in winning World War II—needs a chapter to itself.

3

LESSONS OF THE PAST:
STRATEGIC BOMBING, 1917–1945

Strategic bombing appeared to be the ideal weapon for Britain and the United States after the war. On the one hand it was much more difficult for the democracies than for totalitarian states to keep large armies in existence during peacetime. On the other hand, they much preferred to project their power over long distances and fight wars, if they had to, away from their own territories with relatively small loss of life to themselves. Heavy bombing seemed the most effective way of doing it—a view greatly reinforced by American possession of the atomic bomb and the dramatic conclusion of the war in the Far East.

The development of nuclear deterrence as the chief factor in containing the Soviet Union was in direct continuity with the Western Allies' conduct of the war against Germany and Japan. Nuclear weapons would not have been invented, with such dedication of men and materials, nor would they have been used against Hiroshima and Nagasaki, nor would they subsequently have become the foundation of defence policies, if the moral climate of the appropriate kind had not already existed. This moral climate was created by the theory and practice of strategic bombing designed to destroy civilian life and morale as the way of defeating the enemy in the shortest time.

The Theory: 1917–1939

The theory of civilian bombing preceded the practice by many years. It had been latent in the RAF since its foundation in 1918 and it eventually prevailed over the rival theory of precision bombing against military targets, largely through the unwillingness to develop the means for putting the latter into effect.

In certain military circles the experience of bombing in World War I produced the conviction that this was how wars would be fought in the future and that the only answer Britain had to it was to get its own bomber force as soon as possible. In 1917 and 1918, there seemed to be three possible military solutions to the problem of German bombing: strategic and civil defence, pre-emptive destruction of the German air-force, and deterrence by threat of reprisal. The only one within British military capabilities at the time appeared to be limited reprisals against German towns. 'Reprisals' was in fact a kind of code word for attacks on German towns close to the lines in 1917.[1] The war ended with the newly-formed RAF about to make bombing and gas attacks on Berlin. The idea that the enemy could be deterred from bombing towns by making reprisals had quickly transformed itself into the idea of competitive bombing, with the victory going to the side which could inflict the most damage and for the longest period. By 1918, any ideas of deterrence had passed into a determination to procede with the war by attacking civilians. Sir Henry Wilson, British Military Representative, Supreme War Council, said on 17 January 1918:

The policy intended to be followed is to attack the important German towns systematically . . . It is intended to concentrate on one town for successive days and then to pass to several other towns, returning to the first town until the target is thoroughly destroyed, or at any rate, until the morale of workmen is so shaken that output is seriously interfered with . . . Long-distance bombing will produce its maximum moral effect only if the visits are constantly repeated at short intervals so as to produce in each area bombed a sustained anxiety.[2]

The leading advocate of this policy was Major-General Hugh Trenchard, who was to become the first Chief of Air Staff of the Royal Air Force, which was formed in 1918 from an amalgamation of the Army and Navy air arms. From a very early stage, as shown by his diary entries and dispatches of 1918, Trenchard was dedicated to the idea that the chief value of aerial bombardment was the destruction of civilian morale. He thought it stood to the material effect in a proportion of 20 to 1, and should therefore be the main purpose of the bombing effort.[3] A devastating bombing attack might defeat a country whose civilian population were less

[1] George Quester, *Deterrence Before Hiroshima* (New York: John Wiley & Sons, 1966), 39.

[2] Cited by Gerald Vann, *Morality and War* (London: Burns, Oates & Washbourne, 1939), 48.

[3] H. Montgomery Hyde, *British Air Policy Between the Wars, 1918–1939* (London: Heinemann, 1976), p. 45.

able than the British to 'take it'. While the two other services
continued to maintain, until far into World War II, that an air force
was best employed in giving tactical bombing support in land and
sea battles, Trenchard and his Air Staff maintained very forcefully
that, on the contrary, a future European war would be fought by
direct attacks on enemy cities well beyond the range of other forces.
They maintained in other words, that bombing power was a war-
winning weapon in its own right—hence the designation 'strategic'.
On this concept depended the claim of the RAF to independent
existence—something that had to be fought for throughout the
inter-war years.[4] In Trenchard's mind, strategic bombing was not
merely a new weapon, but an entirely new way of fighting wars,
which was virtually a new concept of war altogether. He summed it
up by saying that it was not the enemy forces that were to be
defeated, but the enemy *nation*.[5]

The aim of destroying civilian morale was not entirely without a
moral purpose: bombing behind the lines was seen as a way of
bringing a war to a quick end and avoiding the carnage of the
trenches. As to the sensitive moral question about civilian casualties: in the opinion of the Air Staff, the 'moral' effect would be more
important than the physical damage and 'in any case' they asked,
'was not this method of warfare more humane than one which
produced starvation or at least malnutrition in the civilian
population by blockade and condemned the youth of all countries
to mass slaughter on the battlefields?'[6] Such was the standard
response to criticisms from the other two services. All wars had
started with the desire and expectation of a rapid victory. Here at
last was a method by which this might be achieved.

The doctrine of the supreme efficacy of strategic bombing was
bolstered by the general belief—strongly propagated by
Trenchard—that there was no reliable defence against the bomber
and that an air force was essentially an offensive force, not a
defensive one.[7] For this reason, the Air Staff continuously played

---

[4] Charles Webster and Noble Frankland, *The Strategic Air Offensive Against
Germany* (London: HMSO, 1961), i. 38.

[5] Hyde, *British Air Policy*, 137, 224.

[6] Webster and Frankland, *Strategic Air Offensive*, i. p. 51, and Noble
Frankland, *The Bombing Offensive Against Germany* (London: Faber and Faber,
1965), 23–5: 'The idea of strategic bombing . . . had its roots in history, in naval
history' (i.e. the naval blockade against civilian supplies).

[7] Webster and Frankland, *Strategic Air Offensive*, i. 62.

down the role of aerial defence and always demanded a high proportion of bombers to fighters. The ratio demanded by the RAF remained as high as 2 to 1 as late as 1938.[8]

The RAF naturally repudiated the stigma that they were in business to bomb women and children, but they themselves are partly to blame for this widespread opinion during the inter-war years. They frequently made alarming and wildly exaggerated predictions about the number of casualties to be expected in the first few weeks of war: 600,000 dead and 1,200,000 injured in the first sixty days, so they said in 1937. Such calculations were based on extrapolation from the Gotha raids and assumed, from these rather freakish examples, that every ton of bombs would cause 50 casualties.[9] The civilian defence committees agreed. They expected that the British people would become so panic-stricken that there would have to be special measures to maintain order.[10] The general opinion throughout the pre-war period, shared well beyond the RAF, was that defence against the bomber was impossible.

The Baldwin speech already mentioned was indicative of a general unwillingness at that time to think about how a future war could be fought. It was easier to dwell rhetorically on its awful effects for the sake of whatever cause one was pursuing, whether it was getting more bombers or abolishing bombers altogether. Such dire predictions had ambivalent effects: they strengthened the case for more bombers as a deterrent to suprise attack, but they also immensely strengthened the peace movement of the time. Trenchard's insistence that the country should prepare, during peacetime, to win a city-bombing war ran up against the powerful anti-war feeling which affected the vast majority of people in Britain during the 1920s and 1930s. Many thoughtful people drew the conclusion that modern weapons were simply too destructive to use in the cause of justice.[11] Through no fault of their own they were not wholly right about this at the time, but what they said was prophetic of what was to come before the next war was over. Thus bombing threats proved to be self-deterring during this period, partly because of the casualty predictions and partly because

[8] Hyde, *British Air Policy*, p. 444.
[9] For the causes of the exaggerations, see A. J. P. Taylor, *English History 1914–1945* (Harmondsworth: Penguin, 1979), 504, 535.
[10] Webster and Frankland, *Strategic Air Offensive*, i. 45.
[11] See the discussion of Vann's views in the chapter on just war.

Britain did not have sufficient confidence that it could match German bombing performances if war came. Hitler exploited British fears to invade Czechoslovakia with impunity. His was a policy of deterrence by bluff which eventually overreached itself and led to war.[12]

Did the RAF really intend to bomb civilians in the event of another war? A belief that a victory could be won through the collapse of civilian morale does not amount to an actual plan to destroy them directly. All that can be said is that Trenchard and his staff were ambiguous about it. As Malcolm Smith points out:

Though in the 1930s civilian morale was to be rejected by the Air Staff as a target in its own right, the speed with which it reappeared once war broke out implies that the importance of the supposed vulnerability of civilian morale remained a powerful underlying assumption in Air Staff minds. Given the prevailing attitudes towards war in the 1920s and 1930s, to have advocated unashamedly a policy of terror bombing would have been a form of political kamikaze on the part of the Air Staff. This aspect of their thinking was therefore played down; they preferred to concentrate on the argument that air power would shorten the war of the future.[13]

The imprecision of their intentions had a direct outcome in the imprecision of the bombing in World War II. The most important evidence for the RAF's intentions lies in the almost total neglect of techniques for precision bombing which would have been necessary if their targeting plans were to be put into effect. Although after the end of World War I at least, the Air Staff seems never to have stated outright that civilians would be indiscriminately attacked, the assumption that they would be was implicit in their concentration on achieving maximum bomb-loads and their failure to develop adequate navigation and bomb-aiming techniques. Early success at the latter by the Royal Naval Air Service was forgotten by the RAF.[14] When, after World War II the RAF was in need of a public explanation for its rapid resort to area bombing, it maintained that precision bombing had always been impractical because of the crudeness of navigation and aiming. But there had been no insistence that these things should be developed. As Webster and Frankland report:

[12] See Quester, *Deterrence Before Hiroshima*, pp. 96, 100, 104.
[13] Malcolm Smith, *British Air Strategy Between the Wars* (OUP, 1984), 63.
[14] Neville Jones, *The Origins of Strategic Bombing* (London: William Kimber, 1973), cited by Geoffrey Best, *Humanity in Warfare* (London: Methuen, 1980), 266.

Before the war, the navigational means by which bombers would find their targets were hardly ever tested in practice and scarcely even considered in theory. The aiming methods by which bombs could find their targets was studied in an inadequate and unnecessarily unrealistic manner.[15]

No priority and very little material assistance was given to the Committee for the Scientific Survey of Air Offence, chaired by Henry Tizard. He later complained that Britain began World War II 'with the most inadequate bombs, with rudimentary ideas of accurate bombing under conditions of war, with little, if any experience of flying in a "Black-out" '.[16]

The fact is, not that the RAF—any more than the Luftwaffe— made a definite choice for area bombing as opposed to precision bombing, but that *no choice was made because no choice was thought necessary*. They were not sufficiently interested in the distinction. This can only be explained by supposing that the collapse of civilian life remained the chief strategic goal of bombardment. No great accuracy would be needed to bring it about. The targets worked out before the war were only notionally precise, merely lists of enemy resources that the Air Staff hoped to put out of action.[17] It was tacitly accepted that the destruction of civilian life and property around the factories, oil-plants and depots that were to be bombed would be the most valuable result. The true nature of this purpose was obscured during the inter-war years—as it continued to be obscured throughout World War II itself—by the use of the indefinitely expandable notion of 'military objective'.

The Moral Background

There is no doubt that the general opinion during the inter-war years was that civilian bombing was immoral and against international law. In 1928, Trenchard defended the legality of his overall strategy in the face of General Staff criticism. In a memorandum on 'The War Object of an Air Force', he described bombing objectives as war-factories, depots, docks and 'in general the means of communication and transportation of military personel and material'. But he then went on to point out that such objectives were often situated in the centres of population and that

---

[15] Webster and Frankland, *Strategic Air Offensive*, iii. 297.
[16] Hyde, *British Air Policy*, p. 385.
[17] Ibid. 466 for such lists.

the resulting casualties ('moral effect') was an inevitable, and legitimate result of a lawful operation of war—the bombing of military objectives.[18] However, in the opinion of the other Chiefs of Staff, this argument was disingenuous, nothing but a rationalization of the real objective: to win the war by direct attacks on civilians. Such attacks could only be justified according to the law of reprisal—strictly limited retaliatory action intended to get the enemy to comply with the law. They said it would be against the accepted principle of international law and 'against our national interest to adopt it' as a policy.

There is no doubt that the open advocacy of the practice of bombing civilians would have transgressed moral limits which were widely accepted among the general public and in government and military circles. There was universal horror and indignation at the German three-hour 'experimental' bombing raid on the defenceless town of Guernica on 26 April 1937. It is widely remembered as the moment when the age-old prohibition was broken and deliberate massacre of civilians became a routine method of war. But the general consensus that the practice was contrary to morality and law went hand in hand with an equally general reluctance to think about the question of restraints. The obverse of the RAF's disinclination to distinguish precision from area bombing—so making an early resort to the latter inevitable—was the public's distaste for measures which would merely make war more 'civilized', when the important thing was to abolish it altogether. This may explain the fact that more hopes were invested in the Geneva Disarmament Conference (1932–4), which tried to ban aerial warfare completely, than in the Hague Draft Rules for Aerial Warfare (1923), which were designed to set legal limits to its scope. The latter were never adopted by states in legally-binding form. However, these rules were frequently recognized as embodying a common moral inheritance, and several states announced that they would comply with them.[19]

The substance of the rules was clearly accepted by the British government on the eve of World War II. On 21 June 1938, Neville Chamberlain enunciated in the House of Commons three fundamental principles of international law applicable to warfare from

---

[18] Ibid. 223 f.
[19] See Adam Roberts and Richard Guelff, *Documents on the Laws of War* (OUP, 1982), 122.

the air, stating that Britain would abide by them: (1) direct attack against the civilian population is unlawful; (2) targets for air bombardment must be legitimate, indentifiable military objectives; (3) reasonable care must be taken in attacking military objectives to avoid bombardment of the civilian population in the neighbour-hood.[20] A year later, the Archbishop of Canterbury obtained from the Secretary of State for Air, Sir Kingsley Wood, the statement that the government accepted the declaration of the League of Nations in 1928, that 'The intentional bombing of civilian populations is illegal.'[21] On 1 September 1939, President Roosevelt appealed to both sides in the coming war not to bomb 'civilian populations or unfortified cities', upon the understanding that the enemy did likewise. The British government accepted this restriction the same day (as did the German government seventeen days later), and the next day issued a statement declaring that Britain and France 'had indeed some time before sent explicit instructions to the commanders of their armed forces prohibiting the bombard-ment . . . of any except strictly military objectives in the narrowest sense of the word'. Neverthless, the 'right' of reprisal was retained explicitly.

That was an important reservation. A paper from the Chiefs of Staff during October 1939 pointed out that the planned British attack on the Ruhr, which was bound to kill many civilians around the industrial targets, *would have to be justified by some previous German behaviour of a similar kind*, such as the unrestricted bombing of France or Britain or the infliction of numerous casualties during an invasion of Belgium'.[22] In other words, a pretext would have to be found for putting into action the chosen plan of war because it was a prima-facie violation of international morality. The first bombing campaigns against cities were deliber-ately planned 'reprisals'. The same appears to have been true of the Luftwaffe's plans in 1938.[23]

[20] Roberts and Guelff, *Documents on the Laws of War*, p. 122.

[21] Alan Wilkinson, *Dissent or Conform? War, Peace and the English Churches 1900–1945* (London: SCM Press, 1986), 266.

[22] Webster and Frankland, *Strategic Air Offensive*, i. 137.

[23] Barrie Paskins and Michael Dockrill, *The Ethics of War* (London: Duckworth, 1979), 17.

The Practice: 1939–1945

The story of the abandonment of bombing restraints and the transition to deliberate attacks on civilian areas during World War II has frequently been told, and there is no need to give a full account of it here.[24] There were three main periods. It was during the first, up to November 1941, that the moral and prudential barriers to terror bombing were effectively breached on both sides, even though the official policy remained that of precise attacks on military targets. It represented a breakdown of deterrence with regard to this method of fighting.

Both sides began the war hoping for restraints: Hitler because he feared the effects of reprisals on German morale, the RAF because it had little confidence in its ability to respond in kind to the threats previously made by the German leaders. However, when the war began in earnest in the spring of 1940, bombing restrictions were quickly abandoned in a chain reaction of retaliations which was not entirely undesired. At the same time, none of the dire predictions of huge slaughter and immediate social collapse were fulfilled. Strategic bombing turned out to be evil enough, but not the decisive knock-out blow that many had feared or hoped for. It soon became another sort of war by attrition, with great losses to bomber crews, but for the most part it strengthened, rather than weakened, the morale of the civilians on the receiving end.

There were several reasons for this failure of expectations. In the first place, it turned out to be a complete fallacy that the bomber would always get through. Both sides greatly underestimated the effectiveness of strategic defence: fast interceptor aircraft assisted by the newly-invented radar early-warning system. The daylight raids in September and December 1939 with which the RAF opened its offensive were disastrous for the bombers, with little damage being done and nearly 20 per cent of the planes being lost. It was this experience which forced Bomber Command to convert its machines to a night bombing force, for which they were ill-designed.[25] Secondly, Bomber Command was for some time almost completely incapable of finding its target areas, let alone the actual

---

[24] Apart from Webster and Frankland's official history in three volumes, the best short account is that of Quester, *Deterrence Before Hiroshima*. See also, Max Hastings, *Bomber Command* (London: Pan Books, 1981).

[25] Martin Middlebrook, *The Battle of Hamburg* (Harmondsworth: Penguin 1980), 20, and Webster and Frankland, *Strategic Air Offensive*, 297–300.

targets, or of aiming its bombs accurately in the night raids which were forced upon it. The extent of the inaccuracy was not appreciated at the time. When, in May 1940, Churchill sanctioned attacks on German industrial centres by night, the targets were still notionally precise: marshalling yards and oil-plants in the Ruhr.

The reasons for the breakdown of bombing restraints may be summarized:[26] (1) The inaccuracies of navigation and bombardment by night obliterated any difference between precision and terror bombing so that the civilian casualties were easily attributed to the latter and reprisals demanded; (2) Churchill, by ordering attacks on Berlin in August 1940, deliberately provoked German reprisal raids on London in order to draw their fire away from Fighter Command bases, which were beginning to collapse under the strain; (3) the fact that the loss of civilian lives was not nearly so great as predicted and that the effect on morale was *absolutely* less than it had been in the raids of World War I, despite the far heavier tonnage of bombs dropped, meant that Britain ceased to be deterred by the prospect of the destruction of its cities.

These factors led to a decisive change in the climate of opinion in Britain towards the end of 1940. As a result of the Luftwaffe's raids on London, Coventry, and other British cities following the attack on Berlin in August 1940, it appeared that Germany was now bombing civilians as a matter of policy and it was felt that Britain could, and should pay Germany back with the only effective weapon left: the bomber force. Meanwhile there was a parallel shift of policy taking place within the Air Ministry. In June 1940, Air Marshal Sir Charles Portal, Chief of Bomber Command, was told that 'in no circumstances should night-bombing be allowed to degenerate into mere indiscriminate action, which is contrary to the policy of His Majesty's Government'.[27] The Air Ministry apparently still believed that precision bombing could be effective at night. However, a Bomber Command memorandum of 30 September shows that they were canvassing the idea of diverting the attack from the enemy's means to fight to the 'will of the German people to continue the war'.[28] They were pressing—in common with Churchill at that time—for counter-city attacks. Meanwhile, it was

[26] The summary largely follows Quester's account, *Deterrence Before Hiroshima*, pp. 105 ff.
[27] Webster and Frankland, *Strategic Air Offensive*, i. 145.
[28] Ibid. 154.

becoming clear that any night-bombing was going to involve large numbers of civilian casualties, whatever the intentions. As Webster and Frankland report it, Portal 'now believed that this by-product should become the end product'. He believed that the time had come to launch a direct attack on the German people themselves, and that this would be justified by previous German action. By October 1940, the Battle of Britain having been won by Fighter Command, the time had come for an offensive against the morale of the German people:

It was suggested that twenty to thirty German towns should be selected, taking into account their size and the importance of the objectives they contained, and that one of these should be attacked by fifty to one hundred bombers every few nights. Thus, what had so recently been no more than a suggestion from Bomber Command, now became Air Staff policy.[29]

This policy had the wholehearted support of Churchill, although his views about the efficacy of bombing remained notoriously changeable throughout the war. On 30 October, the War Cabinet agreed that the 'civilian population around the target areas must be made to feel the weight of the war'.[30] In January 1941 the Chiefs of Staff were in favour of the Oil Plan, reckoned by many advisers throughout the war as the best way of crippling Germany's war effort. But Churchill at this time was for attacking towns as such. He pointed out that the oil-plants were for the most part far removed from the centres of population.[31]

In the light of these events, it is necessary to challenge the judgement of Webster and Frankland that night-time civilian bombing was 'operationally inevitable',[32] if by that it is meant that it was forced upon a reluctant RAF by circumstances wholly beyond its control. Not only were they uninterested in the alternatives at any period before or during the war, but Britain had a positive strategic interest in expanding the scope of the war at a certain stage to include civilian targets.

Precision bombing continued to be tried until July 1941, mainly against oil-plants, but by that time it had become clear that they were 'not tactically vulnerable' with current bombing techniques.

[29] Ibid. 156.
[30] Taylor, *English History 1914–1945*, p. 630.
[31] Webster and Frankland, *Strategic Air Offensive*, i. 161.
[32] Ibid. iii. 300.

There was as yet no capacity for the massive attacks on cities that were being demanded by Lord Trenchard from his retirement. An independent report (the Butt Report) in August 1941 showed that night-bombing had been hopelessly inaccurate. One third of the aircraft did not attack their target areas at all and of those which did only one third got within five miles of it.[33] This caused Churchill to express grave doubts about the usefulness of bombing cities.

The second period of bombing was from February 1942 to mid–1943, when restraints were officially abandoned and there was deliberate adoption of an anti-city policy for beating Germany. Massive attacks on German civilian life became Britain's chosen method of fighting. On 14 February 1942, a directive from the Air Ministry ordering a resumption of bombing after the pause provoked by the Butt Report, stated that the 'primary object of operations should now be focused on the morale of the enemy civilian population and, in particular, of the industrial workers'.[34] Lord Portal, now Chief of Air Staff, made the meaning of this unambiguously clear:

Ref the new bombing directive: I suppose it is clear that points are to be built-up areas, *not*, for instance, the dock-yards or aircraft factories where these are mentioned in Appendix A of the directive. This must be made quite clear if it is not already understood.[35]

This new policy—vigorously pursued by Sir Arthur Harris, the new C.-in-C. of Bomber Command—came to be known as 'area bombing'. To some extent it was still a case of making a vice out of a necessity, i.e. willingly accepting the consequences of being unable to do anything else. But by 1943, when the most massive indiscriminate attacks were being made on Hamburg, precision bombing was becoming a real possibility (practised by the USAAF) and the strategic priority of certain targets such as oil-plants was well understood. However, Harris, with the tacit agreement of many in power, including Churchill, and with much popular support in the country, was ill-disposed to consider the alternatives. He had always adhered to the pure Trenchard doctrine that massive

[33] Hastings, *Bomber Command*, p. 127.
[34] Ibid. i. 232.
[35] Ibid. 324.

and repeated attacks on cities was to be the decisive war-winning strategy.

As Webster and Frankland show, area bombing was not merely the *idée fixe* of Bomber Command executed in the teeth of political opposition and moral revulsion. Some of the leading members of the war administration were behind it, including—rather erratically—Churchill. A notorious memorandum from Churchill's close friend and Principal Scientific Adviser, Lord Cherwell, on 30 March 1942, rationalized area bombing by stating that the only way to win the war was to demoralize the German workers by 'de-housing' them—as if this could be done without killing a very large number of innocent people.[36] And in April of that year, the Foreign Secretary Anthony Eden, wrote to Sir Archibald Sinclair, the Secretary of State for Air, that the bombing should be extended to smaller towns in Germany of under 150,000 inhabitants which were not too heavily defended, even though they contained targets of only secondary importance. The important thing would be the 'psychological effects' of the bombing.[37]

In January 1943, the meeting of the Allied war-leaders at Casablanca ordered the attack on German military and industrial production—and on civilian morale—as the West's contribution to the defeat of Germany, in lieu of opening a second front, for which they were not ready. Harris took the second part of the directive to be a sanctioning of his methods, while the American Air Force—which had never abandoned its attempts at daylight precision bombing, concentrated on the first part with increasing success.

The climax of the 1943 campaign was the Battle of Hamburg, at the centre of which were four major night raids by the RAF and two day raids by the USAAF between 24 July and 3 August. In the words of the Bomber Command Operation Order of 27 May, written by Harris, the purpose of the raids would be 'the total destruction of the city'.[38] As to the method of bombing, the RAF was by this time relying on the phenomenon of 'creep-back'—the natural tendency for the bomb aimers to release their bombs just short of the target—to spread the destruction backwards from the marked aiming point in a 'carpet' across a large residential area of

[36] Ibid. i. 324.
[37] Ibid. iii. 115.
[38] Middlebrook, *The Battle of Hamburg*, p. 95.

the city.[39] The terrible and unexpected climax of the 'battle' was the fire-storm on the night of 17–18 July during which some 44,000 civilians were burned or suffocated to death. Less than 1 per cent of the total death toll was caused by the two American raids which followed the usual practice of precise targeting by day. Relatively little direct damage was done to Hamburg's war industries such as the U-boat yards. The main disruption to life in the city was caused, with intent, by the RAF's 'indirect method', which aimed at the workers themselves.

Hence the RAF proceeded to the third period, from mid-1943 to May 1945: a period of unrestrained bombing which was intended to destroy the heart of as many German cities as possible, in order to bring about total defeat and unconditional surrender.[40] The element of sheer revenge was by now of great importance to the offensive behaviour of both sides. Hitler's response to the destruction of his cities was the bombardment of Britain with the indiscriminate 'Revenge' weapons, the V 1 and V 2 missiles. This so enraged the British, and especially Churchill, that in mid-1944, the latter wanted to respond with chemical attacks on German towns, and probably would have done so if the military had not argued against it on tactical grounds.[41]

The fact that deterrence broke down in the case of civilian bombing but appeared to hold in the case of chemical and bacteriological weapons needs some attempt at explanation. The chief difference between the two methods of warfare is that aerial bombing always had the notional possibility of being precise and discriminate, whereas the other two methods did not. Bombing could be understood as a militarily effective weapon with many different functions, tactical and strategic, whereas chemical and bacteriological attacks would be so uncertain in their effects over space and time that the disadvantages of using them outweighed any military effectiveness they might have had. They might be just as damaging to the attacking side or they might render the conquered land uninhabitable for a very long time. Virtually the only rationale (if that is the right word) which would be attached to their use is that

[39] Middlebrook, *The Battle of Hamburg*, p. 99–100, 283, 301.

[40] As Webster and Frankland point out, it was less 'economical' to try to destroy factories, let alone machinery, scattered in the suburbs of towns than to destroy the town centres, which were areas of congested residential property. *Strategic Air Offensive*, ii. 122.

[41] Robert Harris and Jeremy Paxman, *A Higher Form of Killing* (London: Triad/ Grenada, 1983), 134.

of revenge. Certainly, fear of retaliation was an important factor in the non-use of chemical weapons in 1944—a fear which fed on memories of the gas war in 1914–18. However, this was something which applied to the use of any weapons of mass destruction and in each case it had to be balanced against military usefulness.[42] Both Britain and the United States made sure that chemical and bacteriological weapons were ready for use if the moment came to use them. The military is always willing to forgo the use of inhumane weapons which are in any case not much use for obtaining military objectives, but it is a different matter with weapons which have proved themselves to be useful.[43]

The continued disregard for bombing restraints, even after precision bombing had become a real possibility and when Britain was in no immediate danger, can only be explained as a convergence of the Trenchard–Harris doctrine of the moral purpose of bombing with the growing desire for retribution which affected government, Parliament, and the public generally. The RAF's chosen method of fighting, worked out long before the war began, coincided with the prevailing mood of the nation, so sharply different from what it had been in 1939. Harris was enabled to continue with his massive anti-city bombing campaigns, even when there was serious doubt in the government that any use was being served by them, by widespread public support and satisfaction that Germany was being hit hard where it hurt most. Bombing was more important on account of what it did to boost British morale than on account of what it did to undermine the German morale or war effort, even though this is what the RAF believed was happening.[44] World War II showed that, for a nation to remain in the fight, it was necessary to have some means of hitting back at the

[42] Nuclear weapons exist uneasily between the two categories and there have been continual efforts to make them appear as militarily useful weapons while at the same time stressing their end-of-the-world consequences. The bombs dropped on Hiroshima and Nagasaki were, after all, 'useful'. Contemporary claims for the necessity of tactical nuclear weapons in Europe depend on this ambiguity. See Chapter 9.

[43] For instance, the reason why the British delegation at the Geneva Disarmament Conference was never allowed by its government to accept a total prohibition of aerial bombing was that the practice was far too useful as police bombing when pacifying outlying regions of the empire, such as Iraq and Aden. See the sarcastic account of the episode in the memoirs of Anthony Eden, *Facing The Dictators* (London: Cassell, 1962), 42.

[44] The controversy about its true effectiveness continued for a long time after the war. For a defence, see Frankland, *The Bombing Offensive*. For a critique, see Middlebrook, *The Battle of Hamburg*, p. 336.

enemy *and* to believe that this was just retaliation for past atrocities. It was possible to put up with almost any amount of collective suffering if the enemy was believed to be deservedly suffering even worse. The reflexive function of bombing was of extreme importance, and it continues to be an important part of the psychological climate which sustains nuclear deterrence.

The use of the term 'moral', as in the 'moral effects of bombing', appears to have been a British peculiarity, not used by its allies. It refers essentially to strength of will in combat. It is part of an ethos which values the competitive virtues very highly, as in the British imperial respect for moral fibre. In this ethos, a person's moral character is formed and tested more by what he suffers under attack than by what he does to others. Of course, it does not make the British character any more vengeful than the German or the American, but it does perhaps make it more difficult to think straight about what really matters in morality. Interestingly, an extensive analysis of British morale in relation to morals, compared with those of other nations, was published in the midst of the bombing war by one J. T. MacCurdy, a lecturer in Psychopathology at Cambridge.[45] The book was developed from a series of lectures given to army officers from 1940 to 1942. The author was a firm believer in the superior capacity of the British to 'take it', and he connected this with a variety of moral attributes, including a missionary zeal for universal values spread by means of the Empire, as opposed to the merely tribal beliefs and worship of force shown by the Germans. He predicted that the war would end after a moral collapse of the overdriven and deprived German civilians under British bombing, before the German armies had been broken. Since German ambitions were 'materialistic', i.e. territorial, they would not have the stamina to fight on once this territory was lost, as would the British, who had more transcendent values to defend. The basis of the theory was cultural and historical, not racial.

The final phase of the bombing lasted from November 1944 to May 1945 with Bomber Command at its maximum strength and German defences almost entirely ruined, giving the Allies command of German airspace. By this time, the bombing was certainly having a big effect on the German people's will to fight, largely because the means to strike back had been lost. The United States 8th Air Force

---

[45] *The Structure of Morale* (CUP, 1943).

had also resorted to area bombing by 1945, even though officially it maintained its continued moral opposition to it. From 13 to 15 February 1945 Bomber Command and the 8th Air Force together destroyed Dresden in three massive waves of fire-bombing, killing from 30,000 to 100,000 people. This time the fire-storm was intentional and the city centre, with its population swollen to twice the normal by refugees, was the deliberate target. The action caused immediate revulsion and intense controversy in Britain and the United States and official attempts were made in Britain to disguise the fact that the target had been the people in the city as such. Although they were originally briefed to attack the city centre because it was packed with refugees, on returning from the raid the bomber crews were 're-briefed', for the sake of a Ministry of Information film, to aim at the rail junction east of the city because the city centre was 'full of women and children'.[46]

The US Air Force officially abandoned precision for area targets in the war against Japan, in the first two weeks of 1945, when the decision was made by General Curtis Le May to destroy Tokyo with incendiary bombs. On 10 May a massive low-level attack was made in which 2,000 tons of bombs were dropped creating fire-storms which destroyed 40 per cent of the city in three hours, killing some 125,000 people.[47] Other massive attacks were made on Tokyo and other cities during May and June with the deliberate intention of destroying organized civilian life. It seems that the long-desired goal of strategic bombing—that the civilians should turn against the military and demand an end of the war—did begin to occur in Japan as a result of the American bombing. But it was only when Japanese control of their airspace had been lost, and with it any means of striking back. The job was finished off by the atomic destruction of Hiroshima and Nagasaki, cities which had not previously been severely bombed. The aim of the attacks was to destroy the cities completely, with their inhabitants, in order to shock the Japanese into surrendering unconditionally.

The Official Version

Despite popular knowledge and approval of the real purpose of the

[46] Andrew Wilson, *Observer*, 10 Feb. 1985.
[47] Peter Calvacoressi and Guy Wint, *Total War* (Harmondsworth: Penguin, 1972), 853.

bombing campaigns against Germany, the British government practised a great deal of dissimulation throughout the entire course of the war. The chief purpose of it seems to have been to protect the morale of the bomber crews. At the outbreak of war in August 1939, the instructions issued to Bomber Command accurately reflected the principles enunciated by Chamberlain (see above, p. 54). The instructions defined 'military objectives' very narrowly, so as to exclude civilians who worked assembling tanks in a factory. Sir John Slessor who was to be Chief of Air Staff in 1952, and who was largely responsible for formulating Britain's first nuclear deterrence policy in the Global Strategy Paper of that year, remarks that drafting the rules in 1938–9,

was all an unhappy, tedious and really rather meaningless business . . . In reality, speaking for myself (and I think for the rest of the Air Staff), I regarded it all as a matter not of legality but of expediency . . . We should no doubt have taken a different line if we have believed that, in the near future and with our existing equipment, we could have achieved anything like the decisive results from an unlimited offensive—either to succour our allies or to protect ourselves.[48]

By October 1942, the rules issued to the RAF had been revised to exclude German, Italian, and Japanese territory from the prohibition on civilian bombing 'consequent upon the enemy's adoption of a campaign of unrestricted air warfare'.[49] The pretext of reprisal appears again to have been a powerful facilitating factor in allowing the RAF to do what it had always planned to do, though its acts were, strictly speaking, against the moral and legal norms of the time. However, official answers to awkward questions from important people, both in and out of Parliament, continued throughout the war to repeat that Bomber Command aimed exclusively at 'military' targets—mainly the industrial base of Germany's war effort.[50] The popular press and the radio—both controlled by the government during the war—greatly assisted in propagating the deceitful message that it was Germany's industrial areas that were being aimed at, when, from 1942 onwards it was largely city-centres and densely populated residential areas which rarely contained any industry.[51] On the other hand, the British

---

[48] John Slessor, *The Central Blue* (London: Cassell, 1956), 214.

[49] Hastings, *Bomber Command*, p. 201.

[50] See House of Commons Official Report, 31 Mar. 1943, vol. 338, col. 155, and 1 Dec. 1943, vol. 395, vol. 337–8.

[51] Middlebrook, *The Battle of Hamburg*, p. 344.

public were not particularly sorry that a large number of German civilians were being killed in the process of bringing Germany to her knees. It was generally thought to be well deserved punishment. In parliamentary exchanges, the feelings of both houses were predominantly on the government side and against the making of moral distinctions that might impede the work of flattening German cities and winning the war as quickly as possible. It is clear that those who protested on grounds of just-war morality and international law—such as Bishop George Bell and Richard Stokes MP—were members of a tiny, persistent, and unpopular minority.

The declaratory policy voiced by government spokesmen was sometimes simple lying but more often failure to tell the whole truth by taking advantage of the ambiguities of 'military objectives'. For practical purposes this concept could be expanded to cover any objectives which needed to be destroyed in order to bring the war to a satisfactory conclusion, from a military point of view. When the only satisfactory conclusion was believed to be unconditional surrender, there was in principle no limit to what might be described as a 'military objective'. But when used in replies to those invoking traditional moral restraints, the phrase could still be understood in its narrow sense of 'objectives of a military nature or, at most, contributing directly to the prosecution of the war'. According to the account of Webster and Franklin, Sir Archibald Sinclair, Secretary of State for Air,

usually and, on public occasions, invariably, suggested that Bomber Command was aiming at military or industrial installations as, of course, it sometimes was. He did not conceal that severe and sometimes vast damage was done to residential areas but he either implied, or on occasions said, that all this was incidental and even regrettable. Only in this way, he explained to Sir Charles Portal in October 1943, could he satisfy the inquiries of the Archbishop of Canterbury, the Moderator of the Church of Scotland and other significant religious leaders whose moral condemnation of the bombing offensive might, he observed, disturb the morale of Bomber Command crews. This latter consideration was, the Secretary of State thought, more important than another which Sir Arthur Harris had raised, namely, that the Bomber Command crews might form an impression that they were being asked to perform deeds which the Air Ministry was ashamed to admit. [52]

---

[52] Webster and Frankland, *Strategic Air Offensive*, iii. 116. The policy seems to have had a remarkable success in the Archbishop of Canterbury, William Temple,

Indeed, the official dissimulation did not please Sir Arthur Harris who, in October 1943, wrote to the Air Ministry requesting that, 'the aim of the combined Bomber Command Offensive . . . should be unambiguously stated as the destruction of German cities, the killing of German workers and the disruption of civilized life throughout Germany'.[53] The Air Ministry replied that the current operational directive to Bomber Command, which included as a primary objective 'the undermining of the morale of the German people to the point where their capacity for armed resistance is fatally weakened . . . neither requires nor enjoins direct attacks on German civilians *as such*'. Harris thought this duplicity unnecessary and observed that it was not his policy to attack children, invalids, and old people since they were a handicap to the German war effort:

This however, does not imply, as the Air Minstry seems to assume that it does, that *no* German civilians are proper objects for bombing. The German economic system, which I am instructed in my directive to destroy, *includes* workers' houses and public utilities, and it is therefore meaningless to claim that the wiping out of German cities is 'not an end in itself but the inevitable accompaniment of all-out attack on the enemy's means and capacity to wage war'.

The Air Ministry's response revealed its need for a moral face:

. . . while in the case of cities making a substantial contribution to the war effort, the practical effects of your Command's policy cannot be distinguished from those which would accrue from a policy of attacking cities as such, the Council cannot agree that it is impossible to draw a clear distinction between these two policies. This distinction is in fact of great importance in the presentation to the public of the aim and achievement of the bomber offensive.[54]

How can we explain this care for appearances when the bomber crews, the government, and the nation as a whole, with very few exceptions, had abandoned the idea that restraints were relevant to

who in 1940 thought there would be nothing worth fighting for if the bombing of open towns were to be adopted as national policy, but who by 1943 was accepting everything he was told about military objectives and who thought it would be wrong not to fight effectively, by which he meant the 'dislocation of the whole community engaged in the work' rather than attacking the factories themselves. See Wilkinson, *Dissent or Conform?*, p. 266.

[53] Ian McLaine, *Ministry of Morale* (George Allen and Unwin: London, 1979), 161.
[54] Ibid. 161–2.

the business of winning the war? Ian McLaine believes that the official propagandists, having condemned German terror bombing for three years, could not easily find reasons for Britain's use of the same thing which would be persuasive enough to overcome the moral objections from important sections of the community. 'For everyone concerned it was much more convenient to lie.'[55] But it is also true that, despite overwhelming public enthusiasm for making the German people suffer, there remained a moral contradiction at the heart of bombing which could not be entirely suppressed, and which quickly reasserted itself in people's minds once the bombing was over: that when the 'enemy' was being hit in just retribution, it was in fact innocent people who were paying the price: women, children, old men, invalids, and refugees. Although the men who were doing the bombing had certainly not volunteered for Bomber Command in order to do such things, they were not entirely ignorant of the effects of their work. It was largely these men— whose great personal courage made it possible at all—who would have to pay the price of conscience. Meanwhile, there was a very important job to be done, and they were not to be encouraged to think too deeply about what was happening below them.[56]

Reprisals in Law and Ethics

Reprisal links the conduct of World War II with post-war defence policy in the sense that the practice of it undermined the pre-war moral consensus on civilian bombing, and the threat of it against civilian populations became the basis of deterrence. It is obviously a subject which invites close examination. Are reprisals in any sense a morally acceptable form of behaviour in war? Do the laws of war give us any guide?

Acts of retaliation, as distinct from ordinary acts of war, are immediately suspect for several reasons. First, they carry with them a suspicion of being unnecessary, something superfluous to military necessity, and therefore contrary to the rule of minimum force. Second, they appear to be motivated by the ignoble desire for

---

[55] Ibid. 162.
[56] See Middlebrook, *The Battle of Hamburg*, pp. 347–54 for the varying attitudes of the bomber crews to their task. He points out that, 'The aircrew were subject to the same type of Press influence and conditioning as the general public and what they were told at the briefings about the targets they were to attack was often as limited and selective as what the British public were told by the Air Ministry.'

revenge rather than for justice or peace. Third, they risk inviting counter-retaliation and a spiral descent into savagery which are against the deepest interests of both military reason and justice. On the other hand, retaliation for a particularly damaging act of war may be the best way of showing the enemy that one is still in the fight. In this sense it is unexceptional, just part of the normal conduct of war. But this is not what is normally meant by reprisal. Its normal meaning is retaliation in kind for an act of war that the recipient believes to be unlawful or otherwise 'beyond limits'. The purpose is to demonstrate to the enemy forces that they cannot do such things with impunity, and if possible, to stop them doing them at all. This is the origin of the so-called 'right of reprisal', often invoked before and during World War II. What right, if any, was involved?

In modern times the practice of reprisals has been an issue in four main areas of warfare: the mistreatment of prisoners of war, the suppression of resistance in occupied territory, acts of war that are indiscriminate in their tendency to kill combatants and non-combatants alike, and the use of prohibited weapons or methods of warfare, causing unnecessary or extreme suffering to combatants. These are all rather different issues and only the last two are strictly speaking the subject of *belligerent reprisal*, attempting to control the conduct of war itself.

Belligerent reprisal is an established but highly controversial category of the laws of war. It may be defined as an 'otherwise illegal act of retaliation carried out in response to an illegal act of warfare and intended to cause the enemy to comply with the law'.[57] Belligerent reprisals are a form of deterrent punishment exercised by a state in the absence of a central authority capable of enforcing the international laws of war. The purpose of law enforcement is all-important and distinguishes reprisals, properly speaking, from cruder forms of retaliation. The primary purpose of belligerent reprisals is to bring about a change of policy of the authorities of the delinquent state, so as to prevent future wrongs of the same kind. They consist of prima-facie illegal acts, but these acts must be subject to strict limits which are in accordance with the primary

[57] Roberts and Guelff, *Documents on the Laws of War*, p. 15. Cf. Remigiusz Bierzanek, 'Reprisals as a Means of Enforcing the Laws of Warfare: The Old and the New Law' in Antonio Cassese (ed.), *The New Humanitarian Law of Armed Conflict* (Naples: Editoriale Scientifica, 1979), 232–57.

purpose of the law, and therefore of the acts themselves, namely to put a stop to illegal violence. In this sense, reprisals have drastically ambivalent—even contradictory—character, since they involve perpetrating the very acts which are agreed to be wrong. But, as Geoffrey Best points out, reprisal is an ancient military *practice* before it is anything else, and as such it has always been in need of restraint or, in the judgement of many, outright legal prohibition.[58] The legal category signifies an attempt to bring the practice within certain limits, to curb its inherent tendency towards an endless chain of violence. But lawyers are divided over the question of whether the final objective is to prohibit reprisals altogether, or whether it is to institutionalize within certain limits a right which cannot be denied to states in the absence of an effective international authority. Reprisals in a crude sense are a feature of anarchic international society, where self-help is the only recourse. But where there is a customary law of nations but no international organization capable of imposing sanctions on law-breakers—as in the European society of states after the Middle Ages—reprisals, legally defined, acquire a judicial aspect as well. They may be the only available method of forcing a delinquent state authority to observe the customary limits of war.

However, reprisals always suffered from severe drawbacks when seen from an ethical point of view. They tended to inflict suffering on the defenceless, on easy targets, rather than on the state authority which broke the law in the first place, and—because they involve actions that are prima facie illegal—they tend to lead to a spiral of retaliation with each side claiming the right of reprisal. International lawyers became increasingly critical of the practice which could so easily be used to cover the brutality of the strong against the weak and which so often served as a pretext for the wholesale abandonment of the laws of war. Consequently, efforts began to be made in the nineteenth century towards the statutory limitation of reprisal practices and eventually their abolition. They were seen by some international lawyers as a historical half-way stage from the total barbarism of unrestrained retaliation to the legal control of international conflict.

Criticism of reprisal practices became more severe in the twentieth century owing to their more frequent abuse, to the indiscriminate destructiveness of modern weapons, and to the legal and moral

[58] Best, *Humanity in Warfare*, p. 267.

questioning of the principle of collective responsibility which has made such an unfortunate come-back in contemporary wars.

The notion of limits is essential to the legal idea of reprisal. The limit most frequently mentioned is that of *proportionality*: a reprisal act must be in recognizable relation to the offending act, otherwise it will invite counter-reprisal and escalation of illegal violence will follow. It is here that reprisals are seen to be a form of the ancient principle of *lex talionis*, which is a principle of limitation designed to stem a limitless sequence of revenge killings.[59] Such legal measures are always ambivalent since they can be used for permissive reasons instead of the restrictive reasons for which they were originally intended. Escalating violence is still the major danger. In his review of reprisal practices in modern wars, Frits Kalshoven claims to have shown that 'the only instances having a semblance of efficacy were precisely those which strictly observed the requirement of proportionality to the wrong retaliated against'.[60]

However, the most important limitation is that of *humanity*: there are always some things which must never be done, even if an enemy does them, for instance, killing prisoners of war, or torturing and killing hostages. Consequently, the major question with regard to reprisals in modern war is, how can it ever be right to attack defenceless people in order to get their government to behave? The history of actual reprisals consists largely of attacks on non-combatants, or persons *hors de combat*, intended to persuade the combatants to stop fighting in particular ways or give up altogether. It has been a predominantly unjust practice, the victimization of hostages. This appears to have been true of virtually all reprisals taken in World War II.[61]

Legislation about reprisals has therefore largely been a matter of designating classes of person against whom they may not be made. The process began with prisoners of war, and the sick and others *hors de combat* by land and sea, and progressed to legislation about civilians subject to attack by indiscriminate weapons.[62]

[59] See Exodus 21: 23–4 and Leviticus 24: 19–20.
[60] Frits Kalshoven, *Belligerent Reprisals* (Leyden: A.W. Sijhoff, 1971), p. 341.
[61] Ibid. 210, '. . . the number of reprisal actions justifiable in all respects in World War II appears to be exactly nil'. Not all international lawyers agree with this judgement however.
[62] See the 1949 Geneva Conventions, I, Article 46; II, Article 47; III, Article 13; IV, Article 33; the 1977 Geneva Protocol I, Articles 20 and 51 in Roberts and Guelff, *The Laws of War*.

Thus reprisals and retaliation in general were central to the discussion at the Geneva Disarmament Conference of 1932–4, which debated the best way to prevent chemical, bacteriological and incendiary warfare, as well as civilian bombing. The dispute was between those who thought there should be total prohibition and those who thought that, regrettable as they may be in moral terms, the threat of retaliation in kind is the only effective way of preventing these inhumane methods. The result, as Kalshoven says, was 'a draw'.[63] There was an unresolved tension between the humanitarian and deterrent principles. But no one thought that the right of reprisal should be unlimited, and the limits were normally expressed in terms of humanity and proportion.

On the threshold of World War II four different positions were current with regard to attacks on civilians in wartime. In increasing order of permissiveness, they were:

(1) It is always wrong to do it and therefore wrong to threaten to do it by holding the means in readiness. This position we may call 'abolition', after the position taken by some of the delegates at the Geneva Disarmament Conference, 1932–4.

(2) It is normally wrong to do it, but it may be justified within strict limits in order to get the enemy to comply with the law. This position corresponds to the legal category of 'belligerent reprisal' explained above.

(3) It is wrong to do it first, but if the enemy does it first one is released from responsibility and may respond in kind. This position is normally referred to in legal circles as 'reciprocity', to be explained below.

(4) It is right to do it if military necessity demands it, in order to fight effectively and to finish the war, even if the enemy has not done it first. We may call this 'first-use'.

At the outset of World War II, the majority position in Britain, shared by government and public alike, seems to have been something like (3). Bombing civilians was considered to be a barbaric and immoral thing to do and probably contrary to international law, but if the enemy did it first, one was largely absolved of moral guilt when responding in kind. Unfortunately (2) and (3) were easily confused, and may not in fact be separable in contemporary conditions of warfare between major powers. Where

---

[63] Roberts and Guelff, *The Laws of War*, pp. 101–14.

this confusion prevailed, it was easy to appeal to the supposed legal right of reprisal, while succumbing to the strong emotional demand for revenge. On the British side this was made easier by the fact that the RAF held something like position (4) from the outset, and only required the pretext of 'reprisals' to put it into action.

The practice which seems to have emerged in the long run for governing the use of 'inhumane' weapons—at least among the powerful nations of the world is 'reciprocity'. Use of this word causes confusion among non-lawyers, since it has wider meanings well beyond the narrow one it has in this context, and I will keep it in inverted commas to mark its peculiarity. Historically, there has been an important difference between the notions of reprisal and 'reciprocity', even if they have a common root in military practice. Where reprisal—for all its moral ambiguity—is intended to be a precise legal institution for limiting the use of violence and reasserting the rule of law, 'reciprocity' is not a legal practice in this sense at all. It is a reservation made by a state signing a convention prohibiting the use of certain weapons to the effect that, if an enemy uses them first, it will consider itself free of the prohibition. It is precisely a declared intention to abandon law if the other side does so. For instance, many states, including all the major powers, which were signatories to the 1925 Geneva Protocol on Gas and Bacteriological Warfare, made reservations of this kind.[64] As we have seen, when it came to the threshold of World War II, Britain and France accepted the prohibition of civilian bombing subject to the same conditions of 'reciprocity'. In the event, reciprocal restraint broke down very rapidly, with both sides looking for excuses to make what they called reprisals. From then on, they habitually invoked the legally respectable right of reprisal in order to justify indiscriminate bombing, even though their actual behaviour came nowhere near satisfying the legal and moral requirements. Far from limiting the scope of violence, it became loosely used as an excuse for unlimited violence against non-combatants.

Unfortunately, the circumstances in which reprisals are most likely to be demanded is that in which indiscriminate attacks on non-combatants have already been made, or are thought to have been made. Retaliation is then likely to spring more from a passion to strike back at the enemy where it hurts most—against 'soft'

---

[64] Roberts and Guelff, *The Laws of War*, pp. 144–5.

targets such as civilians—than from a nice calculation aimed at enforcing the law and nothing more. Moreover, in an environment created by the use or the threatened use of weapons of mass destruction, the subject matter for legitimate reprisals tends to vanish altogether. Retaliation in kind with such weapons cannot count as legitimate reprisal according to traditional legal and moral criteria. So the legal category of reprisal collapses into mere reciprocal violence in contemporary conditions and the distinction between so-called 'right of reprisal' and 'reciprocity' cannot be maintained.

What morality says about retaliation is likely to be more exacting than what the law says about it at a given stage in its development. The goal of the law is the peace of an imperfect society, the containment of illegal force. Hence it will tolerate some practices which, from a moral point of view are intolerable while a way is found to get international agreement to their abolition. The criteria of just warfare would appear to rule out categorically the taking of reprisal actions against non-combatants.

Conclusions

Strategic bombing during World War II laid the foundations of post-war nuclear deterrence in several ways. It destroyed the pre-war consensus that bombing civilians was unacceptable behaviour for a civilized nation. The weak link in the pre-war view had been the acceptance that the only foundation of restraint was 'reciprocity', which placed all the blame for a breakdown on the side which first 'fought dirty'. Reciprocal infringements of the laws of restraint was regularly referred to as reprisal, which had a legal status as an otherwise illegal act intended to force the other party back to observance of the law. But under pressure of war, reprisal was nothing more than a pretext for acts of war already planned by air-forces on both sides—something which lent them an aura of justification. This conflicted with legally and morally accepted notions of reprisal, in that it punished large numbers for the crimes of their leaders and, in the final phases of war, led to acts which were grossly disproportionate to any reasonable war aims. These acts in turn fostered the belief—against much evidence to the contrary which emerged during and after the war—that killing large numbers of civilians was an efficient way of shortening a war and so of lessening the suffering in the long run. This view was strengthened by the surrender of Japan after the atomic destruction of Hiroshima and Nagasaki, although this event was very special in a number of ways, not the least being that Japan was at the end of the road and had no means of striking back, and had lost command of the air. For the most part, strategic bombing was much more productive in strengthening the morale of the nation which used it than in weakening the morale of the nation against which it was used. Henceforth, possession of the most powerful strike weapon available became the primary means of the subjective aspect of security. Finally, the pre-war belief that war could be started and won quickly by a devastating surprise attack from the air survived the war, despite the lack of evidence.

Granted that consensus against making war on civilians was not all that secure in 1939, its complete collapse thereafter needs some explanation. The remnant of it in the official care for appearances is not a genuine survival. That depended on a relegation of morals to morale, in which the danger was seen to be a psychological collapse in the individual member of the bombing crew, thus weakening his ability to do his job, rather than a real affront to a shared standard of moral behaviour. It is likely that there were various causes of the eclipse, reinforcing one another. The prior dedication of the RAF to morale bombing caused a swift breakdown in the practical observation of limits, provoking the appeal to reprisal. In war, if not in peace, this appeal was a powerful one which both government and general public could identify. The supposed 'right of reprisal' confused an established legal category with mere 'reciprocity'—a morality of revenge against soft targets. A further blunting of sensitivity would be brought about by the very things people were called on to do. This was particularly so in the case of bombing since it was an imprecise activity, done at a distance to victims who could not be differentiated among the enemy who was being hit in order to force 'him' to capitulate.

Among the correspondence which marked the fortieth anniversary of the bombing of Dresden, a letter from Robert Kee in *The Times*, 8 March 1985, pointed out that Churchill, in the matter of retribution bombing,

as in much else . . . reflected the feelings of the great majority of the British people at the time. On a bomber squadron in the summer of 1941 we were always given as targets of last resort 'anything that opens and shuts in Germany' and the thought was not an unwelcome one.

He wrote that his own view 'of the morality of these things has changed in forty years but that is nothing to do with the history of the time'. We must indeed distinguish between the urgent judgements which had to be made by those involved in winning the war against the Nazis and moral judgements of the acts seen in calm retrospect. The former were complex and heavily dependent on previous policies, such as the RAF's willingness to use strategic bombing as the main weapon of war. In so far as they violated justice and humanity they were wrong, but they were intelligible. However, what may have appeared to some in 1941 as a desperate expedient soon came to be accepted as a wholly justified policy— the *right* thing to do, as some had always believed it was—and the competing claims of international morality were discarded as irrelevant to the situation. Regrets were considered to be out of place. There is an important moral difference between making an urgent decision in an apparent dilemma and perpetuating it as a settled policy, giving up all serious attempts to find a more ethically acceptable alternative.

PART II

BUILDING THE NUCLEAR STATE

4

WEAPON FOR A GREAT POWER
1941–1952

The Decisive Weapon

It was in the midst of the bombing war with Germany that the atomic bomb was conceived and built. Before the war the theory of strategic bombing had fostered the idea of a decisive weapon which would be able to deliver a knock-out blow and defeat a nation with a sudden strike instead of a long-drawn-out war. Ordinary bombing did not fulfil such hopes and fears, which nevertheless survived and were finally given dramatic substance in the destruction of Hiroshima and Nagasaki, even though this happened at the very end of a ferocious conventional bombing campaign and when Japan was on the verge of collapse.

In the decade preceding the war the idea of a decisive weapon was a highly realistic one, based on the widespread belief that scientists were pushing ahead so fast with their discoveries that something earth-shaking was bound to be discovered soon.[1] By one of the great coincidences of history, it so happened that in 1939, the year the war began, nuclear physics was going through its greatest period of discoveries in several different countries simultaneously: Germany, Denmark, France, Britain, Italy, Poland, the United States, and probably also the Soviet Union and Japan. There were few secrets—the nuclear physicists were in fierce competition with one another, and discoveries were published immediately.[2] Fission of the uranium atom was demonstrated by Lise Meitner and Otto Frisch in January 1939 and shown to involve a very high release of energy. By February every atomic physics laboratory in the world was duplicating the results. When the French team proved in April 1939 that a chain reaction was possible—which was the crucial step towards the bomb—they resisted the request of Leo Szilard, a

---

[1] See e.g. the novel by Harold Nicholson, *Public Faces* (London: Constable, 1932), first published in 1932, predicting the atomic bomb as a weapon so devastating that it would make war impossible.

[2] Alwyn McKay, *The Making of the Atomic Age* (OUP, 1984), 28–9, 35.

refugee from Nazism, not to reveal it in case it was exploited in Germany.[3] They announced their results in a letter to *Nature* published in March. Scientists in Britain and Germany immediately alerted their Governments to the danger inherent in this discovery. But there was much scepticism about a military application at this stage. However, in March 1940 Rudolph Peierls and Otto Frisch at Birmingham worked out the conditions for producing a bomb using a chain reaction in uranium 235. The Frisch–Peierls memorandum also proposed a method of separation from U 238 by gaseous diffusion, and foretold the dangers to human life from long-term radiation released from such a bomb. The information was communicated to the Air Ministry scientific committee under Henry Tizard, and in April 1940 the Maud Committee was set up under George Thomson of Cambridge to investigate the possibilities of atomic energy.

The Maud Committee produced two reports, one on the technical feasibility of making a bomb with U 235 and the other on the use of uranium to produce power to drive machinery. The first report, presented to a small Cabinet committee in July 1941 was positive—even enthusiastic—about the chances of constructing a bomb before the end of the war:

In spite of the very large expenditure we consider that the destructive effects both *material and moral*, is so great that every effort should be made to produce bombs of this kind . . . Even if the war should end before the bombs are ready the effort would not be wasted except in the unlikely event of complete disarmament, since *no nation would care to risk being caught without a weapon of such decisive possibilities.* [4]

As to the moral question, Ronald Clark points out that the atomic bomb was not the hydrogen bomb and that, despite its far greater explosive power, it was not seen as morally different from other contemporary weapons of war. It does seem that it was use rather than deterrence which the Maud Committee had in mind:

Although the cost per lb of this explosive is so great it compares very favourably with ordinary explosives when reckoned in terms of energy released and damage done. It is, in fact, *considerably cheaper* but the points

---

[3] Ronald W. Clark, *The Birth of the Bomb* (London: Phoenix House, 1961), 20. Cf. Alwyn McKay, *The Atomic Age*, p. 35.

[4] The text of the Maud Report, presented to a Cabinet committee in July 1941, is given by Margaret Gowing, *Britain and Atomic Energy 1939–1945* (London: Macmillan, 1964), 394 (emphasis added).

which we regard as of overwhelming importance are the destruction which it would produce, *the large moral effect*, and the saving in air effort the use of this substance would allow, as compared with bombing with ordinary explosives. [5]

The quite new scale of blast effects, and the long-lasting danger of radiation were foreseen by the Report, although they must have been difficult to understand by the non-scientists involved. Radiation from fission products and irradiated matter is one of the main indiscriminate effects of nuclear explosions and is consequently an important factor in assessing the morality of using the weapons. The Maud Committee already realized some of the truth:

We have now reached the conclusion that it will be possible to make an effective uranium bomb which, containing some 25 lb of active material, would be equivalent as regards destructive effect to 1,800 tons of TNT, and would also release large quantities of radioactive substances, which would make places near to where the bomb exploded dangerous to human life for a long period. [6]

Nothing was said about genetic effects. Nor was anything said about the moral effects of using it as opposed to the moral effects of having it used upon one. It could have been the vagueness about the future use of the bomb which inhibited anyone from thinking about the moral implications of it. Among the thousands of documents and memoranda through which Margaret Gowing sifted, there was only one which showed any evidence of moral questioning. It was from Dr Charles Darwin, when he read the Maud Report in 1941 and asked whether, if 'the thing' could be made, it would be used:

For example are our own Prime Minister and the American President and the respective general staffs willing to sanction the total destruction of Berlin and the country round, when, if ever, they are told it could be accomplished in a single blow? [7]

So at the time it was accepted that an atomic bomb was a practical possibility, the war was at its most dangerous phase for Britain and everyone concerned thought that the remaining German atomic scientists would already be working to make it for Hitler. However, even if the scientists working in Britain had not

[5] Ibid. 397 (emphasis added).
[6] Ibid. 394.
[7] Ibid. 86, 370.

believed in 1941 that the Germans might be making a bomb, they would still in all probability have pursued it themselves.[8]

On the basis of the Maud Report, Churchill consulted the Chiefs of Staff in August 1941 and they recommended immediate action with maximum priority.

The Bomb is Made and Used

The Maud Report was read with tremendous interest in the United States, which was not yet at war and in which there was as yet no comparable government interest in atomic research for military purposes. An offer was made for a joint project with Britain and was somewhat haughtily rebuffed on the assumption that Britain was so far ahead that it did not need it. But it soon turned out to be quite beyond the capacity of wartime Britain to do the basic research, let alone construct the immensely costly and complex separation plants for U 235. Moreover, the large and conspicuous plant that would be necessary for producing the uranium would have been vulnerable to German bombing.

By mid-1942 those in charge of the British project decided that the best prospect was in asking the Americans for full co-operation and equal partnership. But it was too late. By that time the Americans had established the Manhattan Project on an immense scale under the military command of General Groves and it very soon outstripped the British efforts. The Americans became hostile to co-operation or even exchange of information. Although it had pioneered the theoretical work, Britain was far behind materially and was now in that inferior scientific and military relationship to the United States in which it has ever since remained. The atomic project subsequently became the primary symbol of Britain's ambitions to get as close as possible to the United States, where Western economic and military power now centred. However, despite some American suspicions that the main interest of the British was in obtaining information which could be exploited for commercial purposes after the war, co-operation was restored on 19 August 1943 with the Quebec agreement between Roosevelt and Churchill. The British teams joined the Manhattan project and the post-war British bomb project benefited enormously from the knowledge and experience which had been gained while working

[8] Gowing, *Britain and Atomic Energy*, p. 87.

with the Americans. Gowing shows that the main advantage that the British hoped to gain through participation was quick possession of the decisive weapon. In 1943, Sir John Anderson, Home Secretary, ex-physicist and the member of Churchill's inner circle asked to oversee the British part in the atomic project, wrote that 'we cannot afford after the war to face the future without this weapon and rely entirely on America should Russia or some other power develop it'.[9] Anderson was instrumental in negotiating the Quebec Agreement. In it the leaders of the two countries agreed: never to use nuclear weapons against each other; nor to use them against other countries without each other's consent; and not to pass on information to other countries without each other's consent.[10]

In September 1944 Churchill and Roosevelt met at Hyde Park, the President's home, to discuss post-war atomic collaboration, which was a source of anxiety in Britain. They produced an *aide-mémoire* in which they agreed to full collaboration between Britain and the United States for both military and commercial purposes after the defeat of Japan. They also agreed that Japan was the possible target of the bomb when it became finally available.

In November 1944 an American mission led by the scientist Samuel Goudsmit discovered files in the university at Strasbourg, newly-liberated by the Allies, which showed that the German atomic project, although of high scientific quality, had never got beyond the academic laboratory stage. It is still frequently claimed that the German scientists, led by the great physicist Werner Heisenberg, stalled the project for moral reasons and had no intention of giving Hitler possession of the atomic bomb, keeping the project in their own hands lest others, less scrupulous than they, should succeed with it. This story appears to originate from Robert Jungk's account in *Brighter Than a Thousand Suns*.[11] However, clandestine recordings of the German scientists' conversations on hearing the news of Hiroshima, made during their internment in Britain in 1945, show this not to have been the case. They had thought themselves well ahead of Allied research and were astonished at the American success in making the bomb in so short

[9] Ibid. 168.
[10] The text is given by John Baylis, *Anglo-American Defence Relations 1939–1984* (London: Macmillan 1984), 23.
[11] Robert Jungk, *Brighter Than a Thousand Suns* (London: Gollancz, 1958), 98.

a time.[12] However, the discovery of German backwardness did not mean that the United States would not complete the bomb and use it, as some of the scientists involved in the project hoped. For since the early days of the Manhattan project the military rationale for the weapon had undergone an important change. It had ceased to be seen as purely deterrent, against the possibility of the Nazis acquiring it. Instead, it came to be seen by the American military leadership as simply an offensive weapon of superior power which was to be used in the war. It would be a much more efficient way of doing what was now already being done to German and Japanese cities.[13] 'Isn't it wonderful that the Germans have no atom bomb?' said Goudsmit when he made his discovery. 'Now we won't have to use ours.' 'You don't know Groves,' replied one of its military members. 'If we have such a bomb, then we'll use it.'[14] General Groves was intensely anxious to have the bomb available before the end of the war. There was considerable pressure to use a weapon which had cost astronomical sums to produce. But Germany was defeated too soon for this and attention was turned to Japan.

On the 31 May 1945, the Interim Committee set up by President Roosevelt to deal with the whole range of questions surrounding the bomb, met to consider *how*, not *whether*, it should be used against Japan. By that time it seemed to the participants that it was a foregone conclusion that it would be used.[15] There was general agreement that, if the best way of shortening the war in the Pacific was to use the bomb without warning against a populated target in Japan, then it would be done. The idea of demonstrating the bomb on an unpopulated target was considered and passed over, chiefly because of the fear of what might happen it it turned out to be a dud. Even the proposal that the Japanese should be warned beforehand of the nature of the weapon that would be used against them was rejected in case it should lessen the impact and reduce their will to surrender.[16] There was considerable dissent on moral grounds among some of the scientists working on the project, who continued to see the bomb as a deterrent only and a last chance to

[12] Information from a lecture by Margaret Gowing, Nov. 1987.
[13] Gowing, *Britain and Atomic Energy*, p. 317 and Herbert Feis, *The Atomic Bomb and the End of World War II* (Princeton, NJ: Princeton University Press, 1966), 28.
[14] McKay, *The Atomic Age*, p. 111.
[15] Feis, *The Atomic Bomb*, p. 45.
[16] Ibid. 48.

restructure international relations. They thought that use against Japan would destroy this opportunity and bring nothing but long-term insecurity to the user. At least there should be a purely technical demonstration first. However, the Interim Committee overruled these objections and advised the President that only direct military use against a populated target would give the Japanese a sufficiently severe shock for them to surrender and so save many American lives that would otherwise be lost. Truman wrote in his memoirs that he was advised that at least half a million American lives would be lost in an invasion. Such was the consequentialist argument that prevailed in making the decision. All this rested on the assumption, which remained largely unquestioned at the time, that an invasion was inevitable and unconditional surrender the only acceptable way of ending the war.[17] Whatever the real reasons for using the bomb against Hiroshima and Nagasaki, it seems that in some circles there existed a strong desire to demonstrate both the U 235 and the plutonium bomb against relatively intact Japanese cities before the war ended. Hiroshima and Nagasaki were chosen because they had received little war damage up till then. Before the attacks their people were deliberately accustomed to the sight of small formations of high flying American B–29 bombers, presumably so that they would not take shelter or other avoiding action when the plane which carried the atomic bomb appeared in the sky.[18]

In all this there was no dissent from the British observers and participants.[19] In his memoirs of World War II, Churchill repeats the 'saving lives' argument and records the unhesitating British agreement to what was essentially an American presidential decision:

The decision whether or not to use the atomic bomb to compel the surrender of Japan was never even an issue. There was unanimous,

[17] Ibid. 55.

[18] Cf. Feis, *The Atomic Bomb*, p. 83.

[19] Gowing, *Britain and Atomic Energy*, p. 370; and Feis, *The Atomic Bomb*, p. 58. A British airman who was one of the observers of the atomic bomb attack on Nagasaki, had this to say about it in 1954: 'I may as well confess to you that we were so keen on dropping this bomb on Nagasaki, and would have been so disappointed if the war had ended without our doing so, that we'd quite determined—if Japan did surrender before we flew to Nagasaki—to fly there and drop the bomb just the same!', *Picture Post*, 5 June 1954, p. 33, cited in *Pax Bulletin*, No. 67, Sept. 1954.

automatic, unquestioned agreement around our table; nor did I ever hear the slightest suggestion that we should do otherwise.[20]

Lord Louis Mountbatten, responsible for planning a possible invasion of Japan as Supreme Allied Commander South East Asia, was asked if the atomic bomb was inhumane. He replied,

If the bomb kills Japanese and saves casualties on our side, I am naturally not going to favour the killing of our people unnecessarily. I am responsible for trying to kill as many Japanese as I can with the minimum loss on our side. War is crazy. It is a crazy thing that we are fighting at all. But it would be even more crazy if we were to have more casualties on our side to save Japanese.[21]

Much British opinion was on the same side, and the feeling of many servicemen was one of relief that the war was about to end. The *Manchester Guardian* commented on 17 August 1945 that,

Churchill was surely right in justifying the use of the bomb against Japan. Those—apart from the pacifists—who object to it have no better logic than that it is more wicked to kill simultaneously than successively and that it is better for a million soldiers to die than a hundred thousand civilians. In truth, it is war which is wicked and war which must be prevented.

However, newspaper correspondence in the days immediately following the explosions revealed a considerable amount of moral revulsion at what had been done by the Allies. Several letters in *The Times* for instance, recalled the British moral indignation at the indiscriminate nature of the German V1 and V2 attacks only a year previously and asked where the difference lay. There was a sharp divide between those who continued to adhere to the principle that not any means was permissible to obtain the end, however good, and those who believed that, in the circumstance, such an attitude lacked realism and moral sense. The latter tended to justify the use of the bombs by claiming that not only had it saved lives but that it made war impossible henceforward. Others pointed out that this was by no means certain. This first period of debate on nuclear morality seems to have lasted only a very short time.

[20] Winston S. Churchill, *The Second World War*, vol. vi. (London: Cassell, 1954), 553.
[21] Peter Cole, *Guardian*, 6 Aug. 1985.

Labour Inherits the Bomb

The Labour government came to power just one week before the two atomic bombs were dropped. Throughout the war years, Attlee and his colleagues had been kept out of Churchill's inner circle and knew nothing of Britain's part in the atomic project. When they came to power they maintained the tradition of secrecy. All decisions were made by a small group of ministers in obscurely named Cabinet committees usually dominated by Attlee and Bevin, and the Cabinet as a body was completely excluded from all major decisions on atomic policy.[22] Needless to say, Parliament had even less of a role in these matters. When, from time to time, questions were asked in the Commons as to whether Britain was developing the bomb, the answer was always a frosty one to the effect that it was 'not in the public interest to say yes or no'.[23] It was not until 12 May 1948 that the Minister of Defence, in answer to a planted question, made the briefest of references to the fact that Britain was developing 'all types of weapons, including atomic weapons'. And that was to forestall press enquiries and was laden with D-notices. Attlee's reason for not letting anyone know anything was to keep such knowledge from an enemy, but he also gives the impression of having considered it as some kind of obscenity, which should not be spoken of or put into print, although it was absolutely necessary to get on with it in the dark.[24] He was probably afraid of criticism from the internationalist wing of the Labour party. However, there is no indication that the general public would have been in any way opposed to Britain having its own bomb had it known what was going on. Britain's pioneering role in atomic research had made it extremely unlikely that the fruits of it would be left to others.

Although the final decision to make bombs was not made until 8 January 1947, the project already had considerable momentum owing to the fact that vital decisions about building an atomic pile and supplying it with purified uranium and graphite had been made as early as December 1945, on the advice of the Advisory

---

[22] Margaret Gowing, *Independence and Deterrence* (London: Macmillan, 1974), 20–4.

[23] For instance, Minister of Supply, G. R. Strauss, oral answers, 12 Dec. 1949, House of Commons Report, vol. 470, col. 2337.

[24] Cf. Gowing, *Independence and Deterrence*, pp. 21, 28–9, 279, 408.

Committee on Atomic Energy.[25] This work was given the 'highest urgency and importance', and the Chiefs of Staff were instructed by the small, secret Cabinet Committee dealing with this matter, Gen 75, to submit a report on 'our requirements for atomic bombs and the possibility of making consequential reduction in other forms of armament production'.[26] Attlee noted that 'it was impossible to separate altogether the questions of use for peaceful and for warlike purposes'—which was what made the problem of international security so intractable. At a meeting of Gen 75 on 26 October 1946, Hugh Dalton and Stafford Cripps declared themselves, on economic grounds, against Britain making its own atomic bombs. But Bevin opposed them with the words,

> That won't do at all, we've got to have this . . . I don't mind for myself, but I don't want any other Foreign Secretary of this country to be talked at or by a Secretary of State in the United States as I have just had [sic] in my discussions with Mr. Byrnes. We have got to have this thing over here whatever the costs . . . we've got to have the bloody Union Jack flying on top of it.[27]

In later years, when Attlee was asked what was Bevin's greatest contribution as Foreign Secretary, he replied without hesitation, 'standing up to the Americans'.[28]

The final decision to make atomic weapons was made, not by Gen 75, but by another secret Cabinet Committee, Gen 163, convened specially for that purpose and excluding Dalton and Cripps. At this meeting, Lord Portal and Dr Penney, who were jointly responsible for the project, were simply asking for the go-ahead. They had already decided themselves that the bombs must be made. During the meeting, Bevin said that, in his view, it was important for Britain to have the bomb, since 'we could not afford to acquiesce in an American monopoly of this new development'.

The desire to stand up to the Americans was undoubtedly a major factor in the determination of British public servants and ministers to make a British bomb. Since they still considered Britain to be a Great Power, temporarily in reduced circumstances, it was

[25] CAB 130/2, Gen 75/8, Report from the Advisory Committee on Atomic Energy, 18 Dec. 1945.

[26] Ibid.

[27] Alan Bullock, *Ernest Bevin, Foreign Secretary 1945–1951* (London: Heinemann, 1983), 352.

[28] Ibid. 416.

not easy to put up with American bullying and hostility to Britain's imperial attitudes immediately after the war. The Americans were very suspicious of the Socialist government, and their monopoly of the bomb made them even more arrogant. Clearly, for Britain to survive in anything like its former position meant sharing with the Americans in the secrets of atomic energy. But there was a strong body of opinion in the United States which considered the atomic bomb to be a sacred trust to the American people, to be shared with no one. The Truman administration was ignorant or distrustful of the wartime agreements for 'full and effective co-operation', which had largely been a product of the personal relationship between Churchill and Roosevelt. Despite great personal efforts, Attlee failed to restore the wartime collaboration, and in August 1946, the US Congress passed the McMahon Act, amid rising anti-Soviet feeling. It prohibited the communication of atomic information to any other country on pain of the most extreme penalties. This breakdown was a major stimulus to the independent British atomic project. But it was not, in itself, sufficient reason for the decision to make the bomb.

The two main factors in the decision were: (1) assumptions about Britain's Great Power status, which were shared by almost everyone after the war, including Labour ministers, the churches, and the general public; [29] and (2) claims about strategic necessity put forward by the General Staff.

The war had greatly reduced Britain's real power and influence in the world, especially with respect to the United States and the Soviet Union, but it took a very long time for this to sink in. The real situation was disguised by a number of factors: Britain was the only victorious European power, much less damaged by the war than any of the others; it was a permanent member of the UN Security Council; it was one of the 'Big Three' in the councils of war and in the ministerial conferences which followed the war; the Empire was still a proud and permanent feature of British consciousness, even if about to break up in fact. And there were

[29] Bevin asserted it in Parliament, see House of Commons Report, 16 May 1947, vol. 437, col. 1965. A group of eminent churchmen and women asserted it in the British Council of Churches Report, *The Era of Atomic Power* (London: S.C.M. Press, May 1946). They thought that a Great Power had to possess the principal weapon of the day, or renounce its status: 'An attempt in the atomic age to remain a Great Power while renouncing the use of the atomic bomb would be equivalent to an attempt, in the naval age to wage naval war without the use of capital ships' (p. 41).

other things: a great industrial nation was not easily going to give up the project which seemed to hold so much promise for the future. Unlimited cheap energy was the other face of the atomic project. For some time to come this would make it easy for the collective conscience to be pacified about the bomb by talk of 'atoms for peace': the belief that atomic power could, eventually, be turned into a benefit for mankind rather than a curse. In the event, acquisition of the bomb itself became a primary means of disguising from Britain her loss of world status after the war.

In retrospect, it does seem unlikely that the Labour leaders could have voluntarily taken a step which would have been interpreted both at home and abroad as an abandonment of Britain's historic position in the world. In Socialist eyes, Britain's greatness and power was to be expressed in different ways perhaps—as a moral force in the councils of the world, pioneering a third way between American capitalism and Soviet Communism—but it was not to be abandoned. In the stages leading up to the British decision to make the bomb, there was little or no dissent from the assumption that possession of overwhelming bombing power was an indispensable mark of Britain's true worth. As Gowing remarks, it was something 'fundamentalist and almost instinctive'.[30]

However, to balance the picture, it should be recorded that, between the autumn of 1945 and sometime late in 1946, both Attlee and Bevin invested great hopes and put much effort into achieving international control through the United Nations Atomic Energy Commission. They initially accepted that this would involve sharing the secret of the bomb with the Russians immediately, in order to remove one of the main sources of their distrust of the West. In December 1945, the British ambassador in Moscow, Archibald Clark-Kerr, had sent a long telegram showing what a dangerous and disappointing place the world seemed from the point of view of the Russian leadership. In their everlasting search for secure borders they had—with immense losses—repelled the latest and most devastating attack from the West, only to find in their hour of victory that they were threatened with the atomic bomb, against which their vast land forces were of little value. The failure of the West to share the secret of the bomb aggravated

[30] Gowing, *Independence and Deterrence*, p. 184.

ancient suspicions and added new fears of American intentions.[31] Besides such considerations as these, Attlee sincerely believed that the only hope for the post-Hiroshima world was for an international authority to have the power of using the weapons against an aggressor state.[32] The only alternative seemed to be for each state which could to arm itself as soon as possible with the capacity to retaliate in kind—something that filled Attlee with foreboding and contradicted all the Socialist hopes for a more rational world order. In contrast, Churchill and the Conservatives tended to envisage the morally-reliable United States and Great Britain policing the post-war world with their nuclear monopoly, which they expected to last for some time.[33] It was not until both Bevin and Attlee had become convinced that Russian obstructive behaviour at three-power conferences was not dependent on the atomic factor that they began to abandon their faith in the internationalist solution and go for sovereign-state deterrence instead. Attlee, at least, had a very gloomy view of its chances of success. But it soon became apparent that the Socialist hope—that in the post-war world the old system of power blocs facing one another in armed mistrust could be superseded—was not to be fulfilled in any sense. The world was still stuck with nation states putting their own interests first. Other members of the Cabinet continued to think that sharing was a necessary first step:

If it was our policy to build world peace on moral foundations rather than on the balance of power we should be prepared to apply that principle at once to the atomic bomb.[34]

As for the Chiefs of Staff, they thought it absolutely unacceptable that Britain should place atomic weapon research under the supervision of an international authority even if other governments were ready to do so.[35] For a while it seemed that the Prime Minister was looking in both directions at once: to a new world order to

[31] Ibid. 68. Opinions are divided as to whether the Russian leadership really believed that the West's possession of the bomb reduced the value of their divisions or not. They certainly behaved as if it did not make much difference, which may have been the only sensible thing to do in the circumstances.

[32] CAB 130/2, Gen 75, 12th meeting, PM's memorandum on forthcoming discussions with President Truman and the Canadian Prime Minister, 5 Nov. 1945.

[33] Gowing, *Britain and Atomic Energy*, pp. 95, 154.

[34] Gowing, *Independence and Deterrence*, vol. i, p. 70.   [35] Ibid. 91.

control the awful weapons, and to an independent British capacity
to retaliate in kind. He eventually accepted the position which was
being pressed upon him by his own military and scientific advisers,
that each nation should look after its own interests first and then
perhaps talk about international control.

Strategic Priorities

The Chiefs of Staff had their eyes fixed firmly on what they
supposed to be Britain's permanent strategic requirement—
overwhelming bombing power to be used against a future enemy,
which they had long since identified with the Soviet Union. It is not
easy to ascertain whether, and if so, how they brought their strong
feelings about this to bear on the Cabinet committee which made
the decision to make British bombs, but it is clear that they had
increasing influence thereafter in determining the part to be played
by nuclear weapons in Britain's defence.

The straightforward strategic argument for Britain equipping
itself with atomic weapons originated in the prevailing assumption
that massive bombardment of cities was decisive in modern war. It
was generally assumed that the advantage would lie with massive
surprise attack, a view which originated in the 1930s, which was
not confirmed by anything which happened in World War II, but
which nevertheless survived it. Few people stopped to think that the
destruction of Hiroshima and Nagasaki was something quite
different, namely the final blow at the end of a long war against an
enemy which had lost control of its airspace and was already
effectively defeated. However, military strategists were afraid that
Britain was specially vulnerable to aerial warfare because of its
concentration of military and industrial targets. When the potenti-
alities of the atomic bomb first dawned on those who knew about
it, it was immediately assumed that an enemy possessing the new
weapon would be able to destroy Britain quickly and that there
would be no effective way of protecting the civilian population.
Together with this came the conclusion that a country like Britain
could no longer rely on mobilizing its resources after the start of a
war—which it had just about got away with in 1939–40—but that
some means of offensive war had to be already in place for instant
use. According to Margaret Gowing, nuclear deterrence originated
in British circles as early as June 1945, with a committee of eminent

scientists arguing that, since the population could not be protected from atomic bombs, the only answer they could see was 'to be prepared to use them ourselves in retaliation'.[36] The Chiefs of Staff said the same thing a few months later.

A Chiefs of Staff memorandum to the Prime Minister in January 1946 demanded urgent production of bombs 'in the order of hundreds rather than of scores', so that Britain would 'be prepared for aggressors who have widely dispersed industries and population' (who else but the USSR?).[37] They were quite unwilling to wait for the UN Atomic Energy Commission to try for international control through negotiations. Nor could they accept permanent reliance on supplies of weapons from the United States: an offer made from time to time, in exchange for Britain giving up its own atomic programme. The Chiefs of Staff said that it would not 'appear compatible with our status as a first-class Power to depend on others for a weapon of this supreme importance'.[38] No war was expected during the next five years, after which it was expected that British bombs would be available for equipping an offensive strike force. This would be 'the chief tangible evidence of the intention and ability to retaliate immediately, the chief deterrent to aggression, and *the only effective backing for foreign policy*' (emphasis added). Questions were asked about the use of the bombs. The Chiefs of Staff thought that if a potential enemy did not use weapons at the outset of a war, the political objections against Britain's initiating their use might be insuperable. They agreed that it would be a cardinal principle of policy to be prepared to use such weapons immediately, but no hypothetical sequence of events was established.[39]

At this stage the Chiefs of Staff were extremely vague on the subject of strategy: how many bombs were needed, under what circumstances they would be used and how they would be delivered. But, as Gowing points out, a clear answer would have required a careful analysis of the use of the atomic bombs by Britain in given tactical and strategic circumstances. The Chiefs of Staff organization did not attempt this and was still ill-equipped to do

[36] Ibid. 163–4. Some members of this Committee, notably Sir Henry Tizard and P. M. S. Blackett, were later to change their minds about this.
[37] Ibid. 169.
[38] Ibid. 220.
[39] Ibid. 188.

so.[40] One reason for this incapacity was the military's ignorance about the effects of nuclear weapons.[41] They had no access to details of the Hiroshima and Nagasaki explosions: the Americans were uncommunicative about this and the results of the British scientists' investigation were not published until later in the year.[42] Another reason was that, although the Chiefs of Staff identified the enemy as the Soviet Union, it was not until 1948 that the Government would allow this to be a basic assumption of defence policy. Hence it was some time before a high priority was given to means of delivering the bombs, in contrast to the very highest priority always given to possessing them. In July 1946 the Cabinet Defence Committee gave highest priority to the development of high-performance, long-range bombers but this was allowed to lapse, and it was not until September 1949 that the V-bombers were given equal priority with the weapons programme. This resulted in serious delays, so that the V-bombers, superior to anything possessed by the superpowers, did not become operational until 1957, by which time advances in air-defence and missile technology had undermined their deterrent value. The responsibility for the lack of priority appears to have been shared by the Labour government and the Chiefs of Staff.[43] In any case, the symbolic and psychological value of simply possessing the bombs appears to have outweighed everything else. As we have already seen from the RAF's preparations before World War II, reliance on weapons of mass destruction does not encourage precision of thought about how the next war will be fought. The hope is that a knock-out blow, killing very large numbers of civilians, will make organized life impossible and bring the war to a rapid finish.

So the possession, and declared willingness for immediate use, of weapons of mass destruction was to be the basis of Britain's security. In 1946, in its instructions to the United Kingdom representatives to the UN Atomic Energy Commission, the government, in trying to narrow the scope of the negotiations to atomic weapons, stated that,

---

[40] Gowing, *Independence and Deterrence*, p. 170.

[41] A point recognized by Peter Malone, *The British Nuclear Deterrent* (London: Croom Helm, 1984), 4.

[42] See *The Effects of Atomic Bombs at Hiroshima and Nagasaki*: Report of the British Mission to Japan, published for the Home Office and the Air Ministry (London: HMSO, 1946).

[43] See Gowing, *Independence and Deterrence*, 175, 234–5.

The true weapons of mass destruction . . . are those which *by their nature* are primarily used only for this purpose, namely atomic, bacteriological and other toxic weapons.[44]

In this they were following a Chiefs of Staff definition. After Hiroshima and Nagasaki this was only stating the obvious, but there is no evidence that British officials ever came to regard nuclear weapons in any other way. Reliance on such weapons appeared to the Chiefs of Staff to be the policy most suited to a small, densely populated country like Britain which enjoyed a scientific and technical lead over a vast and still very backward country like Russia, with its enormous preponderance of conventional armaments.[45]

These are the arguments which eventually prevailed with the government and led to the definite decision to make the bomb, although it is not easy to see why they did so as early as January 1947. The environment in which the decision to make the bomb was made was different in most respects from that in which the Maud Committee had done its work. Britain was not at war and, despite the professional need for the military clearly to identify an enemy in order to justify their procurement of the best weapons, none of the political leaders expected a war in the foreseeable future.[46] The Russians did not have the bomb and were— mistakenly to be sure—not expected to acquire one for many years to come. Moreover, early in 1947, when the decision was made, Britain was going through a very severe economic crisis as a result of the hard winter and the difficulties of post-war recovery. Not war but economic collapse was the main danger in 1947. A high priority given to a very expensive programme to manufacture weapons of mass destruction was not the obvious answer to the situation. Rationalizing the decision many years later, Attlee said that not putting 'ourselves entirely in the hands of the Americans' had been the chief concern.[47]

---

[44] CAB 130/2, Gen 75/12, 'Definition of Weapons of Mass Destruction', 20 Mar. 1946; and CAB 130/2, Gen 75/29, Advisory Committee on Atomic Energy, (46)31, 'Draft Instructions to the UK Representatives on the United Nations Commission on Atomic Energy', 14 May 1946 (emphasis added).

[45] Gowing, *Independence and Deterrence*, p. 218.

[46] For Bevin's opinion see Bullock, *Ernest Bevin*, p. 223: 'It is said that we are drifting into war with Russia. I cannot conceive any circumstances in which Britain and the Soviet Union should go to war . . . It never enters my mind and I am certain it does not any of my colleagues.' In 1947 he thought the main danger was not war but Communist subversion of weakened European countries (p. 486). Cf. Gowing, *Independence and Deterrence*, pp. 91, 187.

[47] Bullock, *Ernest Bevin*, p. 353. Attlee added that 'it's all very well to look back and say otherwise, but at that time nobody could be sure that the Americans would

There were some dissenting voices at the time, although it was not moral doubts which prompted them. In November 1945, P. M. S. Blackett presented a very carefully argued memorandum to the Chiefs of Staff and the government in which he maintained that for Britain to become a nuclear power would decrease rather than increase its long-term security.[48] He believed that—since atomic bombs were only useful for attacking cities rather than armies—it would be interpreted in the worst light by the Soviet Union, which would become more aggressive in Europe as a result. The situation was already aggravated by well-publicized demands from certain groups in the United States for pre-emptive atomic war against the USSR. Unfortunately, Blackett's arguments, which were far more thought-out than those of the Chiefs of Staff, were scornfully dismissed by them and by Attlee as being nothing more than an attempted interference by a scientist in affairs of which he knew nothing. Many of Blackett's guesses about the future were inaccurate, but there was a very large grain of truth in his prediction that nuclear weapons will not necessarily enhance the security of the country which has them, because of the counter-measures it is likely to provoke in others and the fear of this which is implanted in the possessor of the weapon.

In 1949, when still Chief Scientific Adviser to the Ministry of Defence, Sir Henry Tizard came to the conclusion that Britain should not be making the bomb at all, but should rely on the Americans for atomic protection. His reason for thinking this was that Britain was no longer a Great Power and would only do itself long-term economic harm if it tried to continue behaving like one.[49] He thought the best approach to security was to concentrate on economic reconstruction and to give the priority in armaments to conventional weapons.

not revert to isolationism—many Americans wanted it, many Americans feared it. There was no NATO then.'

[48] Blackett's memorandum is printed in full in Gowing, *Independence and Deterrrence*, pp. 194–206.

[49] Gowing, *Independence and Deterrence*, p. 229: 'We persist in regarding ourselves as a Great Power, capable of everything and only temporarily handicapped by economic difficulties. We are not a Great Power and never will be again. We are a great nation, but if we continue to behave like a Great Power we shall soon cease to be a great nation. Let us take warning from the fate of the Great Powers of the past and not burst ourselves with pride (see Aesop's fable of the frog).'

The Importance of the Soviet Threat—and the American Presence

Had it not been for the rise of the 'Soviet Threat', would Britain have continued to make its own nuclear weapons? The continuation of the atomic bomb project was still under review until at least 1950, and it would have been possible then to discontinue it without excessive financial loss.

From early 1948 onwards, the Soviet Union behaved in a manner which may have been dictated by its own security needs in the face of what it saw as the increasing American hegemony in Europe, but which appeared to statesmen such as Bevin and Attlee to be aggressive and aimed at extending Soviet power further westward. The Communist coup in Czechoslovakia, which replaced the restored democracy with a Stalinist regime, was a particular shock. Then in March 1948 began the moves which led to the blockade of Berlin. The Western allies responded with the airlift and the return of the United States Air Force to some of its former bases, this time equipped for the use of atomic bombs.

Ernest Bevin's apparent motive for forging the Atlantic Alliance between 1947 and 1949 was the restoration of confidence in Europe to resist the perceived threat of Soviet subversion and intimidation. European countries disunited and weakened by war seemed to be easy prey. But what started off as mainly an economic alliance, to strengthen the social fabric, soon became dominated by military concerns. In 1948 George Kennan pointed out that there was a danger of,

... general preoccupation with military affairs, to the detriment of economic recovery and of the necessity for securing a peaceful solution to Europe's difficulties ... The need for military alliances and rearmament on the part of Western Europe is primarily a *subjective* one, arising in their own minds as a result of their failure to understand correctly their own position. . .[50]

This analysis was accepted by the US government. But so far as Bevin was concerned, an American military guarantee—and actual visible presence in Europe—was a necessary deterrent to Soviet ambitions. It was acting upon the lesson which had been learned in 1939–41. It was not so much a direct military warning to the

[50] Bullock, *Ernest Bevin*, p. 644 (emphasis original).

Russians as a psychological prop for Europeans, which would enable them to resist Soviet pressure in other areas and so avoid appeasement.[51]

The United States on the other hand, had its own purposes to pursue. By this time, it had strongly developed global ambitions, dictated by the ideology of national security. This reversed the pre-war policy of isolationism and posited that the defence of America required a world-wide extension of forces.[52] Containment of Soviet Communism was the main objective, and this was said to require regional military alliances and bases around the world within striking distance of the Soviet Union. By 10 June 1946, the American Joint Post-War Committee had already concluded that:

The principal critical offensive effort against the USSR must consist of an air offensive, utilizing the atomic bomb to the fullest extent, for the purposes of destroying the Soviet war-making capacity. [53]

The United Kingdom was to be crucial in implementing all the short- and long-term war plans of the US Strategic Air Command (SAC) in the 1940s. Although at this stage it had only a few atomic bombs at its disposal, the SAC very soon developed detailed plans for immediate strikes against targets in the Soviet Union should hostilities break out in Europe.[54] Owing to restrictions on bomber range, bases in Britain were needed if Soviet cities were to be attacked. Throughout 1946 and 1947, conversations were held between Air Chief Marshal Tedder and General Spaatz of the SAC for the preparation of bases in the UK and for the rotational tours of American bombers. For the Americans it was an urgent requirement of the forward defence of the United States.[55]

In June 1948, during the Berlin Crisis, Bevin asked the Americans to send to Europe a number of B-29 nuclear bombers on a temporary basis. They responded immediately. Gowing says that the US ambassador,

was anxious to know at once whether the United States might send to

---

[51] Bullock, *Ernest Bevin*, pp. 513–18.

[52] See Daniel Yergin, *Shattered Peace: The Origins of the Cold War and the National Security State* (London: André Deutsch, 1978); and John Lewis Gaddis, *Strategies of Containment* (New York: OUP, 1982).

[53] Cited by Simon Duke, *US Defence Bases in the United Kingdom* (London: Macmillan, 1987) 23.

[54] Ibid. 27–8.   [55] Ibid. 20–5.

Britain three groups of heavy bombers, as a political gesture and a token of interest in the defence of Europe. [56]

In any case, the Cabinet were in favour and agreed the same day. Three groups of B-29s were stationed in Britain by the end of the the year. American officials subsequently expressed surprise that the British government—actually another small secret Cabinet committee—had agreed to it with such apparent lack of concern for the future implications. Bevin was asked by the US Secretary of State whether he had fully considered the implications. Simon Duke comes to the conclusion that,

fear of Russian expansionist aims in Europe following the successful Communist coup in Czechoslovakia, the imminent withdrawal of Russia from the Berlin Kommandatura, fear of an American retreat into isolationism that characterized the inter-war years, and last, but not least, the Spaatz–Tedder agreement effectively made any other decision improbable. [57]

British ministers saw the American presence as a temporary feature prompted by the Berlin crisis. However, this is not the way the Americans saw it. Secretary of Defence Forrestal's diary shows that he saw it as an opportunity to send aircraft immediately, before the British changed their minds, so that they would become 'an accepted fixture'.[58] In 1949 the Americans asked for bases in Oxfordshire and were clearly intending to settle down. In March of that year, the National Security Council determined that 'the development of four airfields in the Oxford area of the United Kingdom was in the national interest', and it brought pressure to bear on the British government to finance the building work required.[59] This was at first resisted by the Treasury because of Britain's precarious economic situation following the war. Moreover, at this time the Foreign Office had no clear idea of 'what the US really had in mind'.[60] The general impression is that a British government decision was being pre-empted by the understanding between the two air-forces. But that is not to say they would have strongly objected had they known of the long-term American

[56] Gowing, *Independence and Deterrence*, p. 310.
[57] Duke, *US Defence Bases*, p. 31.
[58] Andrew Pierre, *Nuclear Politics* (OUP, 1972) 79, n. 1.
[59] Duke, *US Defence Bases*, p. 48.
[60] Ibid. 55.

intentions. By the end of 1949, the American plan was for at least seventeen air-bases and facilities in the United Kingdom, as the minimum to carry out US Emergency War Plans.[61] In March 1950 Air Chief Marshal Slessor put pressure on the Cabinet to arrange negotiations to meet the Americans requirements. The result was an Ambassadors' Agreement in April 1950 by which work on the bases was divided between the United States and Britain. Although there was nothing in the agreement about a permanent US presence, this was now understood on both sides, and the Americans certainly saw it as 'the first phase of a tremendously large expansion of the original USAF plans for operations in the United Kingdom'.[62]

The British government welcomed the agreement, but there were some anxieties. Ernest Bevin wanted to know how Britain would secure its right to bring the arrangements to a close, and what would happen if the United States conducted active operations from United Kingdom airfields before the United Kingdom was at war. He finally managed to get an informal assurance that Britain had the right to terminate the arrangement, but could not obtain any assurance about consultation prior to the use of the bombers. After some ministerial agonizing about the latter, it was decided to let the matter lie for fear of offending the Americans. For their part, the Chiefs of Staff found the situation with regard to prior consultation intolerable, and it was a source of great anxiety for them from 1948 until at least 1953, during which period many unsuccessful attempts were made to achieve an agreement with the United States government on the right to be consulted. In September 1949 the news that the Russians had exploded their first atomic bomb brought with it the certainty that Britain would be in the front line of any atomic retaliation if American bombs were used. But the Americans simply would not discuss the use of the bomb in their meetings with the British Chiefs of Staff.

For some observers, the unexpected arrival of the Soviet bomb removed one of the main strategic arguments for the independent British bomb. Britain could scarcely pit nuclear weapons against Soviet divisions if this would mean the instant nuclear destruction of its own cities. From this time on there was not only a problem of morality attached to the use of British atomic weapons, but also a

[61] Duke, *US Defence Bases*, p. 53.
[62] Ibid. 55.

problem of strategic rationality. However, as we have seen, ideas about how the bomb would be used have always taken second place to the feelings of confidence and status inspired by its possession. Early in 1950 the Chiefs of Staff reviewed both Western global strategy and the arguments for Britain continuing with the bomb project after the Russian explosion.[63] They decided that, since the aim of the Soviet Union was to bring about a Communist world dominated by Moscow, the West needed to retain superiority in offensive air-power—which meant the ability to carry atomic warfare into the heart of Russia. This would provide the backing and confidence that was needed for the West to succeed in the political and economic fronts, where the contest with Communism was being fought. As for continuing with the British project in the face of the enormous American lead—which would seem to have rendered it unnecessary—they argued that there were strong military and political reasons for Britain having a small stockpile of her own. It is not clear what the military reasons were, but the political reasons were largely a matter of retaining influence on the United States, which would evaporate altogether if the atomic project was allowed to die, or so they feared. However, where Britain was concerned, the priority should be the development of *defensive* weapons against atomic attack, i.e. guided missiles.

This was also the Ministry of Defence position. But the Ministry of Supply and the controller of the Atomic Energy Project, Lord Portal, took the opposite position: that priority should be given to atomic weapons, on the grounds that it would be dangerous to run down the project. Again, there were strong political reasons for this: if the atomic bomb teams thought the project was of less than supreme importance, they would lose morale and drain away, and the prospect of getting collaboration with the Americans in atomic matters would fade as they came to see that Britain had less and less to contribute. In Cabinet, Bevin above all was against leaving atomic power to the Americans. The final outcome was a victory for Lord Portal. Never again did strategic defence get a high priority and, in 1958 when the Soviet Union had developed ballistic missiles, it was abandoned altogether.

An intensification of the apparent threat from the East came in 1950 when the Korean War broke out. British ministerial state-ments soon afterwards show that there was a real fear of a Soviet

[63] Gowing, *Independence and Deterrence*, pp. 231–4.

onslaught in Europe, using Korea as a diversion. [64] Memories of appeasement were reactivated and the behaviour of the Soviet Union was likened to that of Nazi Germany in the late 1930s.[65] The deterrent qualities of the (US) atomic bomb were much emphasized in Britain. A strong note of *ideological deterrence* entered into ministerial speeches: the bomb was not simply for the purpose of preventing war, but for stemming the terrible tide of World Communism, described by Attlee in a Commons debate as a 'militaristic and imperialist creed held with fanaticism by its adherents'.[66] At this time, the Labour government initiated a massive rearmament programme, calling up reservists and turning over much engineering industry to armaments production. The programme was so ambitious that it had to be drastically cut back by the succeeding Conservative government. The post-war process of reciprocal threats, fuelled by the atomic bomb and rigidified on both sides by the bitter memories of the appeasement era, was now firmly set on course.

The military crisis of 1950 provoked another kind of panic in the Labour government: that the Americans might use their atomic weapons in Korea and then—if the war spread to Europe—from bases in Britain. High level discussions produced verbal recognition in the United States that British sovereignty was at issue when it was a matter of using bombs from British bases, and that the host country could not be expected to risk annihilation without consultation. But Attlee's attempts to get a written, formal agreement were a total failure. His much-publicized dash to Washington in December 1950 when President Truman was threatening to use atomic bombs in Korea, achieved a verbal reassurance from Truman about consultation. Much later, Dean Acheson, who was Secretary of State at the time of the visit, spoke with admiration of Attlee's success but added that, 'We had to unachieve that.'[67]

The British anxiety about consultation was no sign of loss of confidence in the United States to defend Britain. By this time, the view of the Soviet Union as a direct military threat to Britain,

[64] Minister of Defence Emmanuel Shinwell in the Defence debate, 26–7 July 1950, House of Commons Report, vol. 478, col. 471.

[65] Prime Minister Clement Attlee in the Commons Debate, 12 Sept. 1950, House of Commons Report, vol. 478, col. 951.

[66] Ibid., col. 953.

[67] Gowing, *Independence and Deterrence*, p. 315.

poised to advance wherever it could, had taken a firm hold. Churchill and others sincerely believed that the United States with its atomic weapons had successfully deterred the Soviet army from sweeping across Europe. The Labour leadership was in no position to be less concerned, being always sensitive to accusations of being soft on defence and favourable to Communism—though Attlee and Bevin needed no pushing on that matter. So keeping the Americans in Europe was a major preoccupation of successive Governments. By the end of 1952, the total number of airfields apportioned to the USAF in Britain for one function or another had grown to 43, including 7 main bomber bases, and there were some 45,000 US service personnel.[68] The supposed security advantages came at the price of making Britain subservient to American strategic interests: loss of sovereign control over war preparations made on its territory; establishment as number-one target for early nuclear attack by the Soviet Union—a point emphasized clearly by Churchill himself: 'We must not forget that by creating the American atomic base in East Anglia, we have made ourselves the target and perhaps the bull's eye of a Soviet attack.'[69] Thus the alliance engendered its own insecurities. From this time on the need for an independent nuclear deterrent to Soviet attacks on US bases in Britain became one of the main arguments for continuing with the British bomb. The Americans might be unwilling to put their own homeland in danger by retaliating for a strike on Britain.

Despite the security panics of 1950–1, the answer to the hypothetical question with which this section started is probably 'Yes': those who led Britain at that period (to say nothing of the men waiting in opposition) would have continued with the bomb project in the absence of the 'Soviet Threat'. Great Power status, anxiety about future abandonment by the United States, the desire to deal with American officials on equal terms, and the momentum of the project itself, all appear together to have provided sufficient reason. But it is necessary to remember that it *is* a hypothetical question: the early American monopoly of the bomb, the regional insecurity and aggressiveness of the Soviet Union and its resolve to catch up with the West, and the actions issuing from the US policy of Containment—these created a climate of fear of the immediate

---

[68] Duncan Campbell, *The Unsinkable Aircraft Carrier* (London: Michael Joseph, 1984), 38.

[69] House of Commons Report, 15 Feb. 1951, vol. 484, col. 630.

future. This fear would probably not have been quite so acute for a country with less grand memories and claims to international importance. Other countries with similar capabilities did not feel the same need—Sweden and Canada, for instance. But it was sufficient to make the British bomb a necessary symbol of survival in the minds of those who believed that the country's continued greatness was their responsibility. Threats to status and threats to security are not easy to disentangle—they appear to engender each other.

The British Bomb Becomes a Reality

The policy of the 1945–52 Labour governments had not been to rest Britain's defence solely on the threat to use nuclear weapons, American or otherwise. They were seen by the government, if not by the Chiefs of Staff, as weapons of last resort only, and strong conventional rearmament was thought to be necessary in order to hold back any Soviet invasion. However, it soon became clear that the massive conventional rearmament programme was impossible for the country to sustain. It contributed to a severe economic crisis in the early 1950s. There was a danger that such a situation would undermine security. It was realized that Britain could no longer expect to maintain a large, balanced array of forces on top of the nuclear programme and at the same time try to reconstruct its industries. It was the beginning of those economic ills which became a major factor in the choice of nuclear deterrence as the foundation of Britain's security. When it was realized that not only did Britain not have the means to match Communist forces in Europe, but that—thanks to the destructive power of nuclear weapons—*it did not even need to do so*, then the pathway became clear towards this choice, which was made decisively in 1957.

There were stages in this choice however. In early 1952, the chiefs of Staff produced a Global Strategy Paper which, in the words of Andrew Pierre, 'eventually led Britain to become the first nation to base its national security planning almost entirely upon a declaratory policy of nuclear deterrence'.[70] The key proposal of the paper was that NATO countries should not try to deploy sufficient conventional forces to stop a Soviet advance, since in the end they could not afford to do so. They should deploy just enough to halt a

[70] Pierre, *Nuclear Politics*, pp. 1, 87.

Soviet advance for a period during which the nuclear counter-offensive would make itself felt: the so-called 'trip-wire' strategy.[71] Accompanying this was the assertion that there could be no defence against a Soviet atomic attack on Britain. NATO should therefore be prepared to reply to any aggression with immediate, crushing atomic retaliation.[72] This was seen by the Chiefs of Staff as being in continuity with Britain's successful practice in World War II: 'it has always been a cardinal point in British air policy that the counter-offensive is an indispensable element in air defence,' they wrote. In Lawrence Freedman's opinion, this was primarily meant as a message to the Americans, since any nuclear strike forces would have to depend upon them for some years to come.

Why did Britain need an independent deterrent if the United States could provide it? As we have seen already, the main reason was to obtain leverage within the Alliance. The Chiefs of Staff declared that:

We feel that to have no share in what is recognized as the main deterrent in the cold war and the only Alliance offensive in a world war would seriously weaken British influence on United States policy and planning in the cold war and in war would mean that the United Kingdom would have no claim to any share in the policy or planning of the offensive. [73]

Recent discussion in Washington on the use of atomic weapons had shown the Chiefs that they were at a serious diplomatic disadvantage without actual nuclear weapons of their own.

When, on 3 October 1952, the first British atomic bomb was exploded at Monte Bello, it was hoped that the desired influence would be immediately regained. The event was accompanied with a great display of national chauvinism in the press and statements to the effect that world security was now much strengthened.[74] On 23 October, Churchill made a statement about the test in the Commons, during which he said that he thought it would 'lead to a much closer American interchange of information than has hitherto taken place'.[75]

[71] Lawrence Freedman, *The Evolution of Nuclear Strategy* (London: Macmillan, 1982), 80.

[72] Baylis, *Anglo-American Defence Relations*, p. 68.

[73] Gowing, *Independence and Deterrence*, p. 441.

[74] See Joan Smith, *Clouds of Deceit, The Deadly Legacy of Britain's Bomb Tests* (London: Faber and Faber, 1985), 80 ff.

[75] House of Commons Official Report, vol. 505, col. 1270.

However history had moved on and things were not so simple. Only nine days later, on 1 November, the United States exploded its first true thermonuclear device at Eniwetok in the Pacific. It had a yield of about 10 megatons, some 1,000 times that of the bomb dropped on Hiroshima.[76] So Britain had 'arrived' only to find that there existed a weapon of limitless destructive power which it did not have. Moreover, the Americans, being so far ahead, were not particularly interested in exchange of information. For Britain herself to develop the H-bomb appeared to be the only way of equalizing with the United States and of getting back to the happy state of affairs which Churchill had known during the war.

The Silence of the Moralists

Once the immediate revulsion and soul-searching caused by Hiroshima and Nagasaki in 1945 had died away there was little moral argument to be heard for quite a long period. There were two main reasons for this: the fact that the West had a monopoly—or at least an overwhelming superiority—of nuclear weapons for most of the period, and the fact that there was no general understanding of the evils of radioactive fall-out. One might also add that problems resulting from actually possessing the bomb were felt to be problems for the Americans who possessed it. Britain's problems came from not possessing it and it was generally assumed that the first priority was to catch up and thereby restore something of Britain's former greatness.

As to the effect of Western superiority, it has generally been the case that outbreaks of moral concern over the bomb have followed a renewed fear of a Soviet nuclear threat to the West. The Soviet achievement of the H-bomb in the early 1950s and the achievement of nuclear parity in the late 1970s have preceded the two main periods of moral debate about nuclear weapons—although they are not the only cause of it. As to the second factor, the failure to appreciate the insidious, indiscriminate and transnational effects of fall-out caused nuclear weapons to be seen by many as more powerful versions of World War II weapons, rather than as something entirely different. Consequently, most of the arguments

---

[76] Jack Dennis (ed.), *The Nuclear Almanac* (Reading, Mass.: Addison-Wesley, 1984), 62. The first deliverable bomb was the one used in the *Bravo* test at Bikini Atoll on 1 Mar. 1954.

of the few moralists to discuss the weapons in a serious way during the earliest period were couched in terms of violation of proportionality rather than of discrimination.[77] Despite the publication in 1946 of a detailed report by a British mission sent to study the effects of the bombs at Hiroshima and Nagasaki,[78] parliamentary and public interest in the matter appears to have been nil at this early period. There is no indication that most people thought of the bomb as anything but a device for producing very large explosions which could destroy whole cities at one go. No anxiety was shown beforehand about possible fall-out from the British tests in Australia in 1952 and later. The only questions in the Commons were about possible damage to wildlife from the explosions. Five months before the first test, Churchill assured the House that there would be no danger 'to the health and safety of the people of Australia'.[79] There was very little objection at the time from politicians or public in Australia. At the Australian Commission of Enquiry into the tests in 1984, evidence was given of extraordinary carelessness, or callousness, in testing the immediate after-effects of the explosions, from 1952 until 1958, when they ceased. The Commission concluded that protection and decontamination had been well carried out according to the standards of the time, but that the Monte Bello tests, which contaminated largè areas of the Australian mainland and exposed an unknown number of aborigines to high doses of radiation, should never have been conducted there.[80]

Thus despite the predictions of dangerous secondary radiation which had been made in the Maud Report in 1942 and witnessed at Hiroshima and Nagasaki, this most evil effect of nuclear weapons was forgotten, discounted, or hidden. Politicians of both parties in government must bear some responsibility for this, since it was their stonewalling attitude to all parliamentary questions which

[77] See e.g. Walter Stein, 'A Time for Decision', *Crux*, Easter/Pentecost, ii. (Nov. 1948), 13; and Lawrence McReavy 'The Morality of Atomic Bombing', *Catholic Times*, 17 May 1946.

[78] *The Effects of Atomic Bombs at Hiroshima and Nagasaki*. Report of the British Mission to Japan, published for the Home Office and the Air Ministry (London: HMSO, 1946).

[79] House of Commons Official Report, vol. 499, col. 1658, 2.

[80] Smith, *Clouds of Deceit*, pp. 66, 110. See also, Anthony Tucker, 'Cloud of Unknowing', *Guardian*, 17 Mar. 1983; a report on recent evidence released at the Public Records Office, *Guardian*, 28 Nov. 1984; and the conclusions of the enquiry, *Guardian*, 6 and 13 Dec. 1985.

successfully kept atomic matters out of debate for many years. There are obvious reasons why a government should want to keep the issue out of the public eye. As proved in later years, the invisible and delayed effects of radiation, which make all nuclear weapons 'dirty' weapons, tend to turn civilians against them as nothing else does.

The obscurity of this subject in the early years contributed to the widespread tendency to discuss the moral issues—when they were discussed at all—only in terms of immediate deaths. This narrow approach to the ethics of nuclear war—which has continued in some circles until this day—helps to ensure that government replies to moral criticism can be conducted on the relatively easy terrain of proportionality, where the Soviet threat can be presented in whatever terms are necessary to make nuclear war of some kind a proportionate response.

With very few exceptions, it cannot be said that moralists—either theological or secular—were awake to the real situation in the period during which the vital decisions were being made towards Britain becoming a host to American nuclear weapons and then an independent nuclear power in its own right.

5

JOINING THE 'H-CLUB', 1953–1956

The Year of the H-bomb

The research decisions which led to the British hydrogen-bomb project were made quickly in 1952, after the news of the first American explosion.[1] However, the full destructive power of thermonuclear explosions were not yet appreciated in Britain. This knowledge came as a consequence of the American *Bravo* test at Bikini Atoll on 1 March 1954. It was this explosion, and the series which immediately followed it—rather than the explosions at Hiroshima and Nagasaki—that marked the true revolution in public consciousness caused by nuclear weapons. There was now a weapon that not only caused world-wide fall-out, affecting everyone, but one which could potentially destroy, not merely cities, but the entire human world. It marked the beginning of widespread moral revulsion which gave rise to the anti-nuclear movements later in the decade. The Bikini explosion was twice as powerful as expected—nearly 15 megatons—and, owing to unforeseen changes in the weather, according to the official story, radioactive fall-out contaminated over 7,000 square miles of the Pacific, seriously affecting a large number of Marshall Islanders 110 miles downwind, and the crew of the Japanese fishing boat, *Fifth Lucky Dragon*, one of whom died of radiation burns.

News of this disaster soon became public in Britain, and a few weeks later the government was beginning to get panicky about the possible impact on public opinion. Both the British and United

---

[1] Anthony Eden in *Full Circle* (London: Cassell, 1960), 368, states that the Conservative government 'decided to make the hydrogen bomb in 1952, and so reported to Parliament'. There seems to be no parliamentary record of this and Peter Malone thinks there may have been a secret decision to make the H-bomb in 1952. In 1954, the formal Cabinet decision would be giving constitutional sanction to research and production that had been proceding towards the H-bomb for two years already. See A. F. Allen and I. Bellany (eds.), *The Future of the British Nuclear Deterrent*, Centre for the Study of Arms Control and International Security (University of Lancaster, 1982), 13, 24, n. 38.

States governments were very alarmed at the prospect of political opposition to their nuclear-weapons and nuclear-power pro- grammes. On 13 April, the Home Secretary, Sir D. Maxwell-Fyfe, laid before the Cabinet the draft of a speech he proposed to make in Bristol in which he reaffirmed the importance of the West having the H-bomb, since the only alternative would be surrender:

... it would only be a matter of time before we were obliged to abandon our freedom and hand ourselves over as slaves to a slave state. For that, sooner or later and probably sooner, would be the inevitable result of a decisive inferiority in our defensive equipment. Surely not one of us will give a moment's further consideration to such a fatalistic solution.[2]

He proposed to add that the H-bomb in the hands of the West would make the Soviet Union more vulnerable and therefore more inclined to take arms negotiations seriously.[3] As for Civil Defence, there was to be no change of outlook, and, in the event of a hydrogen-bomb attack, the WVS and the St John Ambulance Brigade were to carry on in their fine tradition of rescue work.

From May to July 1954 the Chiefs of Staff Committee and the Cabinet Defence Committee discussed the future of the British H-bomb programme. On 12 May, the Chief of Naval Staff, Sir Rhoderick McGrigor, argued that:

if we were to maintain our influence on the councils of the world it was essential that we should join the 'H-club'. From the practical point of view we must assess the minimum subscription that would be necessary for us to be recognized as a full member of that club.

To this was added the by-now-familiar argument from influence:

The United States is the most powerful country in the Free World but she is less experienced than we are. Whilst she can launch a nuclear attack on the Soviet Union without effective retaliation it is most important that we should retain and strengthen our influence on her policy.[4]

On 16 June 1954, the Cabinet Defence Committee proposed to a

---

[2] CAB 129/67, C(54). 149, Draft of Home Secretary's speech on Civil Defence, 13 Apr.1954.

[3] This oft-repeated argument seems to me to belong to the self-deceit that is endemic to the situation of those involved in making reciprocal threats. It is sometimes put in cruder terms: 'the only language the Russians understand is superior force'. Historically, the first reaction of the Soviet Union has always been to match the West in nuclear innovation and force levels.

[4] DEFE 4/70, COS (54) 54, United Kingdom Strategy, 12 May 1954.

full Cabinet meeting that Britain should produce the weapon, on which some progress must already have been made at Aldermaston. On 7 July Churchill told his Cabinet colleagues, 'We could not expect to maintain our influence as a world power unless we possessed the most up-to-date weapons.' At the next day's meeting, further arguments were produced to the effect that the thermo-nuclear bomb would be more economical than the atomic bomb and, ' . . . if we were ready to accept the protection offered by the United States use of the thermonuclear weapons, no greater moral wrong is involved in making them ourselves'. [5]

On 24 July the Cabinet Defence Committee, considering future defence policy in the light of revolutionary implications of the H-bomb, thought that Britain needed 'the military means to exert our influence as a World Power and to meet our "cold war" commitments', and that having the most modern weapons should take priority over preparations for fighting a major war, which they did not think was likely. These things were necessary if Britain was to 'hold its place in world councils on the issue of peace and war'.[6] On 26 July the Cabinet agreed that Britain should make the weapons. However, there were clearly some misgivings, since ministers also recognized that their decision would offend the consciences of 'substantial numbers of people in Britain'. But they argued that 'in so far as any moral principle was involved, it had already been breached by the decision of the Labour government to make the atomic bomb'.[7]

It was fall-out that was to cause the major problem. On 2 December 1954, the Minister of Defence, Harold Macmillan, presented a top-secret memorandum on fall-out to the Cabinet based on British scientists' assessment of the American H-bomb tests in the Pacific.[8] They estimated that, as a result of a 10 megaton explosion, fall-out would cover an area of 5,000 to 6,000 square

[5] Information on the meetings of 16 June and 7 July is from Richard Norton-Taylor's account of recently-released Cabinet papers in *Guardian*, 2 Jan. 1985. My search among the Cabinet papers in the Public Records Office has so far failed to discover the sources of these interesting remarks. It is possible that the papers containing them have since been withdrawn.

[6] Report by the Committee on Defence Policy, 24 July 1954, CAB 129/69, C(54) 250

[7] Ibid. n. 5.

[8] CAB 129/72, C(54). 389, Memorandum on Fall-out from the Minister of Defence, 9 Dec. 1954.

miles, and that there would be an inner zone of approximately 270 square miles (larger than Middlesex) in which radiation would be so powerful that all life would be extinguished, whether in the open or in houses. This information seemed to come as a powerful shock to the MOD. The memorandum speaks of 'a revolutionary effect over a wide range of our war plans, both military and civil'. However, there is anxiety lest the necessary changes in policy reveal to the public what lies behind them. Macmillan foresees that 'much of the present indifference of the public would vanish if they found that the government had adopted this basis for their defence plans'. The memorandum, and the accompanying assessment, make clear that the government was well aware even before Britain had the H-bomb that the effects of nuclear war would be much worse than those subsequently described in its own civil defence propaganda. The Cabinet was well aware too, that 'the man in the street' is more likely to worry about fall-out than about bomb damage. On 5 May 1954 it had been argued at a meeting of the Cabinet Atomic Energy Group that,

damage to the defence interests of ourselves and the Americans [changed in a later draft to the ideological category of 'the free world'] might possibly be caused, not by the disclosure to the Russians of information not otherwise in their possession, but from the effect of publicity on public opinion. It might be argued that public opinion might be so alarmed by official publicity that the Government would be handicapped in the pursuit of a policy of nuclear weapons development if that appeared to be the right course.[9]

For the first time then, serious political opposition to nuclear weapons was beginning to be feared, just when Britain was launching its own H-bomb programme. The government's reaction was to minimize the effect of radioactivity, setting up misleading safety standards and recommending quite unrealistic Civil Defence plans, which were not to be seriously challenged until many years later, when accurate knowledge became widespread, largely through independent American studies.[10]

The fear of domestic opposition was well founded. At the end of

[9] CAB 130/101, Gen 465, 4th meeting of the Atomic Energy Group, Nuclear Weapons Publicity, 5 May 1954. The meeting discussed a draft paper, 'Nuclear Weapons Publicity' in response to a request from Indian Prime Minister Mr Nehru.

[10] Cf. *The Medical Effects of Nuclear War*, The Report of the British Medical Association's Board of Science and Education (London: John Wiley, 1983), 31–91.

March 1954 Labour MPs—with some sympathy from the Conservative benches—introduced a motion in Parliament asking the government to seek a summit meeting with the Soviet leadership to arrange an end to all nuclear testing. It was defeated, but the warning had been given and Churchill promised to seek a summit meeting in the near future. The government was now in a dilemma: they felt it to be imperative that Britain should have its own H-bombs, but also realized that it would have to face heavy domestic and international pressure to accept a superpower agreement to halt testing before that goal was achieved. It was this situation that motivated Britain's very rapid development of thermonuclear weapons, from 1954 to 1957.[11]

There were also problems for the notion of deterrence. By 1954, it was known by the government that the West had lost its technological lead over the Soviet Union on which its previously reassuring concept of deterrence had rested. After the first Soviet thermonuclear test in August 1953, it was deduced that they had discovered how to make relatively cheap, easily-deliverable H-bombs using solid lithium deuteride. For critical thinkers like Blackett, this made the 'Great Deterrent' problematic, to say the least. It was little use threatening instant nuclear devastation of Soviet cities in response to a Red Army attack if this would provoke the immediate destruction of British cities.[12]

In the shadow of the reciprocal threat—and with the new, though confused, knowledge of the dangers of fall-out—the full implications of nuclear policies for civilian populations were at last beginning to be appreciated in Britain. Use of the H-bomb would not simply kill a large number of people at one go, as the atomic bomb had. It could also mean the end of human life on the planet. The official reaction—followed by much of the popular press—was to suggest that those who brought the matter up as an argument against the H-bomb were being disloyal, even pro-Russian agitators.[13]

---

[11] See John Simpson, *The Independent Nuclear State* (London: Macmillan, 1986), 104. Where the United States had taken 76 months from decision to first explosion, Britain took only 28. Of course, more things were understood by the time British scientists set about it.

[12] P. M. S. Blackett, 'British Policy and the H-bomb', in *Studies of War* (London: Oliver & Boyd, 1962), 39.

[13] Cf. Joan Smith, *Clouds of Deceit: The Deadly Legacy of Britain's Bomb Tests* (London: Faber and Faber, 1985), 94–6.

However, so far as the Chiefs of Staff were concerned, nothing but a renewed emphasis on immediate and overwhelming nuclear retaliation against Soviet territory would meet the new situation. In their opinion, there could be no mutual restraint if war came:

... the Allies would have to make immediate use of the full armoury of nuclear weapons with the object of countering Russia's overwhelming superiority of man-power.

Repudiating an entire moral and legal tradition of warfare, they concluded that:

The employment of nuclear weapons will at once become general. It is of vital importance that the Allied strategic and tactical air forces should be capable of hitting back immediately *without any limitation on targets or weapons.* [14]

In their opinion, war with Russia in the near future was unlikely, and the best way to keep it so was to build up stockpiles of strategic and tactical nuclear weapons at airfields widely dispersed round the periphery of the Communist bloc, 'from all of which the attack can be concentrated on pre-selected targets'. In their estimation, 'the greater the deterrent the less the risk', meaning by this, the more powerful the stockpile of ready-to-use weapons close to the borders of the Soviet Union, the less the latter will be inclined to misbehave.

These recommendations probably influenced the formulations of the *Statement on Defence* published in February of the following year, 1955. It announced publicly for the first time that the government 'have thought it their duty' to proceed with the development and production of the British H-bomb, in view of the fact that the Soviet Union had already made it:

In the hands of the free world, which at present has a marked superiority both in the weapon itself and in the means of delivering it, and which has no thought of aggression, it is a most powerful deterrent ... In these circumstances our immediate duty and our policy are clear. To build up our own forces, in conjunction with those of our allies, into the most powerful deterrent we can achieve. By these means to work for peace through strength. Thus we shall hope to obtain real disarmament and relaxation of tension. [15]

Perhaps the contradiction inherent in this Statement could not be

[14] Memorandum from the Chiefs of Staff on United Kingdom Defence Policy, to the Cabinet Defence Committee, 23 Dec. 1954, CAB 131/14 (emphasis added).

[15] Cmd. 9391, *Statement on Defence: 1955.*

perceived by those who assumed that, while the Soviet Union was wholly aggressive in intent, NATO was wholly defensive, *and seen to be so by the Soviet Union*. Those who drafted the Statement do not appear to have reflected on the extraordinarily aggressive appearance that such a policy would present to those at the receiving end—especially in view of the much publicized recent talk in the United States of pre-emptive nuclear war against the Soviet Union, and of the idea of the 'roll-back' of the Soviet frontiers, much discussed on both sides of the Atlantic since 1952.

Several features of the 1955 Statement betray a moral unease about the H-bomb decision. One of them is the unusually frequent use of the language of duty. Another is the deliberate association of appeasement with any idea of giving up the option of having the H-bomb, as in the following somewhat browbeating set of unsupported assertions:

The consciences of civilized nations must naturally recoil from the prospects of using nuclear weapons. Nevertheless, in the last resort, most of us must feel that determination to face the threat of physical devastation, even on the immense scale which must now be foreseen, is manifestly preferable to an attitude of subservience to military Communism, with the national and individual humiliation that this would inevitably bring. Moreover, such a show of weakness and hesitation to use all the means of defence at our disposal would not reduce the risk. All history proves the contrary.[16]

Yet another sign of bad conscience is the rhetorical inflation of the Soviet threat. The Soviet Union is described as having 'six million men under arms backed by enormous reserves', which sounds somewhat like a European folk-memory of Asiatic hordes about to descend on civilization.

The use of nuclear weapons is the only means by which this massive preponderance can be countered . . . If we do not use the full weight of our nuclear power, Europe can hardly be protected from invasion and occupation, with all that this implies both for Europe and the United Kingdom.

Studies conducted in the early 1960s showed that the magnitude of Warsaw Pact conventional superiority had been grossly exaggerated, and that it would have been possible for NATO to match it in the 1950s, with its larger population and resources. NATO itself

[16] Ibid. 8.

had some 6 million persons under arms, and the WP some 1.5 million less.[17]

As Blackett once remarked, 'Once a nation pledges its safety to an absolute weapon, it becomes emotionally essential to believe in an absolute enemy.'[18] It may be that the inflation of destructive power now possessed in the H-bomb contributed to an inflation of rhetoric about Soviet capabilities and intentions. It is common for people to end up believing their own propaganda about enemies. This means that the inherent ambiguity of the 'deterrence through strength' stance is ignored. It is an aspect of that failure of objectivity that is endemic to those involved in reciprocal violence, even when this is only a matter of verbal threats and weapons deployments.[19] Each side pretends to a knowledge of the *real* situation that it does not have, convincing itself that it judges from an objective standpoint, from outside the situation. From there it can see clearly that it is innocent of aggressive intent and is only responding to threats from the other side, as any rational agent would do in the circumstances. It just knows that the enemy is innately aggressive and the only real threat to peace. In this way, each side is likely to become a mirror image of the other with regard to its perceptions. Thus for those who accepted the official rhetoric, it would have been much easier to justify the possession of thermonuclear weapons. Some kind of moral status was thereby given to a decision about which many people had an uneasy conscience.

In the Commons defence debate of 1 March 1955, Churchill defended the H-bomb decision in a highly emotional and apocalyptic speech. The chief danger in his estimation was a Soviet pre-emptive attack. Although no war was foreseen in the next three to four years (the Soviet Union could not yet deliver its weapons), if it should come after that he believed that both sides would certainly use thermonuclear weapons. The danger justified American superiority—reinforced by Britain—so that an immediate and far larger

[17] See Alain C. Enthoven and Wayne K. Smith, *How Much is Enough? Shaping the Defense Program, 1961–1969* (New York: Harper and Row, 1971), cited by David N. Schwartz, *NATO's Nuclear Dilemmas*, (Washington, DC: Brookings Institution, 1983), 148–9. For a similar estimation, see also Robert McNamara, 'The Military Role of Nuclear Weapons, Perceptions and Misperceptions', *Survival*, Nov.–Dec. 1983, 261–71.

[18] Blackett, *Studies of War*, p. 94.

[19] See René Girard, *Violence and the Sacred* (London: Johns Hopkins University Press, 1977), 69.

retaliation would be delivered. Besides airfields, administrative and industrial targets behind the Iron Curtain would have to be paralysed at the outset of war. Churchill wholeheartedly supported the global spread of US Air Force bases taking place at that time, from which the attacks would be made. Paradoxically, the West's development of the H-bomb did not, according to Churchill, add to the dangers, but diminished them, because it was now able to threaten the widely scattered population of the Soviet Union, and not only with enormous explosions, but also with radioactive contamination. As for the British H-bomb, it was necessary because,

Unless we make a contribution of our own . . . we cannot be sure that in an emergency the resources of other Powers would be planned exactly as we would wish, or that the targets which would threaten us most would be given what we consider the necessary priority, in the first few hours. [20]

The danger was presumably that the United States forward bases in Britain would be an early casualty of any war with the Soviet Union—taking Britain along with them—unless, that is, we had our own deterrent. This was the first public appearance of a long-lasting argument: the *American* nuclear presence makes the independent British bomb necessary.

Apart from a handful of radical critics, the Labour party as a whole did not dissent from the government's policy, or the H-bomb decision. The main criticism of the policy made by Shadow Defence Secretary Emmanuel Shinwell was that the Tories were putting the whole burden of deterrence on the bomb and were greatly weakening conventional defence. A National Executive Committee policy statement in 1955 formulated the Labour position:

Hitherto, only the United States of America and the USSR have possessed the hydrogen bomb. Labour believes that it is undesirable that Britain should be dependent on another country for this vital weapon. If we were, our influence for peace would be lessened in the councils of the world. It was for that reason that the Labour Government decided on the manufacture of the Atom bomb and that we support the production of the hydrogen bomb in this country. [21]

Although the Labour party under Hugh Gaitskell remained in

[20] House of Commons Official Report, 1–2 Mar.1955, vol. 537, col. 1897.
[21] Quoted by Minister of Defence Duncan Sandys in the defence debate, 16 Apr. 1957, to embarrass the Labour Party, which was by then deeply split on the issue: House of Commons Official Report, vol. 568, col. 1758 ff.

favour of possessing the bomb during the following five years, it became increasingly opposed—along with very many other people—to actually testing it. In the months leading up to the first test, in May 1957, there was almost daily pressure on the Prime Minister in Parliament to postpone it until efforts had been made to obtain an international test ban, separate from a general disarmament agreement. The coming British tests had become the focus of a world-wide protest—particularly from Asian governments— against contamination of the atmosphere and sea by radioactive fall-out. The main danger—already being realized as a result of American and Russian tests—was a buildup of strontium 90 in the bones of children, which would result, so many scientists predicted, in large numbers of bone cancers and leukaemias in the future.[22] Thus an entirely new ethical dimension was added to the possession of nuclear weapons—the first one really to touch the citizens of the nuclear states, who were affected by the danger as much as anyone else. It was this development more than any other which was a spur to the anti-nuclear campaigns that were to be such an important feature of British and American political life in the following years. However, the government was determined to make sure that Britain possessed a usable hydrogen weapon before any international test ban was signed. All protest, both domestic and diplomatic, was consequently ignored until this goal was achieved. The United States administration was at this time putting pressure on the Macmillan government to take part in a test moratorium by 1 July 1958 and in a cessation of the manufacture of fissile material in 1959. In June 1957 the Chiefs of Staff had told the government that from the point of view of Britain's standing as a world power and from a military point of view the proposal was unacceptable— Britain would not have built up a sufficient stockpile of its own weapons by then.[23] The government was in a dilemma on the issue, since it did not wish openly to dissent from the American view and show a split in the Western Alliance. Instead it pinned its hopes on a refusal of the Soviet government to accept the conditions which the Americans were insisting on for a test moratorium: verifiable

[22] See Robert A. Divine, *Blowing on the Wind*, (New York: OUP, 1978), 123–5.
[23] DEFE 4/97 Chiefs of Staff Committee, COS (57) 64, Confidential Annex, 5 June 1957; and DEFE 5/76 COS (57) 134, Disarmament: United States Informal Memorandum to the Soviet Delegation, Memorandum by the Chiefs of Staff, 6 June 1957.

control of the production of fissile material. The British government did not want such a thing any more than the Russians did, since it believed that such a condition would undermine its new defence policy.

The Labour leadership was not in a strong position to protest, being in favour of the British H-bomb in principle, and it was a simple matter for Macmillan to sow confusion among them.[24] He defended the coming British test by minimizing the fall-out danger and declaring that the whole of Britain's defence plans depended on it.

The first British H-bomb was exploded high over Christmas Island in the Pacific on 15 May 1957 releasing comparatively little fall-out into the atmosphere, but destroying vast numbers of sea birds which inhabited the island. The testing continued, with six further explosions, until September 1958, when a moratorium on all nuclear testing was arranged between the two superpowers and Britain. The purpose of the test series was to develop a reliable weapon in the megaton range which could be carried by the Blue Streak missile, i.e. to be a junior member of the same nuclear club as the US and the USSR. Since, further to the test moratorium, there was a probability of a comprehensive test ban and a halt to weapons production, the aim was also to build up as soon as possible a stockpile of operational nuclear bombs. To this end several of the newly constructed civil nuclear power stations were modified in 1957 to enable them to operate on a military fuel cycle. The object was not only to provide material for strategic weapons, but also for a new generation of tactical nuclear weapons.[25]

Once Britain's military/political status was assured, the government felt it could show some enthusiasm about a test ban treaty. John Simpson points out that the Conservative government's vigorous pursuit of internationalist disarmament and arms control measures after 1958 did not in the least contradict the aims of building up a credible stockpile of weapons. There were the same positive national security objectives inherent in both. The government believed that, once Britain had successfully joined the

---

[24] Macmillan's own account of the argument is in *Riding the Storm, 1956–1959* (London: Macmillan, 1971), 261 f.

[25] Cf. Simpson, *The Independent Nuclear State*, pp. 108–9. Simpson points out that the process of arming Britain with a substantial stockpile of nuclear weapons took place while the CND campaign was at its height and at a time of intensive international negotiations to halt the nuclear arms race. (Ibid. 157.)

thermonuclear club, it was in her interests to bring about international agreements which would inhibit the development by the superpowers of new weapons which would threaten the effectiveness of her existing weapons and once again relegate Britain to an inferior military position. [26]

Massive Retaliation and Tactical Nuclear Weapons in Europe

Churchill's statement in the 1955 debate that, 'Should war come . . . there are a large number of targets that we and the Americans must be able to strike at once',[27] was a reflection of the current American doctrine of Massive Retaliation (MR). MR was the name for a strategy by which, if war broke out with the Soviet Union, NATO would rely on immediate and massive use of American nuclear firepower in order to counteract what was thought at the time to be a very large Soviet advantage in conventional weapons. Conventional-force goals set at a meeting of NATO ministers at Lisbon in 1952 were soon abandoned as it became clear that none of the countries involved wanted to bear the extra expense. Instead, the Alliance turned to nuclear weapons as a substitute for the financial and manpower sacrifices which would have been necessary to mount an adequate conventional defence.[28] The result was a declaratory policy formulated by the American Secretary of State, John Foster Dulles, which sought to contain Communist expansion by taking advantage of the virtual American monopoly in nuclear weapons:

The basic decision was to depend primarily upon a greater nuclear capacity to retaliate instantly by means and at places of our own choosing. As a result it is now possible to get and to share *more basic security at less cost*. [29]

The purpose of the reduced conventional forces would be to contain the attack long enough for effects of NATO's immediate nuclear retaliation to be felt. This would include attacks on Soviet industrial centres, using American nuclear bombers from British

[26] Simpson, *The Independent Nuclear State*, p. 145.

[27] House of Commons Official Report, 1 Mar.1955, vol. 537, col. 1895.

[28] McNamara, 'The Military Role of Nuclear Weapons', pp. 261–71.

[29] John Foster Dulles, 'The Evolution of Foreign Policy', Department of State Bulletin 30, no. 761, 25 Jan. 1954, 108, cited by McNamara, 'The Military Role of Nuclear Weapons', p. 262 (emphasis added).

and Continental bases.[30] Deployed since 1948, the bombers were organized according to World War II concepts of strategic bombing. Most of their targets were in cities, and the destruction of Soviet civilians which would result from attacking these targets was treated as a bonus.

However, Lawrence Freedman shows that the US administration's actual policy was far more like graduated response than was usually thought to be the case, especially in Britain.[31] Deliberate ambiguity was promoted by Dulles's conduct of brinkmanship, which gave the impression that the United States just might reply to anything with an all-out nuclear attack. In 1953—the closing stages of the Korean War—the United States had several times used nuclear threats for diplomatic purposes.

However, British ideas of MR were less nuanced and British defence policy continued to incorporate the threat of immediate nuclear response throughout the 1950s, well past the time that the Americans had begun to look for options which would mean less than the end of the world if the Soviet Union made a mistake. One of the features of British policy which prevailed during these years was a certain innocence about the effects that threats of instant, overwhelming nuclear attack must have on the potential objects of it. A sentence from the 1956 Statement is typical:

'The objective of the Western Powers is defensive. They will never be the aggressors, but they must have and be known to have, the power of instant and overwhelming retaliation if attacked . . .'[32]

Until about 1954, few Europeans had thought what it would mean to be defended by nuclear weapons and, since the USAF had a preemptive function and there was no fear as yet of a Soviet nuclear retaliation, it did not seem necessary to do so. In 1953 and 1954 however, the US Army began to add an entirely new element to Europe's armoury: tactical nuclear weapons in the shape of artillery and short-range rockets. Freedman traces the source of these weapons to developments in American strategic thinking, among which was a move by the US Army to harness nuclear technology to fight land battles and to increase its fire power while making cuts in

[30] See Anthony Cave Brown, *Operation: World War III* (London: Arms and Armour Press, 1979).

[31] Lawrence Freedman *The Evolution of Nuclear Strategy* (London: Macmillan, 1981), 84.

[32] Cmd. 9691, *Statement on Defence: 1956*.

manpower.[33] In the following years large numbers of tactical nuclear weapons were brought to Europe, rising to a peak of about 7,000 in the mid-1960s. This fitted well enough with the preoccupations of the European members of NATO: to have US nuclear weapons committed to their defence and to counterbalance Soviet conventional forces as cheaply as possible. Reliance on cheap explosive power became central to NATO plans from this time onwards.

In December 1954, the NATO Council announced that it was reducing its force goals from 96 to 30 active divisions and that it was basing all of its future planning on the assumption that atomic weapons would be used in war. Ideas were moving in the direction of an actual nuclear defence of Western Europe. But this had the almost immediate effect of waking up some Europeans to the suicidal consequences of such a strategy. Much alarm was caused in Britain towards the end of 1954 by Field Marshal Lord Montgomery's characteristically blunt explanation of what NATO's tactical nuclear weapons were for:

> I want to make it absolutely clear that we at SHAPE are basing all our planning on using atomic and thermonuclear weapons, in our defence. With us it is no longer, 'They may possibly be used'. It is very definitely, 'They will be used, if we are attacked' . . . The reason for this action is that we cannot match the strength that could be brought against us unless we use nuclear weapons; and our political chiefs have never shown any great enthusiasm in giving us the numbers to be able to do without using such weapons.[34]

This amounted to the first public declaration of NATO's first-use policy. It caused Labour MP's to claim that control over nuclear weapons had passed from the political to the military—to their minds a very dangerous development.

Public reaction to the policy was even more alarmed in Germany, as might be expected. It was compounded in 1955 by the outcome of a major military exercise, *Carte Blanche*, which was designed to test the NATO Council's decision on early use of nuclear weapons. Three hundred and thirty five simulated atomic weapons were 'dropped' on more than a hundred targets during the exercise.

[33] Cmd. 9691, *Statement on Defence: 1956*, p. 68.
[34] Field Marshal Lord Montgomery, 'A Look Through a Window at World War III', *Journal of the Royal United Services Institute*, 99: 596 (Nov. 1954), 508.

These resulted in an estimated 1.7 million Germans killed and 3.5 million wounded—more than five times the German civilian casualties in World War II. Casualties from fall-out were not computed, so the total was very much on the conservative side.[35] This result caused Helmut Schmidt to remark that the use of tactical nuclear weapons 'will not defend Europe but destroy it'.[36]

However, the attitudes of the American administration towards nuclear war-fighting were a lot more sanguine. In April 1955 the British government received a communication from the ambassador in Washington to the effect that the US government wished to educate the world public on the difference between the massive H-bombs it had recently been testing, and the,

smaller and more precise tactical atomic weapons, which can legitimately be used in the framework of conventional armaments and minor wars, and are indeed less destructive of civilian life and property than the mass pattern bombing of the last war. The Administration considers this particularly important, both in the context of the decision to supply NATO forces with tactical atomic weapons, and also of their possible use in the Far East. [37]

Both Secretary of State Dulles and President Eisenhower had stated in press conferences to launch this PR campaign that tactical nuclear weapons could select and destroy military targets and produce no radioactive fallout: 'Just as bullets would be used', Eisenhower had said. What the US administration wanted the British government to do was to make clear to its own people *the technical and moral justifications* of the tactical nuclear weapons with which allied forces are now being equipped'. Dulles pointed out for good measure that 'Reliance on conventional weapons would be hopelessly costly'. The Foreign Office and Defence Ministry reaction to this campaign was wholly negative. They repudiated the attempt to make a moral distinction between larger and smaller nuclear weapons:

[35] These details are from Paul Bracken, *The Command and Control of Nuclear Forces*, p. 161. He gives no reference for them. See also McNamara, 'The Military Role of Nuclear Weapons'.
[36] McNamara, 'The Miltary Role of Nuclear Weapons', p. 266.
[37] *Distinction Between Large and Tactical Nuclear Weapons*, memorandum by the Secretary of State for Foreign Affairs and the Minister of Defence, CAB 129/74, C (55) 95, 5 Apr. 1955. The memorandum followed the advice of the Chiefs of Staff and Sir William Penney.

The possession by the West of a stock of nuclear weapons of all kinds and the ability to deliver them is at present the most important factor in achieving our aim of preventing war. *An attempt to divide them into those which are small and therefore morally justifiable and those which are large and therefore immoral would inevitably reduce their deterrent value as a whole.* It would be fatal to give the impression that as long as no hydrogen bomb was dropped on Allied territory, none would be used against Russia, or that the only likely victims of nuclear weapons in a new global war would be the armed forces and not *the civilian populations* or centres of government and industry. [38]

This response encapsulates the difference between British and American thinking on nuclear weapons at that time. It was a conflict to be repeated several times in the Alliance, notably in the early 1980s over the question of limited nuclear war in Europe. It is of course largely based on the very different geopolitical situations of the two countries. The United States wanted to be able to use nuclear weapons in the Far East in its 'minor wars' against the Communists, and also in Europe, without necessarily putting its own cities at risk from retaliation, whereas the British government was thinking only about not fighting wars in Europe. Nevertheless, the express rejection of any moral use of nuclear weapons in official policy has seldom been put so plainly.

Nuclear Revisionism: Graduated Deterrence

Not everyone in the British military establishment thought that moral distinctions were out of place in nuclear strategy. Some thought that a more moral use of nuclear weapons, based on the principle of minimum force, could be combined with a more effective deterrence. Early in 1956 Rear-Admiral Sir Anthony Buzzard was arguing vigorously against MR in favour of 'graduated deterrence'.[39] He proposed a new declaratory policy for the West based on 'a clear distinction between a tactical and a strategic use of nuclear weapons, so that we can use our atomic weapons tactically without provoking the strategic use of hydrogen

[38] *Distinction Between Large and Tactical Nuclear Weapons* (emphasis added).
[39] Rear-Admiral Sir Anthony Buzzard, Marshal of the RAF Sir John Slessor, and Richard Lowenthal, 'The H-bomb: Massive Retaliation or Graduated Deterrence', *International Affairs*, 32/2 (Apr. 1956), 148. The ideas are developed by Richard Goold-Adams, *On Limiting Atomic War* (London: Royal Intitute of International Affairs, 1956). They are critically discussed by Freedman, *The Evolution of Nuclear Strategy*, pp. 112–17.

weapons'. By 'tactical' he meant the use of weapons against armed forces and by 'strategic', their use against centres of population. He believed that MR as defined by Dulles was 'too drastic and inflexible' to obtain the objectives of defence policy: to prevent all wars, to ensure that the H-bomb is never used, to strengthen the West's hand in negotiations and in blocking Communist expansion and power politics around the globe, among other things.

If threatened with aggression which, though limited, was too powerful for our conventional forces to combat, we should have the option of saying to the aggressor: 'If you use aggression we will, if necessary use atomic and chemical weapons against your armed forces. But we will not, on this particular issue, use hydrogen or bacteriological weapons at all, unless you do, and we will not use mass destruction weapons against centres of population—regardless of the targets they contain—unless you do so deliberately.'

Strategically, the object would be 'to plug the gap between small conventional defence and major all-out war with the use of all-out nuclear weapons'. The aim was to develop a form of warfare that would be 'sufficiently costly to an aggressor to make local aggression not worthwhile' but not 'automatically so terrible that any threatened country or its allies would shrink from using atomic weapons to defend itself'. Deterrence was to come as much from the threat of making any aggression too costly to the enemy's armed forces as from the threat of ultimate punishment to its homeland. It would exploit Western assets, which at this time were believed to include a superiority in tactical atomic weapons for use on land, sea, and air; a technical superiority in making precision attacks; and an ability to deliver strategic weapons by bombers against the Soviet homeland greatly superior to anything the Soviet Union could do against the West, certainly against the United States, given the 'extremely advantageous geographical location of American advanced air-bases'. The tactical weapons could not deter on their own: the threat of the Western ultimate deterrent would serve to compel the aggressor to accept the West's distinction in the use of nuclear weapons. In order to make the strategy effective, tactical nuclear weapons would need to be used early rather than late, before things got entirely out of hand and distinctions became impossible. Then there would be a mutual interest in limiting nuclear use.

The moral argument depended on the absolute necessity of limitation in war if it was going to achieve its objects:

The moral standards which we propose to defend demand not only this action in the event of aggression, but the pursuance of long term policies which will enable us to conform to these standards to the best of our ability in the future. Massive retaliation hardly passes this test, nor indeed does it square with the moral standards we professed to uphold at the Nuremburg trials. Graduated deterrence on the other hand, at least aspires to pursue these principles so far as is possible, and it seeks to restore moderation and the rule of law in the future conduct of war, without which we will surely never succeed in abolishing it.

However, the strategy was still to depend on the ultimate threat of city-destruction, to be put into practice if the Soviet Union failed to observe the distinctions. The reciprocity rule was still thought to allow the threat of ultimate violence as a kind of necessity existing somehow outside morality.

A response to these proposals representing nuclear orthodoxy came from Sir John Slessor,[40] who had been one of the chief architects of British nuclear strategy. Like the government, he opposed the limitation of any particular weapons in war between the Great Powers. He believed that Buzzard's scheme would suit the Russians very well, by making their homeland virtually immune from attack. Destruction would be confined to NATO soil, particularly Germany, and possibly also the Soviet satellites like Poland and Czechoslovakia. Here he put his finger on the permanent weakness of all graduated deterrence strategies in the European context. They threaten to do more damage to the defended territory than to the aggressor. This objection would become even more potent once the Soviet Union had its own tactical nuclear weapons. An early exchange of tactical nuclear weapons on European soil would hardly be any different in its effects from an all-out nuclear war. So far as the Europeans were concerned limited nuclear war was a contradiction in terms. Other critics pointed out that this would be self-deterring. A threat to use tactical nuclear weapons at an early stage would be no more credible than MR itself. Hopes of precision attacks using nuclear weapons were unrealistic, given their immense destructive power and the effects of fall-out. Thus the principle of minimum force,

[40] See n. 39, above.

taken on its own, without other moral principles which might dictate, for instance, an absolute restraint on weapons with indiscriminate effects, did not appear to lead to a rational strategy. In the eyes of most observers, the most important distinction to be observed in all conflicts remained that between nuclear weapons and non-nuclear weapons. Few believed that, once nuclear weapons were used, the relevant distinctions could be observed.

Buzzard's proposals came about eighteen months before the launching of Sputnik, which somewhat altered Western perceptions in this matter. Clearly, conditions in 1956 were very different from those in which the otherwise similar strategy of flexible response was to be adopted more than ten years later, by which time the Soviet Union was not only able to deliver its strategic weapons wherever it chose, but had also deployed its own tactical nuclear weapons in Europe. The hope of compelling a low level of nuclear use depended on Western nuclear superiority. The achievement of parity by the Soviet Union would make it a far more dubious proposition.

Conclusions

During the post-war period covered in the preceding two chapters, 1945–56, there were two chief factors determining the attitude of British officials to nuclear weapons: the desire to maintain Britain's high position in the league table of nations by obtaining the weapons which were appropriate to its status; and the belief, firmly established in World War II and vigorously promoted by the Chiefs of Staff, that Britain needed to open any future war with massive atomic attacks on enemy resources—including the civilian population—in the manner of World War II campaigns. The Chiefs of Staff Committee had a very strong influence on the developing policy of the Attlee government in particular.

The status motive was automatic and shared by everyone, except a few far-sighted individuals who realized the truth about Britain's permanent political and economic decline. The assumptions of Great Power status, together with the American withdrawal of co-operation, ensured that the British bomb would be made, whoever the next enemy might be. It was absolutely necessary to be able to stand up to the Americans. The Soviet threat was of secondary importance in the decision to become an independent nuclear power. Britain saw itself, by right of history and scientific achievement, as the number two partner in the world's most powerful military alliance. This factor also ensured willing co-operation with the re-establishment of American forward bases once the Soviet Union emerged as the enemy.

As for the Chiefs of Staff and their ideas about how the next war would be fought—no kind of moral restraint or limitation of weapons or targets was considered relevant to them. Throughout this period, neither politicians nor the military considered nuclear weapons to be anything other than weapons of mass destruction, and their immediate and massive use inevitable in any war with the Soviet Union. It was not nuclear deterrence as it later featured in moral argument. American suggestions in 1955 that smaller atomic weapons might be thought of as capable of moral or conventional use was decisively rejected by the Churchill government.

Moral reflection figured hardly at all in all this. After the Cold War set in and the myth of the 'Soviet Threat' was firmly established, a view of East–West relations emerged which seriously inhibited objective ethical analysis. The Soviet Union was seen to be innately aggressive, as well as vastly superior in everything except nuclear weapons. The Western Alliance was declared to be wholly defensive and its nuclear threats purely deterrent. Whatever its objective reality, the Soviet threat was interpreted as the ultimate evil kept at bay only by the ultimate weapon. They needed each other. No account was taken of the fact that the Soviet Union too had lessons to learn from the war with the Nazis and that it was in the highest degree unlikely to see a nuclear threat from the West as anything but provocative and highly threatening to its continued existence.

However, the world-wide alarm caused by the testing of H-bombs put moral questions back on the agenda in the mid-1950s, as the publics of nuclear nations themselves began to feel menaced by the long-term effects of fall-out. This threatened to destroy public apathy about nuclear weapons and to lead to an inter-national test ban before Britain had the chance to make and test its own H-bomb. For this reason, the unprecedented effects of nuclear warfare were played down in official publications. Despite the efforts of the government to dampen and control the alarm, nothing could prevent the H-bomb being seen as qualitatively different from anything preceding it. Not only did it have world-wide indiscriminate effects, but its destructive power was potentially unlimited. It destroyed all conventional notions of civil defence. The government of Winston Churchill, which made all the vital decisions leading to the British H-bomb, was acutely afraid that knowledge of these matters would turn public opinion against the plans to make Britain an independent nuclear power. These fears were partially fulfilled in the next period to be considered.

6

DETERRENCE ON THE CHEAP, 1957–1964

The New Defence Policy of 1957

Making bombs in secret and testing them in faraway places was one thing: a lot of things could be taken for granted when it was the common opinion that Britain's status in the world demanded the possession of the most powerful weapons available. Actual strategic questions did not have to be thought through with any precision. But making Britain's defence depend almost wholly on nuclear weapons as was done in the 1957 and 1958 Defence White Papers was quite another thing: it had to be done politically in the open and it brought into the light awkward questions about nuclear status which the country as a whole—as distinct from professional groups with their own interests—had not had to face before. In ascending order of importance, the leading questions were: (1) a matter of *policy*: did it make economic sense for Britain to continue with its independent strategic nuclear force? (2) a matter of *strategy*: could it ever be rational for a British Prime Minister to order the use of nuclear weapons? (3) a matter of *morality*: was it tolerable for Britain to base its defence on the threat to destroy Soviet cities?

A number of factors made nuclear weapons one of the most important political issues during this period. Among them was the aftermath of the Suez defeat. On the strategic side it had exposed Britain's vulnerability to pressure from the superpowers: the United States had been hostile and obstructive and the Soviet Union had made nuclear threats. On the political side it had revealed to many just how far down the scale of powers Britain had slid since the war. It was clearly no longer the world power which could get political results by the use of force, and it was not able to stand up to its main ally in a serious clash of interests. The event caused a fresh economic crisis at a time when Britain was still trying to recover from World War II. It was generally agreed that, since

1950, the country had been attempting to do too much in the way of defence and that this had contributed to the very slow recovery and periodic crises of the economy.

As a result of these set-backs, the Conservative government under its new leader, Harold Macmillan, was much in need of a political recovery. A brand new defence policy was part of the recovery plan. Macmillan gave the new Defence Secretary, Duncan Sandys, a free hand in formulating a policy which he afterwards described as 'the biggest change in military policy ever made in normal times'.[1] The result was the 1957 Defence White Paper, which promised a much cheaper defence force, and at the same time promised to restore some of Britain's lost status, by staking everything on its nuclear weapons.[2] To the strategic and status arguments for nuclear independence was added a third—the economic. But this meant that independence was increasingly compromised by a deepening dependence on the United States for the supply of delivery vehicles, which Britain found itself unable to produce, mainly because of economic reasons.

The other major factor responsible for bringing the nuclear issue to the centre of public consciousness has already been introduced: the increasing public awareness of horrific effects caused by fall-out from H-bomb explosions and the total destruction that would be caused by an H-bomb war. This was aggravated by a new perception of the Soviet threat: the launching of Sputnik in October 1957 revealed the advances made by Soviet rocketry and the fact that the Soviet Union was able to send its nuclear weapons anywhere it chose, with no chance of defence against them. This factor contributed powerfully to the growth of anti-nuclear sentiment and the first real political challenge to the post-war consensus.

Deterrence or Defence?

The 1957 White Paper proposed to almost halve the size of the armed forces by 1962; to reduce the manpower of the BAOR and to make up for it with the fire-power of atomic artillery; to reduce the number of aircraft in Germany and offset this by providing

[1] Harold Macmillan, *Riding the Storm, 1956–1959* (London: Macmillan, 1971), 263.

[2] Cmnd. 124, *Defence: Outline of Future Policy: 1957.*

some of the squadrons with atomic bombs; to abandon the advanced bomber then being developed and to rely on ballistic missiles to be bought from the United States or developed with its help. Politically speaking, the most important move was the huge reduction in manpower which would come about through the abolition of National Service. Macmillan was able to put this before the country as a straight choice, knowing very well which would prove to be the popular alternative:

The fundamental question . . . is whether or not the nuclear deterrent is to form the basis of British defence planning. If this is not faced, no one, except perhaps a genuine pacifist, has a right to urge the ending of National Service. There can be no doubt at all about this. Short of general disarmament—which is the ideal that we all seek—the end of conscription must depend upon the acceptance of nuclear weapons.[3]

A major, fateful option was taken in this exchange of manpower for firepower. It did not merely take place at the level of strategic forces, but also at tactical levels. It meant that there would be an eventual reliance on the enormous firepower of nuclear weapons at many different levels of all three armed services, and a consequent development of battlefield and tactical nuclear weapons of several different types, to be used by British forces.

The declaratory policy of 1957 was not as new as it was made out to be, since it was a direct continuation of the policy put forward by the Chiefs of Staff in 1952. Its significance lay in restructuring the armed forces for greater dependence on nuclear weapons, and in the economies of manpower and conventional weaponry which this allowed. In doing this it deepened Britain's commitment to early use of nuclear weapons in any future war. By 1958, BAOR was being trained in the use of nuclear weapons in the early phases of battle.[4] It is clear that this choice had more to do with domestic political and economic ambitions than with any sound strategic arguments, which were very thin on the ground. It was one thing to argue—as was done in the 1940s—that Britain needed nuclear weapons to compensate for Soviet predominance in conventional weapons. But it was another to argue that nuclear weapons deployed at all levels would allow the country to dispense with much of its manpower and conventional forces. Harold

---

[3] Defence debate, 16 Apr. 1957, House of Commons Report, vol. 568, vol. 2040.

[4] Andrew Pierre, *Nuclear Politics* (London and New York: OUP, 1972), 167.

Macmillan wrote in his diary, ' . . . the Defence White Paper makes it clear that *all* our defence—and the economics of defence expenditure—are founded on nuclear warfare . . .'.[5]

A further significant aspect of the Sandys policy was the final abandonment of the concept of strategic home defence by the RAF. The White Paper of 1957 declared that it was useless against the virtual certainty of some enemy bombers with megaton weapons getting through.[6] Sandys added in a speech in August 1957, in Australia:

That is why we have taken a very bold step in deciding not to do the impossible. We decided not to defend the whole country, but to defend only our bomber bases. I must pay tribute to the people of Great Britain for the readiness with which they have accepted these harsh but inescapable facts. [7]

It was for this reason, the White Paper says, that the purpose of the military plan was to *prevent* war rather than to *prepare* for it. But such a simplified concept failed to satisfy a great deal of public and expert opinion—the two purposes could not be so easily separated when it came to deploying the weapons.

The 1958 Defence White Paper was a follow-up and confirmation of the new policy. It set off the 'Great Nuclear Debate' in earnest by putting forward a strong and rather crude statement of massive retaliation:

The West relies on its massive stockpile of nuclear weapons and the capacity to deliver them. The democratic nations will never start a war against Russia. But it must be well understood that, if Russia were to launch a major attack on them, even *with conventional forces only, they would have to hit back with strategic nuclear weapons*. The strategy of NATO is based on the frank recognition that a full-scale Soviet attack could not be repelled without resort to a *massive bombardment of the sources of power in Russia*. In that event the role of the allied defence forces in Europe would be to hold the front for the time needed to allow the effects of the nuclear counter-offensive to make themselves felt. [8]

The open statement of what the service chiefs had been saying for

---

[5] Macmillan, *Riding the Storm*, p. 266.

[6] Cmnd. 124, *Defence Outline of Future Policy: 1957*, para. 12.

[7] Cited by Stephen King-Hall in *Defence in the Nuclear Age* (London: Gollancz, 1958), 87 (source not supplied).

[8] Cmnd. 363, *Report on Defence: Britain's Contribution to Peace and Security, 1958*, par. 12 (emphasis added).

some years sent shock waves throughout Parliament and the nation, and gave a considerable boost to the Campaign for Nuclear Disarmament which had been formed a few weeks previously. In the Commons defence debate, Sandys said that there was nothing new about the policy and—less justifiably—that it had kept the peace for the past decade and that there was no alternative. He backed this up with a ritual reference to appeasement. Since Britain did not have the capacity to deliver the kind of threat described in the Statement—the V-bombers not being yet fully operational—he must have been referring to the long-established American policy and the use of American bombers from British bases. As to there being no alternative—Britain and the other European members of NATO had simply chosen not to try to meet the Soviet Union at the conventional level but to rely on American tactical nuclear weapons, largely for economic reasons. Among Opposition MPs in the 1958 defence debate, Sydney Silverman picked up this point and suggested that the government was saying that massive retaliation was cheaper against anything but a 'border incident'.[9]

The radical critics of this policy found two main grounds for attack: (1) it did not amount to a real *defence* policy, since it posed only the two unacceptable alternatives of suicide or surrender, and (2) it was *immoral*, since it proposed to incinerate millions of innocent Soviet citizens in the event of a war. Both arguments contributed to the rapid rise of the anti-nuclear movement, which was a response partly to a moral crisis and partly to a crisis of reassurance. Deterrent policies that are incredible as *defence*, especially in the face of growing Soviet power, have more than once resulted in a surge of anxiety and protest from large sections of the public. 'Deterrence-only' fails to satisfy the basic security needs of very many people.[10] Subjective security needs cannot be based entirely on the prevention of trouble by threatening to 'produce the end of the world at the first stage', as John Strachey put it in the 1958 defence debate.[11] Citizens need to envisage that something can be done to secure a future, even if an attack comes. The reaction to the Sandys policy showed that staking everything on the

[9] Defence debate, 26 Feb. 1958, House of Commons Report, vol. 583, col. 389.

[10] Perceiving this, Michael Howard has introduced the category of 'reassurance' as essential to any successful security policy and has demonstrated its systematic neglect in Western strategy. See 'Reassurance and Deterrence: Western Defence in the 1980s', *Foreign Affairs* (Winter 1982/3), 309–24.

[11] House of Commons Report, 27 Feb. 1958, vol. 583, col. 656.

threat of nuclear annihilation failed to take account of those subjective security needs of the British public.[12] At least, this was true while the fear of Soviet nuclear attack lasted. Later, when this fear receded in the time of *Détente*, so did much of the objection to deterrence.

Throughout 1957 and 1958, the Opposition attempted to call the government's bluff on its threat of massive retaliation with thermonuclear weapons against a conventional act of aggression from the East. But repeated questioning in Parliament and in the media did not bring forth any coherent ideas. Indeed, Macmillan attempted to make a virtue out of the vacuum at the heart of the policy by stating that to answer questions about the circumstances in which the British government would resort to the use of nuclear weapons would be 'very dangerous' and that it would 'incite and invite aggression'.[13] Many critics thought that the policy would be self-deterring: that the Soviet Union could proceed by nibbling advances into Western Europe in such a way as to make a nuclear response absurd and ineffective. This was also the fear of the Kennedy administration, which prompted the shift away from MR to multiple options and eventually to Flexible Response.

In subsequent Defence White Papers, the Conservative government backed-off from the extreme position of 1958, although this was more a matter of changing *declaratory* policy in the face of public anxiety than of any real change in strategy. The 1959 Defence White Paper contained no statement on deterrence policy, and in the 1960 White Paper it was stated that the nuclear power of the West,

. . . is only one component of the deterrent. Because of the need to meet local emergencies which could develop into a major conflict, conventionally armed forces are a necessary complement to nuclear armaments.[14]

By 1961, the Defence White Paper was telling the nation that,

[12]　For a professional view, see Basil Liddell Hart, *Deterrent or Defence* (London: Stevens, 1960), 91: The Sandys policy meant that Britain now had no operational defence: 'The prevailing view of the Western leaders that a serious invasion cannot be repelled without using nuclear weapons, and framing their plans on that basis, amounts to nothing better than a despairing acceptance of suicide in the event of any major aggression. Nothing could be more expressive of hopelessness, and more damping to the spirit of their people.'

[13]　Commons debate, 16–17 Apr. 1957, House of Commons Official Report, vol. 568, col. 2042.

[14]　Cmnd. 952, *Report on Defence: 1960*.

The primary purpose of our defence policy is . . . that it should protect us, our allies and our friends against the whole spectrum of possible aggression and military threats, from the small local action which might be the beginning of larger and more dangerous adventures through 'nuclear blackmail' to nuclear war. [15]

The 1962 White Paper, outlining the policy for the next five years, proposed a return to the idea of a conventional force capable of meeting acts of aggression without bringing about the rapid end of Britain.[16] In addition to the return to a broader notion of deterrence, away from exclusive reliance on massive, instant nuclear response, there was also a recognition that an era of strategic balance between West and East was being entered, in which that kind of threat was no longer rational in a military sense. It is probable that the 1962 Statement reflects changes in thinking which had been occurring in the United States since the beginning of the Kennedy administration. If this is so, the reflection is not a copy but a mixed reaction, for the British position was still dominated by European, not American anxieties, and the foremost European anxiety was the possibility of the United States nuclear guarantee being withdrawn. An adequate conventional defence might make this guarantee appear redundant. The new doctrine promoted by US Defense Secretary, Robert McNamara—the need for multiple options to be available to an American president—was interpreted in some quarters as an attempt to reduce the nuclear risks to the United States only at the cost of increasing the risk of conventional war in Europe—of which the Europeans had bitter memories and for which they had no real intention of equipping themselves. For the European members of NATO, including Britain, the cardinal principle of deterrence, which has remained unaltered till this day, was that any military 'adventure' by the Soviet Union in the NATO area would risk bringing down American strategic weapons on their cities. Conventional armies were to be nothing but trip-wires, ensuring an early entry of American tactical nuclear weapons into the conflict, which in turn would provide the essential linkage with the strategic weapons. The basic British objection to McNamara's call for a conventional buildup in Europe to the point where a Soviet conventional attack could be resisted by non-nuclear means was that it would degrade

[15] Cmnd. 1288, *Report on Defence: 1961*.
[16] Cmnd. 1639, *Statement on Defence, 1962: The Next Five Years*.

the credibility of the nuclear deterrent.[17] It is important to understand that nuclear deterrence has been a fundamental preference of the European members of NATO, and not something forced upon them by the United States or by an incapacity for any other type of defence.

As a consequence of this choice, in the succeeding years no serious effort was made to build up an adequate European conventional defence, despite the declaratory commitment to it in Defence White Papers. First and early use of nuclear weapons remained at the centre of British and NATO action policy, despite all the studies which had shown the immense destruction it would cause to Europeans on both sides of the border if tactical nuclear weapons were used in battle. Investigations in 1961 by Sir Solly Zuckerman, Chief Scientific Adviser to the MOD, found that, with current assumptions about troop deployments and use of the weapons, 'the damage in the battlefield areas would be as great as would occur in an exchange of strategic nuclear weapons'.[18]

A Say in the End of the World: Britain's Independent Contribution

Exactly what Britain's independent contribution to the deterrent amounted to was a matter of great uncertainty from 1957 to 1962, when the Polaris decision was made. The days of manned strategic bombers were coming to an end owing to the increased efficiency of Soviet air-defences and to their vulnerability to missile attack on the ground. This meant that the V-bomber force was beginning to be obsolete almost as soon as it was fully operational. Foreseeing this, the Conservative government in 1957 made the decision to develop a British ballistic missile, Blue Streak, to carry the British H-bomb. But by 1960 it was clear that Britain could not hope to keep an independent place in the missile race and the project was cancelled before it swallowed up too much money. As a result many people concluded that Britain was too poor a country to remain a nuclear power. But there were other reasons for the cancellation, as Macmillan reported to the Sovereign at the time:

[17] Cf. Pierre, *Nuclear Politics*, pp. 259–60.
[18] See especially S. Zuckerman, 'Judgement and Control in Modern Warfare', *Foreign Affairs*, 40/2, 196–212, summarized in S. Zuckerman, *Nuclear Illusions and Reality* (London: Collins, 1982), 62–9.

For political and morale reasons I am very anxious to get rid of these fixed rockets. This is a very small country and to put these installations near the large centres of populations—where they have to be—would cause increasing anxiety to Your Majesty's subjects. A bomber is somehow accepted on its bombing field; and a mobile weapon, either on a truck or better still in a submarine, is out of sight . . . [19]

The government already had some experience of fixed missiles and their problems, with the arrival of a squadron of US Thor missiles in 1959 under a dual-key arrangement. Their vulnerability to Soviet intermediate-range ballistic missiles caused their early with-drawal.[20] After the cancellation of Blue Streak, the government decided to purchase the more advanced air-launched ballistic missile, Skybolt, from the United States: a move which would prolong the life of the V-bomber force at the same time. In exchange for this access to much-needed American missile tech-nology, the United States was offered the Holy Loch base for its Atlantic Polaris force.[21] The exchange of base facilities for nuclear weapons technology has been the main factor ensuring the permanence of the special nuclear relationship between Britain and the United States ever since co-operation was restored via amend-ments to the McMahon Act in 1958.

However, in November 1962, the Americans suddenly cancelled Skybolt. This took the British government entirely by surprise, thus betraying a serious lapse of communication within the special relationship, and Britain was left without a plan for its future strategic delivery system. But only a week or so after the cancellation, Macmillan met Kennedy at Nassau and—indignantly rejecting the option of a Skybolt kept going purely for British needs—played on the past British contribution to the nuclear partnership and said that if he returned to London without an independent deterrent, Anglo-American relations and his leader-ship would collapse. He asked for Polaris and got it, only not without conditions. The American dislike of small independent nuclear forces caused Kennedy to put pressure on Macmillan to

[19] Harold Macmillan, *Pointing the Way, 1959–1961* (London: Macmillan, 1972), 253.

[20] Pierre, *Nuclear Politics*, p. 140.

[21] Ibid. 227, and John Baylis, *Anglo-American Defence Relations, 1939–1984* (London: Macmillan, 1984), 99. Pierre says that the British felt 'morally obliged' to offer the base; Baylis suggests that they wanted to do a deal. Macmillan reminded Kennedy of the Holy Loch offer when he was asking for Polaris at Nassau: See Pierre, pp. 233, 235, and Macmillan, *Pointing the Way*, p. 254.

agree that the purpose of the British Polaris force would be to act as a contribution to a 'multilateral NATO nuclear force in the closest consultation with other NATO allies'. To save the independence principle however, Macmillan had the following clause written into the Nassau Agreement:

The Prime Minister made it clear that except where Her Majesty's Government may decide that *supreme national interests are at stake*, these British forces will be used for the purpose of international defence of the Western Alliance in all circumstances. [22]

Macmillan himself records that, in July 1962, during the crisis over the Skybolt cancellation, he was worried about loss of nuclear status:

it was difficult to suppress the suspicion that the failure of Skybolt might be welcomed in some American quarters e.g. the Pentagon as a means of forcing Britain out of the nuclear club.[23]

This problem was solved by his forceful bargaining at Nassau and the purchase of Polaris. The Polaris agreement solved many problems for the Tory government. Strategically, Polaris was invulnerable, and it had none of the special disadvantages for Britain of bombers and land-based missiles. Moreover, Macmillan had been right about the political and moral effects of weapons kept 'out of sight'—it is a reasonable conjecture that the non-visibility and invulnerability of Britain's strategic deterrent throughout the 1970s played some part in making people forget its moral implications.

Macmillan and the Test Ban

During the period 1960 to 1964, the Macmillan government not only worked vigorously to make sure that Britain was equipped with a range of nuclear weapons, but it also put a great deal of effort into halting the nuclear arms race. This sounds less contradictory when it is recognized that both activities were designed to preserve Britain's place in the nuclear club, and through this to ensure its long-term security from attack. On the one hand it

[22] The Nassau Agreement, text in Pierre, *Nuclear Politics*, p. 347 (emphasis added).
[23] Harold Macmillan, *At The End Of The Day* (London: Macmillan, 1973), 343.

was thought necessary to have an independent nuclear force as an insurance against American withdrawal and a measure of Britain's international standing. On the other hand there was a fear that the nuclear competition between the superpowers was about to begin a new, uncontrollable stage in the arms race. Not only would this create fresh dangers for world peace and seriously distort the world economy, it would leave Britain so far behind that its small nuclear forces would count for nothing.[24] The particular danger in the early 1960s was the possible development of anti-ballistic missiles which, even if only partially effective, would seriously threaten the deterrent effects of Britain's strategic weapons.

In the autumn of 1961, and after a sequence of diplomatic disasters including a new Berlin crisis and the failure of the 1960 summit due to the U-2 incident, the Russians brought an end to the test moratorium with a series of multi-megaton explosions in Siberia. These were described by Macmillan as 'peculiarly dirty'.[25] The biggest was a 50 Mt bomb, and Khrushchev boasted of a 100 Mt bomb to be added to the Soviet stockpile. One of them exploded high in the atmosphere would be able to destroy half of Britain. The combination of this dire news and the information that the Russians were pushing ahead with their anti-missile missile, Macmillan found particularly threatening to his plans to make Britain an effective nuclear-deterrent state. He wrote to President Kennedy about the anti-ballistic missile race in terms such as critics now use of SDI:

the purpose of the private approach to Kruschev would be to indicate that we were genuinely concerned to save humanity from the threat and the wastage of a new competition designed to provide immunity against nuclear attack, a competition which we believe would almost certainly be fruitless and which could distort the whole economic life of the world.[26]

Concurrent with this, the new American administration was decidedly hostile towards the British nuclear deterrent, claiming that it was a major incitement to proliferation, particularly with regard to the French.[27] They were alarmed at the possibility of Britain offering nuclear information to de Gaulle as part of the

[24] For a record of Macmillan's anxieties at this time, see *At The End of the Day*, chap. VI.

[25] Ibid. 142.

[26] Ibid. 162.

[27] John Simpson, *The Independent Nuclear State* (London: Macmillan, 1983; 2nd edn. 1986), 158.

price of entry into the Common Market. At the same time the Americans were exerting pressure to use the Christmas Island site for further atmospheric testing. Although the British government was publicly opposed to atmospheric tests, Macmillan saw an opportunity to bargain with the Americans: in an exchange for the use of Christmas Island for a series of tests which they said was necessary for security rather than merely retaliatory, he got the Americans to agree (1) to share any results of the tests, and (2) to make further efforts to negotiate a test ban with the Russians. At the same time he was negotiating for the use of the Nevada testing grounds to resume the testing of British weapons, cut off in 1958 by the moratorium. There is no doubt that Macmillan was deeply alarmed at the prospect of a nuclear arms race and wished to do everything to stop it—provided that Britain herself was safely across the deterrence threshold. This was seen to be a matter of historic right, given the fact that Britain had been in the nuclear business from the very beginning.

Macmillan was largely successful in these ambitions. He played an active part in the negotiations towards the Partial Test-Ban Treaty, signed in July 1963, which, by prohibiting atmospheric testing, removed a major source of public and international protest over nuclear weapons and at the same time allowed Britain to continue to develop its nuclear arsenal, currently in a delicate state of transition from bombers to missiles. It also effectively prevented the high-yield, high-altitude nuclear explosions which were necessary for the development of an anti-ballistic missile system. The future of the British deterrent was assured.

The Question of Strategy

Macmillan had obtained Polaris on extraordinarily cheap terms— the United States having borne virtually the whole burden of research and development of the missiles. The agreement solved the economic problems of Britain's nuclear force for a long time to come. However, the questions of strategy and morality were never satisfactorily answered and continued to aggravate British political life until they became dormant in the mid-1960s because of an altered international climate.

Strategically, the independent deterrent was supposed to make Britain independent of the United States in a moment of national danger when Britain might be subject to nuclear blackmail by the Soviet Union. The launching of Sputnik in 1957 had rendered the United States vulnerable to direct attack and had raised doubts as to the willingness of an American president to risk the destruction of his own cities in the cause of European freedom. The French under de Gaulle decided straightaway that he would not, and that no country would do anything but use strategic weapons in its own defence—a position which led them out of the NATO deterrence structure altogether to a position of complete nuclear self-reliance. However much of this anxiety was felt in Britain, it was not something that Conservative politicians wanted to state outright. There was too much to lose by real independence from the United States. But it was implicit in Macmillan's Commons speech of 30 January 1963 that Britain might find herself isolated and facing a life-and-death situation with which the United States was out of sympathy. But this sort of thing had to be stated in a roundabout way. It was suggested that, rather than this uncertainty of American support being well-founded, it was a miscalculation that the *enemy* might make. The *Statement on Defence* of 1964—the Conservative Government's last—expressed it thus:

To suggest that the independent deterrent might be abandoned in the interests of non-dissemination overlooks the fact that if there were no power in Europe capable of inflicting *unacceptable damage* on a potential enemy he might be tempted—if not now then perhaps at some time in the future—to attack in the mistaken belief that the United States would not act unless America herself were attacked. The V-bombers by themselves are, and the Polaris submarine will be, capable of inflicting greater damage than any potential aggressor would consider acceptable. For this reason British nuclear forces make a unique contribution to the main deterrent. [28]

This contains the beginning of what later came to be known as the 'second centre' doctrine—a concept put forward by Denis Healey in explaining the strategic reasons for Labour's acceptance of Polaris after the 1964 General election:

If you are inside an alliance you increase the deterrent to the other side enormously if there is more than one centre of decision for the first use of nuclear weapons. [29]

---

[28] Cmnd. 2270, *Statement on Defence: 1964*, par. 7 (emphasis added).
[29] See Lawrence Freedman, *Britain and Nuclear Weapons* (London: Macmillan, 1980), 26.

That version—which has remained official policy until the present—was politically more acceptable since it concentrated on the neutral notion of *uncertainty* in the mind of the enemy rather than on possible desertion by the United States.

However, these ideas did not solve the outstanding questions being asked about the *use* of the British nuclear force: was it really conceivable that it would be used for the defence of Europe in the absence of American nuclear engagement, knowing that it would provoke the immediate destruction of Britain? From 1958 until 1965, critics of nuclear independence found it impossible to imagine any circumstances in which it would be rational for a Prime Minister to order the use of British Polaris missiles against Soviet cities. It would never make sense to go it alone, and if America were already fighting a nuclear war, all that Britain would get would be a say in the end of the world.

The Symbolic Value of Possession

In the face of such criticisms, the government resorted more and more to arguments from sovereignty, Great Power status, and 'influence': advantages which could be derived from the mere possession of the weapons without having to work out an answer to the embarrassing question of their use. In 1958 Macmillan had claimed that,

The independent contribution . . . gives us a better position in the world, it gives us a better position with respect to the United States. It puts us where we ought to be, in the position of a Great Power. The fact that we have it makes the United States pay a greater regard to our point of view, and that is of great importance. [30]

The leader of the Opposition, Hugh Gaitskell agreed with him. He thought that Britain's nuclear role brought 'influence and prestige and a measure of independence *vis-à-vis* the United States'.[31] In the 1961 Defence White Paper, the government produced another argument: that it substantially increased British influence in negotiations for a nuclear test agreement and for disarmament.[32] However, although Macmillan had worked hard for the Partial

[30] *The Times*, 24 Feb. 1958.
[31] House of Commons Report, vol. 582, col. 1241, 19 Feb. 1958.
[32] Cmd. 1288, *Report on Defence: 1961*.

Test Ban Treaty, it remained an open question as to whether the persuasive influence of Britain's advice was really due to her independent ownership of nuclear weapons.[33] A serious blow to the theory of Britain's influence on the United States was received during the Cuban missile crisis in October 1962. Although President Kennedy did inform Macmillan of the onset of the crisis, and although the latter maintained afterwards that Britain was intimately involved in the decisions taken,[34] the actual amount of influence that Britain was able to have on the highly dangerous confrontation between the superpowers was minimal. The disparity of power was too great to allow anything else.[35]

The definitive Conservative reply to criticisms of independence came from Macmillan during the Commons debate on the Nassau Agreement in January 1963. Then it was made clear that the possession of an independent deterrent was thought to be a prerequisite of *national sovereignty*. He said that 'the most vital argument of all' was that Britain needed the capacity to make sovereign decisions in time of war, though without at any point enlarging on how a sovereign decision to use nuclear weapons would make any sense. He then claimed that President Kennedy had agreed with him:

He told me beforehand how he would explain to his own people our insistence upon the right to use these weapons in matters of supreme importance, because—and these are the words he used—they are 'the necessary requirement for any sovereign nation'.

MR SYDNEY SILVERMAN: Any sovereign nation?

PRIME MINISTER: Any sovereign nation which has them and which can contribute them to the NATO Alliance must also have this sovereign right . . .[36]

Macmillan's spontaneous reply shows just how the sovereignty argument came down to a matter of Britain's historic status and freedom of action: it was *British* sovereignty that demanded possession of nuclear weapons, rather than sovereignty in general. The symbolic value of possession remained the most powerful

[33] A query of Pierre, *Nuclear Politics*, p. 254.
[34] Harold Macmillan gives an account of his role in the crisis in *At The End Of The Day*, p. 219.
[35] Cf. Baylis, *Anglo-American Defence Relations*, p. 106–7.
[36] House of Commons Official Report, vol. 670, col. 962, 30 Jan. 1963.

aspect of the independent deterrent. For Macmillan, the British nuclear force was 'a symbol of independence and showed that we were not just satellites or clients of America. This was one aspect and a vital one.'[37] The increased actual dependence on American nuclear weapons programmes could be forgotten for a long period, until Polaris itself became obsolete. Status in Europe also played a part: France could not be allowed to be the only independent European nuclear power.

It is noteworthy that, in the speech referred to above, Macmillan presented no arguments against unilateralism, still strong in 1963. He rejected it as a mere 'moral gesture'. He considered the deterrence question to be not a moral issue at all, but purely a practical one. By this time, the government, with help from a section of the Labour party, had won the argument (in electoral terms) that Britain's possession of its own nuclear weapons was a purely practical matter of survival, in which moral considerations were irrelevant.[38]

Labour and Unilateralism

In 1958 began a sequence of events which would, a few years later, present a British government for the first time since 1947 with the opportunity to take Britain out of independent nuclear status, if not to get rid of American nuclear bases.[39] The Great Nuclear Debate which began in 1958 deeply divided the Labour party, with the leadership supporting the independent deterrent in a policy not much different from that of the Conservatives, while the pacifist–unilateralist wing marched with CND and demanded a non-nuclear NATO or else complete withdrawal from it. In 1958 the only differences between the Labour front bench and the government were over declaratory policy: where the Government believed in massive retaliation using H-bombs against any Soviet attack, the Labour leadership espoused a graduated-response strategy, with first use of tactical nuclear weapons, even against a conventional

[37] Macmillan, *Pointing the Way*, p. 257.
[38] Cf. Christopher Driver, *The Disarmers* (London: Hodder and Stoughton, 1964), 77.
[39] This section is based largely on two works: Philip M. Williams, *Hugh Gaitskell, A Political Biography* (London: Jonathan Cape, 1979), chaps 18, 22, and 23; and Janet Morgan (ed.), *The Backbench Diaries of Richard Crossman* (London: Hamish Hamilton and Jonathan Cape, 1981), 833 ff.

attack. There was considerable pressure within the party for a no-first-use declaration, but Hugh Gaitskell would not accept it, claiming that it would eliminate deterrence.[40] At this time he and the other Labour leaders were also opposed to Britain joining a non-nuclear club on the grounds that it would force all other countries to shelter behind a superpower, dangerously increasing polarization. The non-nuclear club (NNC) concept, which was vigorously promoted by such organs of liberal opinion as the *Manchester Guardian*, proposed that Britain should give up her own nuclear weapons if all other countries apart from the two superpowers agreed not to make or acquire nuclear weapons. It was the idea which eventually led to the Non-Proliferation Treaty of 1968. Gaitskell was sceptical on the grounds that it would mean a loss of British influence over the US and a loss of insurance in case the US eventually backed out of its European commitments. But by mid-1959 he reversed his opinion on this and the NNC became official Labour policy. The non-nuclear club idea should not be confused with full-blooded unilateralism as promoted by CND, which demanded immediate renunciation of British nuclear weapons and withdrawal of Britain from any nuclear alliance, without conditions. When, for the first time, unilateralism was proposed as Labour policy at the party conference at Scarborough in 1958, Gaitskell maintained that such a gesture would have no effect; that to stay in NATO would mean sheltering behind American bombs and that to withdraw from it would endanger peace. The unilateralist motion was lost by 6 to 1 in 1958.

However, by early 1960 unilateralism had made great strides in the country and in the PLP, and 48 Labour MPs signed a unilateralist motion. It so happened that at that time, having lost three general elections in a row and with a disastrous defeat in municipal elections, the party was going through one of its near-suicidal conflicts, and the unilateralist cause served to focus opposition to Gaitskell's brand of authoritarian social democracy, which in many people's eyes was little different from the welfare-capitalism of Macmillan. The anti-nuclear issue was undoubtedly seen by some as a vehicle for ousting Gaitskell from the leadership. Institutions like 'Victory For Socialism' aimed to restore the Socialist gospel to a party that had grown too like its opponents to be a real alternative. As at other times, the campaign centred on

[40] Williams, *Hugh Gaitskell*, p. 494.

trying to force the leadership to follow conference majority decisions. To some extent the new movement represented a resurgence of the traditional Labour Left anti-militarism and pacifism which had been in eclipse since the 1930s. Gaitskell now represented continuity with the post-war Attlee–Bevin policies of bipartisan consensus over Britain's nuclear role and the necessity of a nuclear-armed NATO. The great shift in public awareness caused by the anxiety over the H-bomb had for the first time produced a substantial opposition to this within the party. Gaitskell's position on nuclear weapons was middle-of-the-road so far as Labour opinion was concerned. He was strongly in favour of Britain remaining within a nuclear-armed NATO so long as the Russians had the bomb, but gave the independent British deterrent only tentative support, less enthusiastic than George Brown or John Strachey.[41] But he had nothing but contempt for CND. It was natural that he should draw the fire of those who were hoping that the Labour party would be the instrument of a radical change in Britain's defence posture. The time seemed to have come for such a change in the spring of 1960, with the anti-nuclear movement at the height of its popular appeal. There was 33 per cent support for unilateralism in the opinion polls, and some of the largest and most powerful trade unions had passed unilateralist resolutions at their conferences.

Meanwhile, as an attempt at party unity, an in-between position on nuclear weapons had been formulated by Richard Crossman and George Wigg, in which Britain was to abandon its independent nuclear pretensions, take a conventional role along with the other Europeans in NATO and leave deterrent protection to the United States. Since 1954 Crossman had been highly critical of the independent nuclear force, which, he charged, was being built for reasons of prestige rather than security, and he continually opposed the Labour front bench on this issue, earning himself dismissal from the Shadow Cabinet in March 1960 for his failure to vote with the others in the defence debate. This position got nowhere with the leadership of the party until 13 April the same year, when the Government suddenly announced the cancellation of Blue Streak, amid charges of gross mismanagement from the Labour front bench. There had been rumours of the cancellation since February and Gaitskell had been urged by such senior figures as Anthony

[41] Ibid. 577.

Crossland and Roy Jenkins to give a clear lead and repudiate the British bomb explicitly in view of the fact that even among the Conservative party there was doubt as to whether Britain could continue with it. But he resisted, claiming that he could not overrule George Brown, who was Defence spokesman. When the cancellation of Blue Streak was finally announced, Gaitskell was out of the country and otherwise unprepared to take the initiative. Some senior members of the Shadow Cabinet, notably George Brown and Harold Wilson, abruptly abandoned their support of the independent deterrent which, they argued, had never really existed. They considered that the failure of Blue Streak had made any dreams of future nuclear independence quite unrealistic. When he heard of it, Gaitskell was furious at this exercise in independent policy making, although it may be discerned from statements made at the time that he had no real enthusiasm for the British deterrent and shared the view that it was rapidly becoming obsolete and impossible to maintain. He managed to put on a show of unity for the press and his redraft of party policy at that time showed that his presumption was no longer for keeping the British bomb, but for abandoning it as a contribution to non-proliferation. But he would not publicly state this because he feared its unpopularity with the electorate. He was thinking as a future Prime Minister rather than as a Leader of the Opposition and he did not like making future commitments which might be hostage to changing conditions. In the circumstances, this was undoubtedly a weakness, as even Gaitskell's sympathetic biographer points out.[42] He missed a golden opportunity to steer the Labour party into new, more realistic policies in regard to the independent deterrent and to give it the initiative in defence at a time when the Conservative government was in confusion and trouble over it. Around that time Denis Healey likened European independent deterrents to virility symbols compensating for political impotence after Suez. Gaitskell's biographer even suggests that for a time he saw adherence to the British bomb as a safeguard against his own political impotence.[43]

Meanwhile the annual party conference was approaching and there were signs that unilateralist and anti-NATO motions would be passed, which Gaitskell was determined to head off. After further argument, and resistance from Gaitskell, a high level

---

[42] Williams, *Hugh Gaitskell*, 577–9.
[43] Ibid. 583.

conference drafting committee, which included Denis Healey, managed to stitch together a compromise policy which was essentially the same as the Crossman–Wigg line. It reaffirmed allegiance to NATO, accepted American bases in Britain for the present, insisted that Germany remain non-nuclear and that NATO reduce its reliance on nuclear weapons, while Britain should stop doing what in any case was impossible for it. Nuclear deterrence was to be left exclusively to the United States while Britain's contribution was to be in conventional weapons only. As Andrew Pierre points out, this meant that British strategy was to be based on military rather than prestige considerations: 'we must accept the truth that a country of our size cannot remain in any real sense of the word an independent nuclear power'.[44] With this policy it was hoped to avoid a split between the party leadership and increasingly unilateralist unions and constituency Labour parties at the party conference at Scarborough in October. Gaitskell's opinion of unilateralism at this time showed little sensitivity to the real moral issues and the crisis of reassurance that had brought it to the top of the political agenda. At about this time he wrote:

Renunciation by Britain alone was ofen based on the desire to contract out . . . associated with a vague though violent distaste for nuclear weapons. While . . . supported by the high-minded through the doctrine of example, it is popular with others for purely escapist or beatnik reasons, and with others, again, because they are fellow-travellers, if not avowed Communists.[45]

The attempt to head off unilateralism at Scarborough was a failure, but only just. There was much bitter hostility within the party where Gaitskell was seen by many as the chief obstacle to a new policy that would take Britain out of the dirty and dangerous business of nuclear defence and help break the international deadlock. It should be recognized however that Gaitskell was by no means the most attached to British nuclear status and that there were many in the PLP to the right of him. But his failure to come clean on the subject of the British bomb caused his enemies— including, by now Harold Wilson—to consider all compromise policy statements unacceptable because the untrustworthy leader

---

[44] Pierre, *Nuclear Politics*, p. 202. The text of the new policy is in the *Report of the Fifty-Ninth Annual Conference of the Labour Party* (London: Transport House, 1960), 13–16.

[45] Williams, *Hugh Gaitskell*, p. 579.

would interpret them in such a way that he could continue with the policy—support for the British bomb—to which they thought him committed.[46] However he clearly identified the main point of dispute with the unilateralists: it was not the British bomb, which he now considered to be a minor issue, but membership of the NATO alliance. He believed that, whatever happened to the British bomb, which he was willing to renounce in favour of a NNC, Britain should remain within a nuclear alliance so long as the Soviet Union had nuclear weapons. He considered that, although the Soviet Union was not rashly aggressive like the Nazis, it would expand in Europe if it could do so without cost. He thought that NATO without Britain would either break up or fall under German domination. It was his insistence on having this clearly spelled out against all attempts at fudging for the sake of unity that led to the bitter conflict before and at Scarborough.[47] However, he was by this time willing to concede that Britain should cease further tests and make a no-first-use declaration in respect of the H-bomb. The central issue at the conference then was not that of the independent deterrent, but that of a non-nuclear, neutralist status for Britain. This, at least, was how Gaitskell saw the alternative to full membership of a nuclear NATO, and he attacked the opposition for not drawing this conclusion. It would do as a moral aspiration for CND but not as a programme for a future government of a country where unilateralism had never been a majority position. Whether this was the only realistic alternative is perhaps something that some of his opponents—like Frank Cousins of the TGWU—did not want to think about, or—like Harold Wilson, who agreed with Gaitskell in substance on that issue—did not want to be spelled out for political reasons, while others continued to ignore the political gap between the moral position of CND and the conditions for a Labour success in the next election. [48]

The successful resolution at Scarborough, proposed by the Amalgamated Engineering Union, called for 'a complete rejection of any defence policy based on the threat of the use of strategic

[46] Williams, *Hugh Gaitskell*, p. 599.

[47] Ibid. 589.

[48] Cf. ibid. 617: 'Unlike the CND rank and file, the Left politicians preferred to have these unwelcome implications clothed in discreet obscurity—rather as their pre-war predecessors had tried to embrace collective security without quite renouncing pacifism, thus paralysing Labour's opposition to Hitler and denying it either immediate influence or subsequent credit.'

nuclear weapons'. It was opposed to the production, testing, or first-use of these weapons, and to having bases in Britain either for missiles or for patrolling aircraft with H-bombs. This meant a rejection of the presence of United States nuclear arms in Britain under any form. But it did not draw the conclusion that Britain should leave NATO altogether and terminate the alliance with the United States, although many resolutions that had done so had been withdrawn in its favour. But for Gaitskell the implications were obvious and he spelled them out amidst uproar from his opponents. The atmosphere was not made any more friendly by his reference to 'unilateralists, pacifists and fellow-travellers', which caused lasting offence in the party. He particularly emphasized the point that unilateralism equalled neutralism and total withdrawal from American protection, which he guessed, probably rightly, many of the unilateralist supporters at the conference had not seriously thought about and did not want to face. The 'real decision facing the country' he claimed, was the choice between NATO with American protection and neutralism with complete vulnerability to Soviet threats. This may have been an over-simplification but it was an effective one. Although the unilateralist motion was passed, Gaitskell's speech was very effective in rallying waverers to his side, and his defeat was not nearly so great as had been expected. It was seen by himself and most of the media as a great personal victory and he forgot his threat to return to the back-benches if defeated on this issue.[49] There is no doubt that his leadership was greatly strengthened from this time forward.

Subsequently, it was by presenting neutralism and the abandonment of NATO as an inevitable outcome of unilateralism, and by organizing his counter-attack at local level throughout the following year, that Gaitskell was able to win back enough party support to have the resolution reversed at the 1961 conference at Blackpool.[50] By that time the political climate had changed away from CND, with only 19 per cent support for it in the country by April 1961. In the run-up to the conference in October, agreement was maintained over renunciation of the British bomb—even

[49] Ibid. 613.
[50] As Gaitskell wrote in Oct. 1960: 'The issue is clear-cut and straightforward—on the one side, unilateralism on principle equals neutralism; on the other, collective security with Britain ceasing to be an independent nuclear power but remaining an important and loyal member of the alliance.' But he would not commit himself publicly on the British bomb. Williams, *Hugh Gaitskell*, p. 620.

though Harold Wilson continued to misrepresent Gaitskell's opinion on this for his own ends.[51] By representing himself as the leader most likely to get rid of the British bomb, he sought alliance with the unilateralists in order to replace Gaitskell in the leadership election of October 1960, but he was heavily defeated.

The unilateralist motion at Blackpool was defeated by a 2 to 1 majority. On the other hand the conference voted against the Polaris deal by 4 to 3, thus giving a clear path for the leadership to abandon it when it had the power and opportunity to do so—as Wilson was to have three years later. It also passed a resolution condemning the American Polaris-submarine base at Holy Loch. Gaitskell was not in agreement with these two latter decisions, but his leadership did not depend on it as it did with the unilateralist issue and he viewed them as a small price to pay for winning the main contest. There is no doubt that Gaitskell stood in the way of the Labour party adopting a radical anti-nuclear policy, but he was not the completely stubborn wrecker of all anti-nuclear hopes that subsequent myth has portrayed him as. There had been a considerable shift on Gaitskell's part since 1958. He would not oppose bases on principle, but he continually found practical arguments against them. Moreover he accepted several commitments that he had previously refused: to stop all British tests, to promise no first use of the H-bomb, to abandon the separate national deterrent, at first if others did so, later unconditionally. However, he was in no sense a radical either, for in 1961 so precarious did the independent deterrent seem that even prominent Conservatives were stating aloud that it was pointless and wasteful and that something had to be done about the hazards of tests and proliferation.

As a result of his strengthened position, Gaitskell was most probably heading for an election victory in 1964, but he died unexpectedly in January 1963, leaving the way open to Harold Wilson, who had coveted the leadership and presented himself for that purpose as a resolute opponent of the British bomb and the one most likely to bring about party unity over the issue.

[51] Wilson said: 'I believe the crisis of confidence arises from the feeling that some of our leaders do not unequivocally reject the idea of the independent British bomb, and that they are waiting for Skybolt or Polaris to come along, with the idea of returning to the notion of a separate British deterrent, with an American rocket to deliver it. I believe it is essential that the Leader of the party states beyond all doubt that, as the policy statement intended, he accepts that there will be no British H-bomb.' Williams, *Hugh Gaitskell*, p. 625.

Labour Accepts Polaris

In the run-up to the general election of 1964, the Tories under Douglas-Home tried to capture the patriotic vote by emphasizing the independent deterrent as a symbol of British political and military power. They stated that the Labour party wanted to throw these things away, and that the result would be to 'surrender all our authority in world affairs and hand over the decision about the life and future of Britain to another country'.[52] Labour fought the election with a promise to renegotiate the Nassau Agreement, with the implication that the independent deterrent might be abandoned, together with the promise of building up conventional defence. It was a very vague project, which was intended to win the support of both those in the Labour movement who were for the deterrent, and those who were against it, and to keep every option open for the future. This was something Harold Wilson was especially skilful at doing, and the Labour leadership successfully managed to keep its divisions on this question out of the election, which was won on other, domestic issues.

After a month in office, an inner Cabinet, argued round by Denis Healey, the new Secretary of State for Defence, decided to continue with Polaris after all.[53] It is well worth asking how this reversal of party policy happened so easily. The Conservatives had believed in the independent deterrent because it was a symbol of greatness and an ultimate safeguard if Britain should have to go it alone in wartime. But the Labour leadership apparently did not believe this and continued to ridicule it even when in office. [54] What was the rationale for their change of attitude? The ostensible reason, given by Harold Wilson in his memoirs, is that when he, Healey, and Gordon Walker looked at the information which became available to them, they saw straight away that the Polaris project was 'well past the point of no return; there would be no question of cancelling the submarines, except at inordinate cost'.[55] But a more positive reason appears to have been its *cost-effectiveness*, which

[52] Sir Alec Douglas-Home in a television speech, cited by Pierre, *Nuclear Politics*, p. 256.
[53] Freedman, *Britain and Nuclear Weapons*, p. 32. Wilson in his memoirs implies that there was no argument at all and that it was endorsed by the Cabinet and not even discussed at the first full defence meeting: see *The Labour Government, 1964–1970* (London: Penguin, 1974), 40.
[54] Ibid. 56.
[55] Ibid. 40.

particularly impressed Denis Healey.[56] There is no doubt that the *cost* was extraordinarily low: around 5 per cent of the defence budget while it was being built and under 2 per cent when it was operational.[57] The *effectiveness* was the ability of one British submarine on patrol to deploy more explosive power than was used in the entire Second World War, and to destroy a number of key Soviet cities without fear of interception by defence forces. The only concession to Labour's previous reformist arguments was to cancel the fifth boat—a decision made upon the calculation that the minimum of four boats would allow at least one to be on patrol at any given time. The Labour government, having decided to retain Polaris, had to show that it was making do with the minimum effective force and saving as much money as possible.[58]

But cost-effectiveness can never be a sole motive—there has to be a basic desire for the thing itself. Andrew Pierre suggests a number of other reasons for Labour's reconciliation with Polaris, some of them unstated at the time.[59] The most important of these was probably the feeling that Britain needed nuclear weapons in order to 'make her voice heard'—a constant preoccupation of all post-war Labour governments. It was once again a matter of prestige and influence in foreign affairs, particularly within NATO. Not only the Tories, but also the Socialists believed that possession of the bomb would give Britain access to the 'top table'—a hope which was never fulfilled. Finally, Harold Wilson gave reasons for the decision when interviewed in June 1985. One of them was financial help from the Americans if Britain continued with its independent deterrent—which is presumably a reference to the American subsidy of Polaris. The other was freedom of choice in some ultimate crisis: 'I didn't want to be in the position of having to subordinate ourselves to the Americans when they at a certain point, would say, "Oh, we're going to use it", or something of that kind.'[60]

We should not discount the probability that members of the new

[56] Lawrence Freedman, *Britain and Nuclear Weapons*, pp. 32, 39.

[57] Pierre, *Nuclear Politics*, p. 287; cf. Freedman, *Britain and Nuclear Weapons*, p. 32.

[58] Freedman (pp. 33–6) calculates that it was, within the terms of the enterprise, a false economy, which seriously reduced the reliability of the force.

[59] Pierre, *Nuclear Politics*, pp. 283–9.

[60] Richard Norton-Taylor, *Guardian*, 27 June 1985.

Labour administration—very few of them with any experience in office—came under very great pressure from the MOD, from service chiefs, and possibly from the nuclear weapons teams, not to abandon the British nuclear project, for fear of never being able to restore it. Evidence for this may not be forthcoming until 1994, when some Cabinet papers relating to this matter may be released.

Unacceptable Damage: How Polaris would be Used

Whether the British independent nuclear force really amounted to a *deterrent* to the Soviet Union had always been a question of its targets and its ability to get through to them in time of war. The periodic debates on modernization have revolved around the question of the least expensive way of continuing to make sure that the British strategic weapon could penetrate whatever defensive barrier the Soviet Union might put up in order to protect its vital centres. The deterrent rationale of the British force has depended wholly on the capacity to cause unacceptable damage to the enemy's society. It is time to consider what this phrase amounts to.

Never possessing anything but a relatively small strategic nuclear force, which would not have a plausible counter-force role in the event of war with the Soviet Union, Britain could not indulge in anything but the simplest intentions with regard to targets: they had to be those the destruction of which would cause maximum injury, given the size of the force and the probability that not many of the delivery vehicles would get through the Soviet defences. This was particularly true of Britain's first strategic nuclear force, the V-bombers. This force began to be obsolete as soon as it became operational (1958–61), owing to Soviet missile advances threatening to destroy it on the ground, and to the fact that the Soviet Union had concentrated on efficient air defences. It was assumed that the attrition rate of the V-bombers would be very high, possibly involving the loss of 70–90 per cent shot down.[61] It was mainly this factor which prompted the experiments with various missile systems before 1962. At this time there is no evidence of any refined targeting doctrine for the V-bomber force and it is generally assumed by commentators—without official denial—that the 'unacceptable damage' and the 'massive nuclear bombardment of

[61] Pierre, *Nuclear Politics*, p. 306.

the sources of power in Russia' spoken of in the official documents refers to the destruction of Russian cities, especially Moscow.[62] The fact that in the later debates on modernization at the end of the 1970s it clearly did mean this lends weight to the judgement. The declaratory policy of the late 1950s—massive retaliation—could scarcely involve anything more refined than simple all-out attack on large city targets by those few bombers which were expected to get through the defences. It would be a direct continuation of area bombing as developed in World War II by the same men who were the architects of the 1952 Global Strategy Paper and the Sandys policy which gave effect to it.

The adoption of Polaris submarine-launched ballistic missiles to replace the V-bombers by the late 1960s did not involve any greater accuracy or refinement of targeting. On the contrary, the missile fired from the ocean was not likely to be as accurate as the manned bomber, and it was not chosen for such reasons. It was chosen because of its far greater invulnerability to counter-force attack, for its immunity to ordinary air defences and for its invisibility to the public. The Polaris A-3 missile, which Britain purchased, was a warhead capable of dividing into three, each with a yield of some 200 Kt. As Freedman describes it,

These warheads are released in a shotgun effect and can be distributed around a target, with some 10 miles between each explosion. They lack the accuracy and wider separation of the more advanced multiple independently targeted re-entry vehicles . . . As a rough guide one could assume that each Polaris missile hitting a city centre could kill directly or indirectly, some quarter of a million people. [63]

The effect then would be a scatter of nuclear explosions, each some thirteen times the explosive power of the bomb which destroyed Hiroshima, over a very wide area of Soviet industrial, military, governmental and—unavoidably—civilian locations. The destruction of people would be indiscriminate and immense—even without taking into account the long-term effects of radiation over a much wider area.

[62] See for instance, P. M. S. Blackett: 'There is no room for doubt that in practice, if not in intention, the phrase "sources of power in Russia" was a euphemism for Russian cities'. ('Thoughts on British Defence Policy, 1959', *Studies of War* (London: Oliver and Boyd, 1962), 88.) Cf. Pierre, *Nuclear Politics*, p. 295, and Lawrence McReavy, 'The Morality of the NATO Deterrent Policy', *Clergy Review* (Oct. 1960), 615.
[63] Freedman, *Britain and Nuclear Weapons*, p. 36.

Freedman also reports that, when the new Labour leadership decided after their success in the 1964 election to endorse the Polaris programme, they arranged a briefing for the whole Cabinet in order to explain its cost-effectiveness:

To bring home the fact that, in spite of being small compared with the superpowers' strategic force, the British Polaris fleet would still be able to pack a punch, the Ministers were told that missiles from three of the submarines would be able to destroy 15 to 24 cities and up to 25 million of the Soviet population. [64]

Of course, the Defence Ministry's boast about the capabilities of its most precious piece of hardware, made in order to impress politicians who might want to scrap it on economic grounds, does not amount to an operational policy for the weapon. However, there is no good reason to believe there was a secret operational policy that would involve city-avoidance. The British Polaris missiles were assigned targets by the Joint Strategic Nuclear Targeting Committee in Omaha, Nebraska, but there are presumably separate targeting plans in case 'supreme national interests are at stake'. The 'Moscow criterion' was always used in subsequent discussions to assess the deterrent efficiency of the British nuclear force. By 1964 then, it was agreed by both major political parties that Polaris was the cheapest, most publicly acceptable way of being able to do the maximum damage to the people of the Soviet Union, and that Britain's security should be founded on this capability.

Moral Critique, 1957–1964

The economic and strategic arguments against Britain's nuclear independence—such as those presented by the Labour party in 1961—were the easiest to put forward in a practical way. However, the moral argument against British nuclear policy was a great deal more radical in its implications, and correspondingly more difficult to present in a practical way. It implied not just renunciation of nuclear independence, but an end to the nuclear alliance and the expulsion of American bases. It meant a non-nuclear NATO or no NATO at all. This was a course which

[64] Ibid. 32.

probably no politicians of the day had the resources for. This is perhaps why—with the moral arguments being presented in very forceful ways all around them—the politicians of both main parties preferred not to engage with them and to present nuclear questions as purely practical ones, to be solved on a basis of economics. The literature on the morality of nuclear deterrence produced during this period is immense and, by 1961, very sophisticated. But there is no evidence that any of it had the slightest influence on British nuclear policy. It was a process which tied up the moralists in argument with themselves more than it tied up the politicians in argument with the moralists.

In Britain the debate among moralists evolved by 1961 into a debate about deterrent intentions. The central question was: if the indiscriminate destruction of Soviet cities threatened by NATO policy would be mass-murder and morally unjustifiable, even in retaliation for nuclear attack, is the threat itself immoral, given that the primary intention is to prevent aggression by the Soviet Union? Much of the argument proceeded on an abstract level with very little knowledge of the realities of NATO nuclear weapons policy or of the effects of nuclear weapons. For instance, Lawrence Mc-Reavy, the most eminent Roman Catholic moralist of the time, thought that there were probably very few legitimate targets for megaton H-bombs, but that, in spite of this, it was still possible that restraint could be observed. The only logical course, he wrote, was to 'reserve one's final judgement of these possible issues until they became actual' [65]—a manifestly absurd position for a moralist to take which, however, one still hears from time to time from moral leaders. As for the deterrence posture itself, McReavy wrote that no government is morally bound 'per se and in principle' to declare antecedently to the world that it will in no circumstances misuse the weapons: 'There is therefore nothing intrinsically immoral in leaving potential aggressors to guess. If this uncertainty serves to deter them, well and good.' When challenged on these points he went further in justifying co-operation with deterrence by making a distinction which was to become a favourite of some pro-deterrent moralists twenty years later: there is no *necessary* connection between the intention to use the weapons and the intention to deter

[65] L. L. McReavy, 'The Debate on the Morality of Future War', *Clergy Review* (Feb. 1960), 77; also, 'The Morality of the NATO Deterrent Policy', *Clergy Review*, (Oct. 1960), 615, and the ensuing correspondence.

with them. Therefore, so far as the individual conscience is concerned,

It is . . . logically and honestly possible for those engaged in the making or storing of nuclear weapons to limit their intention as co-operators to this primary purpose and withhold their approval from a mass-murder which they have reason to hope self-interest, if not morality, will prevent. [66]

This argument was answered by a number of other Roman Catholic adherents of just war doctrine, of whom Robert Markus was one of the most effective. He pointed out that this kind of argument rests on a confusion between (1) a future intention which can only be formed under certain conditions, and (2) a present intention to do something if certain conditions arise. Deterrent intention, being an instance of (2), is frequently confused with (1). Thus one is able to delude oneself into acting in the present as if no decision had been made while claiming, at the same time, that one has already rejected the morally repugnant course of action: even though one knows that, were the presently-held weapons to be used, it would almost certainly be in an immoral way. The question remains whether, in simply *possessing* nuclear weapons, one is committed to the immoral intention of type (2). Is not possession itself a guarantee of non-use? This, says Markus, makes too large an assumption about rationality prevailing in all circumstances. Deterrence is always a gamble which, when it is based upon the indiscriminate H-bomb, necessarily involves one in the possibility of committing criminal acts. There is, of course, no such thing as 'simple possession'. An elaborate structure of deployments, targeting and readiness to fire, involving a large number of individuals in commitment to obey orders to use the weapons is always required by deterrence. The claim that deterrence could be a bluff could not be sustained for this reason alone. [67]

But another argument was always available to pro-deterrent moralists: what if deterrence could be based, not on the threat to destroy cities, but on the threat to destroy enemy forces? Even though there would be very great collateral damage, the principle of discrimination might be observed and, given the nature of the

[66] McReavy, 'The Morality of the NATO Deterrent Policy' (correspondence), *Clergy Review* (Jan. 1961), 53.

[67] R. A. Markus, 'Conscience and Deterrence' in W. Stein (ed.), *Nuclear Weapons and Christian Conscience* (London: Merlin Press, 1961; repr. 1981), 65–88.

Soviet threat, the use of nuclear weapons might be proportionate to the evil. The US Defense Secretary McNamara's speech on 16 June 1962, announcing a preference for counter-force targeting by American strategic forces, led some British moralists to think that the required shift to a morally acceptable deterrence was taking place. However, as Anthony Kenny pointed out, this was no real change in fact.[68] Not for the last time, churchmen were liable to be taken in by a mere change of declaratory policy, when the substance of deterrence remained the same as before. On the one hand, the counter-force strategy was merely the insertion of 'another stage in the inevitable escalation of nuclear warfare before cities are destroyed'.[69] On the other hand, the estimated death toll from a counter-force war remained immensely high—high enough to make nonsense of any claims that discrimination could be observed. In any case, the MacNamara proposal was not well received by the British Defence Ministry and it was pointed out that British nuclear targets were too close to civil centres for the theory to work. In Kenny's judgement, it was not the threat of lawful use of nuclear weapons, but the threat of their murderous use which remained the basis of deterrence. The experience of the last war had demonstrated that neither the American nor the British governments would be restrained by morality when it came to a fight. Whatever the shifts of American targeting doctrine, any talk of counter-force targeting in the British context could only be academic since, as explained above, the British nuclear force had always been targeted on Soviet cities.

Conclusions

In a major development of policy in 1957–8, the Conservative government proposed to exchange manpower for nuclear fire-power and make nuclear weapons the foundation of defence. From then on, Britain would have to base its security on a willingness to

---

[68] A. Kenny, 'Counterforce and Countervalue', *Clergy Review* (Dec. 1962) repr. in W. Stein (ed.), *Nuclear Weapons and Christian Conscience* (1981), 153–65.

[69] See report in *Times*, 12 Sept. 1962. The fact is that, neither at this time nor in later counter-force declarations, did the United States ever give up targeting cities. The purpose of the 'no-cities' option was to hold them in reserve for later in the hope that the threat to destroy them would be a powerful bargaining lever to end the war quickly on terms favourable to the West. See David N. Schwartz, *Nato's Nuclear Dilemmas* (Washington, DC: Brookings Inst., 1983), 139, and Ian Clark *Limited Nuclear War* (Oxford: Martin Robertson, 1982), 207 ff.

use tactical nuclear weapons in the early phases of battle and on a capacity to destroy key Soviet cities, especially Moscow, in a final act of retaliation.

Of the three important questions mentioned at the beginning of this chapter, only the *policy* question received a positive answer in the following six years. The nuclear option was economically highly advantageous. Through the abandonment of conscription, of much conventional armoury, and of home defence, the policy allowed a much cheaper defence and may have been an important factor in allowing the post-war economic boom to resume after Suez. In one sense it was a demilitarization of society. It appeared to give the best of both worlds: a country enjoying the fruits of peace while ready for immediate devastating military action. Further political benefit came from the fact that the independent deterrent restored some sense of importance to a country that was in conspicuous decline as a world power. Although this enhanced status was subjective and illusory, the economic advantages were probably real enough.

Arguments for economy and prestige masked the question of *strategy,* which never received a satisfactory answer: no one was able to say under what circumstances it would be rational for a Prime Minister to order the use of nuclear weapons of any kind. Everything depended on preventing war. The argument that emerged most prominently for the independent deterrent was that it presented a second centre of decision-making for the Russian leaders to take into the calculations. It was a source of reassurance in the face of the frighteningly ambivalent presence of American nuclear forces in Britain.

As for the *moral question,* it was for the most part not even admitted as relevant by the Conservative government which was in power for most of the period. The intense moral debate which went on in some circles had no effect whatever on the development of policy. British governments have always preferred not to speculate about possible moral arguments for nuclear weapons, but to claim instead that war is prevented by them. There is no alternative for a country which has a nuclear force targeted on cities. But this should not be seen simply as an operational necessity (see Chapter 3). It is a deliberately chosen policy. Thus the moral question, which hinges on future use of the weapons against civilian populations, which may result from unforeseen circumstances, was marginalized as people were presented with the questionable choice of nuclear deterrence or no defence at all against an enemy poised to attack them. The Labour party after Gaitskell—for which the moral question did have some meaning—was contemptuous of the status argument and could have renounced the independent deterrent and allowed Britain to become a non-nuclear member of NATO with a stronger conventional force. The option of a break of this kind was clearly present in 1964. However, this course was not taken for a number of reasons, among which the cost-effectiveness of Polaris and British political influence seem to have been decisive.

They were right who said that renouncing the British bomb for moral reasons but remaining under American nuclear protection was morally incoherent. The fundamental moral question revolves around the hosting of American nuclear bases. Britain would share the responsibility for any use of nuclear weapons from the bases. And the 'independent' deterrent, which exists in a symbiotic relationship with the bases, would lose much of its strategic purpose without them.

7

POLARIS AND *DÉTENTE*,
1965–1976

The Changing Outlook on Defence

The Great Nuclear Debate petered out by 1965. The reasons were both domestic and international: the Labour government's accept-ance of Polaris and its successful defusing of the issue; the successful handling of the Cuban missile crisis in 1962, followed by the first signs of *Détente* (the 'hot-line' and the Partial Test-Ban Treaty). It appeared that the world was learning to live with nuclear weapons without catastrophe after all. The 'Soviet Threat' seemed to be receding and the major threat to world peace was now officially identified as the uncontrolled expansion of the nuclear club.[1] In its defence review of 1964–5, the Labour government announced a major change in Britain's strategic role: its declining power and its economic difficulties indicated a staged withdrawal from 'East of Suez' and a concentration on European defence. Considerably more thought was now being given to the political and military demands of Britain's European situation than had been given to it by previous governments since the World War II. This had important effects on the way the nuclear deterrent force was seen and described. More thought went into assessing the true nature of the 'threat' and the most appropriate response to it.

In the judgement of the 1965 Defence White Paper, major conflict between East and West in Europe could be almost entirely excluded from consideration. This was credited to the effectiveness of the nuclear deterrent, but also to an evolution of both Soviet and Western thinking resulting from a better understanding of the consequences of nuclear war. The security goal in Europe now came to be defined as avoiding 'war by mistake', i.e. a local conflict inadvertently escalating into a nuclear exchange. The major threat to peace was not Soviet territorial ambition or even Communist

[1] Cmnd. 2592. *Statement on the Defence Estimates: 1965.*

subversion, but the spread of nuclear weapons to other countries. The recent explosion of a Chinese bomb had emphasized how proliferation could upset the precarious stability achieved between the Soviet Union and the Western Alliance. However, the major worry appears to have been the possibility that West Germany might seek to acquire a nuclear force of its own if it did not feel itself to be adequately covered by the nuclear powers of NATO. France had already set the example. This spread of independent national deterrents was identified as the most dangerous development on the horizon; the one which could provoke the Soviet Union into a preventive war in Europe.

The Labour government's answer to the proliferation problem was a proposal for an Atlantic Nuclear Force (ANF), in which the non-nuclear powers of NATO would have some collective authority over planning and deployment of nuclear weapons in the European area. When asked in Parliament whether or not the government was about to abandon the independent deterrent, the Defence Secretary, Denis Healey, answered that the intention was not to abandon it but to 'internationalize' it.[2] In any case, so the Labour government maintained, the so-called 'independent' deterrent was not independent at all since it relied heavily on the Americans for supply and operation, including targeting. The Prime Minister, Harold Wilson, went on to demolish the Conservative claim that independent control was necessary in case Britain should find itself in a 'go-it-alone' war with the Soviet Union—a situation he considered to be impossible.[3] But he sidestepped the issue of whether it would ever be rational to use it at all, with or without allies. It appears that what was happening in the debate was one of those shifts of declaratory policy designed to yield political results, while the hardware and operational policy which governed it remained unchanged. Wilson afterwards declared that Britain would retain the right to withdraw the force for her own use in extreme circumstances: basically the same claim that Macmillan had made at Nassau.

But the main purpose of the ANF scheme was almost certainly to torpedo the schemes for a Multilateral Force (MLF), with mixed

[2] Commons Defence Debate, 1 Mar. 1965, House of Commons Official Report, vol. 707, col. 1327 f.

[3] See Harold Wilson, *The Labour Government, 1964–1970* (London: Penguin, 1974), 56.

nationality crews, put forward with great persistence by the US State Department, which was still strongly opposed to small, independent nuclear forces. None of the European members of NATO thought such a plan to be workable. The Labour government's move was successful, after which the ANF itself was quietly abandoned and Britain returned to its former position, with an 'independent' strategic nuclear force, supplied and targeted by the United States. On the political level, various things had been achieved besides the containment of dissent at home: further proliferation in Europe had been avoided, the Labour government with its rhetoric of internationalizing appeared to be renouncing old-fashioned 'virility symbols' (Wilson's phrase), and the United States gave up trying to obtain a nuclear monopoly in NATO. The whole issue was then laid to rest for over ten years, when the question of modernization again surfaced. The United States was eventually persuaded to share some of the nuclear planning responsibilities with non-nuclear NATO countries, including West Germany, through the Nuclear Planning Group (NPG), set up in 1967.

Flexible Response

The concentration of British defence effort in Europe, which was well under-way by 1967, was accompanied by a new strategic doctrine, designed to replace the much-criticized Massive Retaliation of the 1957/8 Sandys defence plan. This was Flexible Response (FR), conceived in 1962 by Robert McNamara as a means of giving a US president other options in Europe than immediately ordering the use of nuclear weapons.[4] Its immediate stimulus was the Soviet blockade of Berlin in 1961. McNamara later stated that the experience of thinking through the response to successive Soviet moves in that crisis convinced him that under no circumstances could NATO initiate the use of nuclear weapons without catastrophic results.[5] Massive Retaliation was bankrupt. When scrutinized by the incoming Kennedy administration it was found to be based on an unduly pessimistic estimate of the balance

---

[4] See McNamara's own account of the reasons for the change in 'The Military Role of Nuclear Weapons: Perceptions and Misperceptions', *Foreign Affairs* (Fall 1983), 59–80, repr. in *Survival* (Nov.–Dec. 1983), 261 ff.

[5] BBC 2 programme, 'A Question of Defence', 5 Aug. 1986.

of conventional forces in Europe and on an unduly optimistic view of the possibilities of using nuclear weapons to NATO's advantage.

FR in its original McNamara version involved raising the nuclear threshold by 'planning for the critical initial responses to Soviet aggression to be made by conventional forces alone'.[6] Implicit in the proposal was the belief that NATO both could and should improve its conventional arms so as to be able to halt a conventional attack by the Warsaw Pact without resort to nuclear weapons. The onus of escalation would be on the other side. This ought to be a strong deterrent to any nuclear use by the WP, owing to the massive superiority of the United States in terms of strategic nuclear weapons. But also implicit was the recognition that this superiority did not translate into usable military power, and that the use of even a small part of it would put the United States itself in peril.

It was this kind of reasoning that upset the European members of NATO, for it seemed to them like an attempt to 'decouple' the United States from the defence of Europe. To the French, it confirmed what they had always suspected—the unreliability of the American nuclear guarantee. The Germans had similar suspicions, and eventually proposed an alternative, more belligerent version of FR: that it should carry a threat deliberately to escalate to the nuclear level at an early stage in the conflict, as a warning of NATO's resolve to engage American strategic systems if necessary. Anything else might lead the Soviet Union to think that it could safely fight a war in Central Europe. None of the European member governments of NATO had any intention of making Europe safe for conventional war. It always seemed safest never to have to fight at all. And apart from anything else, they believed that the cost of an adequate non-nuclear defence would be a major threat to the continuation of their post-war prosperity.

A 'passionate and acrimonious dispute' (McNamara) about FR and the early use of nuclear weapons continued between NATO members for the next five years, until 1967, when a compromise was adopted by the NATO Council. It was a declaration that NATO would deter aggression by maintaining forces adequate to counter an attack at whatever level the aggressor chose to fight. If this 'direct defence' proved unsuccessful, NATO would 'never

<hr>

[6] McNamara, 'The Military Role of Nuclear Weapons', p. 263.

admit defeat, but go to another level' (Healey).[7] If this process failed, the end-result would be a general nuclear response of massive nuclear strikes against the full range of military targets in the Soviet Union and Eastern Europe.[8] Two concepts were central to the strategy—escalation, and control of the scope of the combat. McNamara's account of FR emphasizes the latter, whilst the Europeans tended to lay stress on the former. They do not sit easily together, especially when the escalation in question is a matter of using nuclear weapons at an early stage in the combat, knowing that this would result in the deaths of millions of Central Europeans on both sides. The European members of NATO hoped that this in itself would prevent any war at all.[9]

The final shape of FR was thus much nearer to the West German version than it was to the original McNamara version. The nuclear threshold was not raised, and the European members never paid anything but lip-service to the conventional force improvements that it would have required. From 1967 onwards, a major task of the NPG was to find ways in which NATO might credibly use tactical nuclear weapons at an early stage in a conflict without either totally destroying the area to be defended or provoking an immediate response at strategic level. The explanation which eventually emerged was that the weapons were not for fighting war-battles with, but for maintaining 'escalation dominance' by showing 'resolve' to proceed to strategic level unless the enemy backed off. It was epitomized in the West German formula, 'as late as possible and as early as necessary'. It is essentially this which has remained NATO's official doctrine until now.

The British government's version of FR was presented by Denis Healey in the Defence White Papers of 1968 and 1969, and argued for against various critics in the defence debate of March 1969. He maintained that the important thing was for NATO to have an appropriate response ready and not to make things infinitely worse by hasty resort to nuclear weapons if a conflict originating in Eastern Europe were to spread across the border. His language in

[7] In the BBC programme mentioned above in n. 5.
[8] This description of FR is from James A. Thomson, 'Nuclear Weapons in Europe', *Survival* (May–June, 1983), 98–110.
[9] The Europeans have remained committed to threatening holocaust in order to avoid a war on their own territory—see Paul Bracken, *The Command and Control of Nuclear Forces* (New Haven, Conn. and London: Yale University Press, 1983), 162–4.

the debate departed widely from the usual 'Soviet aggression' model which had served the defence fraternity for so long:

> ... we must avoid surrendering to the temptation, to which so many academic strategists sometimes fall victim, and isolating the military problem from the political context in which it is presented in real life. We must not assume that we are dealing at all times with an enemy who has an absolute will to destroy us and an infinite capacity for calculating the military means to that end. The real world, thank God, is not a Manichaean struggle between Good and Evil; our political adversaries are usually ordinary men subject to ordinary temptations, and often facing predicaments from which they may be as anxious to escape as we are.[10]

He pointed out that the 'trip-wire' concept, to which many Conservatives were still attached, could have been fatal if it had been activated by the various Soviet actions in Hungary, East Berlin, and Prague, in which direct aggression against the West was never part of the Soviet plan.

However, when Healey went on to describe what was being done in the way of strengthening conventional defence, the result was not so radical as might have been expected, given the new theory of East–West conflict. There was absolutely no intention of building a conventional force capable of repelling a full scale attack. One of the main reasons offered for this was the enormous increase in the defence budget that this was said to entail. Another was political and strategic: in Healey's opinion the likely result of British reliance on conventional forces would be for Germany to acquire nuclear weapons once she lost confidence in collective nuclear strategy. And that would invite pre-emptive war from the Soviet Union. The main purpose of an improved conventional force is to 'win sufficient time to enable diplomatic action to bring the aggressor to his senses, or failing that, to enable the awesome decision to cross the nuclear threshold to be taken in full knowledge of the facts'. In answer to possible criticism on moral grounds, Healey asks the critics to consider first, that the use of nuclear weapons would never arise unless the Warsaw Powers launched a large-scale deliberate invasion or aggression against Western Europe, and second, that the thought that they might be used will *prevent* such a thing.

There was little public controversy over Flexible Response at the

---

[10] Defence Debate, 4 Mar. 1969, House of Commons Official Report, vol. 779, col. 238.

time of its introduction, but thirteen years later its weaknesses became the subject of bitter strategic and moral controversy. This will form the subject matter of Chapter 9.

Détente and 'The Continuing Threat', 1970–1976

During the period which began with the return of a Conservative government under Edward Heath in 1970, a number of factors ensured a continued public lack of concern on the nuclear question, among them, the Vietnam War, Northern Ireland, and the apparent success of Détente. The Non-Proliferation Treaty (1968), the German Ostpolitik (1968 ff.), the Biological Weapons Convention (1972), the SALT I Agreements (1972), and finally the Helsinki Accord (1975) and SALT II, all gave the impression of a steady historical progress towards the management of nuclear weapons in a rational process of co-operation. Nevertheless, not far under the surface, processes were at work which would bring that optimism to an abrupt end in 1979.

The main factor was the apparent relentless increase in size and capabilities of Warsaw Pact forces at virtually all levels throughout the 1970s.[11] The Ministry of Defence presented it solely in terms of a military threat. In Defence White Papers from 1971 onwards increasing prominence is given to selected details of 'The Threat', followed by sections on the 'NATO Response'. Through the 1970s the comparison took on a life of its own, and from 1977 onwards there appeared simplified, eye-catching charts for quick comparison of NATO and WP force levels, the former shown as consistently lower in almost every respect. These charts suffer from the usual faults of such comparisons: it is too easy to select forces and figures which produce the desired result and to ignore those which do not, and to leave out things more difficult to present in graphic form, such as quality and readiness for combat of men and machinery. Undoubtedly there was taking place a real, and partially successful, effort of the Soviet Union to gain parity with the United States in matters of military forces and to project itself as a world power.

---

[11] For an account of the Soviet buildup of nuclear forces, see Gregory Treverton, 'Nuclear Weapons in Europe', Adelphi Papers, 168 (Summer 1981). For a political analysis see Jonathan Steele, World Power: Soviet Foreign Policy Under Brezhnev and Andropov (London: Michael Joseph, 1983); and David Holloway, The Soviet Union and the Arms Race (New Haven Conn. and London: Yale University Press, 1983).

This was seen by the Soviet leaders as a condition of *Détente* rather than a contradiction of it. But of course for NATO it contained all the ambiguities of the power–security dilemma mentioned in Chapter 2. One of its consequences was an apparent imbalance of forces in Europe which was alarming to the European members of NATO. As a result of the Soviet achievement of parity with the US, doubt was cast on the latter's readiness to keep sufficiently powerful forces in Europe to meet the local increase in Soviet capabilities. Whatever truth the MOD charts contained, the comparisons they put forward were clearly part of a prolonged public relations effort in the cause of certain policies internal to NATO and the British defence fraternity.

One of the functions of the 'Threat' sections in defence statements may have been to show just how necessary for Europe's security was the American nuclear guarantee. Thus the 1971 Conservative White Paper has not only the 'Threat' in mind, but also the Mansfield Resolution before the US Senate, which proposed to reduce drastically the size of American forces in Europe, partly because of a feeling that the prosperous Europeans were not doing enough for their own defence and partly because of a belief that the danger of a Soviet attack on Western Europe was now greatly reduced.[12] Eventually a bargain was struck between the European members of NATO and the American administration to increase the former's share of the conventional force burden in exchange for an assurance of maintaining current US force levels, which would assure linkage with the US strategic nuclear forces. Armed with the European commitment to a 'defence improvement programme', the Nixon administration was able to stave off the threat from Congress. However, as a response to the 'Threat', the British contribution was not very convincing: some augmentation of surface ships in the Atlantic, some increase of army manpower and a few extra Buccanneer and Nimrod aircraft.

At this time the NPG was undertaking a review of the 'possible defensive employment of nuclear weapons in the context of NATO's strategy of flexibility of response'.[13] This was a matter of

---

[12] Cmnd. 4592, *Statement on the Defence Estimates: 1971*. See also *Strategic Survey, 1970* (IISS, issued 1971), 18–20, and *Strategic Survey, 1971* (issued 1972), p. 21.

[13] *Strategic Survey, 1979*, p. 19.

first-use (studied in 1970) and the nuclear follow-on if this failed to halt the aggressor (1971–2).

The defence review of the new Labour government contained in the 1975 *Statement on Defence* at one and the same time presented a detailed and pessimistic description of the Soviet military buildup *and* announced extensive cuts in Britain's conventional force levels, many of them directly affecting Britain's contribution to NATO.[14] It is worth asking how these could appear together without any sense of total contradiction. Charts are presented to show that in every major department (soldiers, battle-tanks, field-guns, and tactical aircraft) the balance is very much in favour of the Warsaw Pact, and that similar advantage is enjoyed by the Soviet Northern Fleet in the East Atlantic. The overall Soviet military buildup is then detailed as the achievment of nuclear parity with the US, the achievement of maritime superpower status and an increase and improvement in the capability of its forces 'much greater than in any previous five years of peacetime'. Meanwhile, the government was to reduce the UK armed services strength by 38,000 men (11 per cent), with a reduction of 30,000 (10 per cent) in civilian support. By no means all of this could be accounted for by redundancies caused by the withdrawal from east of Suez and the Caribbean. Much of the manpower and equipment reduction was to be through cuts which directly affected Britain's contribution to NATO, especially cuts in Specialist Reinforcement Forces, and a complete withdrawal of the Navy from its regular Mediterranean operations on NATO's southern flank. The RAF would lose half its transport fleet and a quarter of its helicopter force, a quarter of its Nimrod maritime patrol force and some twelve airfields. The Navy was to lose one seventh of its surface ships as well as other extensive losses. Meanwhile the Army was to undergo a thorough restructuring which would result in a manpower reduction of 15,000. This was ingeniously described as an 'improvement of the man-to-weapon ratio'.[15] The government was quite aware that Britain's NATO allies considered these changes to be 'damaging'. The hidden factor was that NATO was seen by the government to be relying on its increasing nuclear strength, on land and at sea, to make up for the disparity of conventional force levels, which it had given up any hope of improving, ostensibly for economic reasons.

[14] Cmnd. 5976, *Statement on the Defence Estimates: 1975*, 6.
[15] Cmnd. 5976, *Statement on the Defence Estimates: 1975*, 42.

American Threats—British Responsibilities

In October 1973, during the Yom Kippur War between Israel and the Arab states, Egypt, and Syria, the British right of joint decision on the use of nuclear weapons from American bases on British soil was discovered to be non-enforceable. Since the Churchill–Truman meeting of January 1952, successive British governments, when questioned about their right to be consulted before the use of the bases, fell back on the vague formula which was used in the final communiqué of that meeting: that it would be a 'matter for joint decision by His Majesty's government and the United States in the light of the circumstances prevailing at the time'.[16] There had been considerable scepticism in the following years over what this would amount to if it were ever put to the test in a real emergency. Both at the time of the Thor missile emplacements in 1957–8, and during the establishment of the Holy Loch base in the mid-1960s, many voices from both left and right in British politics had protested that Britain had surrendered its sovereign right to decide the course of a future war fought from its territory by the United States. There was plenty of evidence coming from public figures in the United States that a British veto over American freedom to do what they pleased with their overseas forces was out of the question. In any case it might well prove to be impossible to consult the British government in an emergency before the weapons had to be used. Some British ministers thought that the presence of the bases rendered the United States a greater danger to the security of the United Kingdom than the Soviet Union.

It was the 1973 Middle East War that dramatically confirmed these fears. Believing that the Soviet Union was about to make a military intervention on the side of Egypt to save her from defeat, President Nixon approved an order putting all American conventional and nuclear forces on alert. This included the F-111 nuclear bomber squadrons at Upper Heyford and Lakenheath, and presumably also the Polaris fleet operating from Holy Loch. The British ambassador in Washington was informed of the order after it had been made. Simon Duke, in his study of the Anglo-American base agreements, says that:

American documentation from National Archives makes it plain that the United States Administration believe that their only obligation toward their

[16] Simon W. Duke, *US Defence Bases in the United Kingdom: A Matter for Joint Decision?* (London: Macmillan, 1987), 80.

allies in time of emergency was to 'notify' them of developments. As it happened, other American allies hosting their forces were not even notified of the alert. Henry Kissinger, in his memoirs, justified the American action by writing that 'there was no middle position between alert and no alert . . . to be frank, we could not have accepted a judgement different from our own'. [17]

The Prime Minister, Edward Heath, apparently refused to endorse the nuclear alert when he was at last informed of it: an action which was not well-received in Washington. It seems clear that Britain could not expect anything like a joint decision in such an instance, even though—as host to American forces—she would share in the moral responsibility for attacks made from the bases, as was discovered in April 1986 after the American raid on Tripoli.

Would Polaris Always Get Through?

Throughout the period covered in this chapter, there were official anxieties about whether Britain's Polaris force remained a real deterrent or not—i.e. whether it would get through to its designated targets if sent. In 1967, it was believed that the Soviet Union was constructing an ABM system around Moscow and perhaps around other cities which Britain might wish to attack. If this were a success it would severely curtail the ability of the missiles to get through, and Britain would have another obsolete system on her hands just when it had become fully operational. It was feared that the force would cease to be a deterrent by the mid-1970s. In May 1972 the United States and the Soviet Union signed the ABM Treaty, which allowed for 100 ABMs apiece, the Soviet Union's to be deployed around Moscow. This token defence still raised problems for the British strategic planners, who were not certain that a retaliatory attack from their Polaris force would be sure to penetrate it. That is, there was a problem if it was assumed that Moscow was the principal target. Evidence given to the House of Commons Expenditure Committee in 1973 and then again in 1978–9 amply confirms that it was. [18] One way of coping with the

---

[17] Ibid. 185.
[18] See Lawrence Freedman, *Britain and Nuclear Weapons* (London: Macmillan, 1980), 47, and 'The Future of the United Kingdom's Weapons Policy', *The Sixth Report from the Expenditure Committee*, Session 1978–9, no. 348 (London: HMSO, 1979), 73.

problem would have been to purchase the Poseidon SLBM system from the United States, with its multiple independently targeted re-entry vehicles (MIRVs). However, this option was conclusively rejected by the Wilson government in 1967. There were no tests of British weapons for many years, and no plans for a new generation of strategic weapons. If the remaining members of the nuclear weapons team at Aldermaston were not to become completely demoralized and even redundant, they needed to work on improvements to the existing Polaris warheads and re-entry system. The rationale for this work was the threat that Soviet ABMs would eventually make it too difficult for Britain to destroy Moscow with certainty. The work on new warheads continued in complete secrecy, although it was known well enough to a small group of initiates in the Wilson government.

In 1973 the government of Edward Heath initiated the Polaris Improvement Programme, which would continue to work at Aldermaston on improving the penetration ability of the Polaris warheads. The product of this progamme was code-named Cheval-ine, and was eventually described publicly in 1980 by Defence Secretary Francis Pym as,

A very major and complex development of the missile front end, involving also changes to the fire-control system. The result will not be a MIRVed system, but it includes advanced penetration aids and the ability to manœuvre the payload in space. [19]

It should be noted that, according to this description the result would not be accurate independent targeting suitable for counter-force strikes, but the scatter effect thought most efficient for the extensive and complete destruction of urban areas.

When the Labour party was returned to power in February 1974, a small Cabinet committee was informed of the improvement programme and it decided to continue with it in secrecy, not wishing to stir up a fresh controversy about the deterrent, always damaging to the Labour party.[20] Since there was to be no switch to

[19] See Freedman, *Britain and Nuclear Weapons*, p. 48. The preoccupation with 'penetration' backs up Harold Wilson's description in 1964 of Polaris as a 'virility symbol'.

[20] Harold Wilson later gave a reason for the secrecy: 'It isn't a question of not trusting. It's more a question that the more people you have, the more people can be got at, for example by back-benchers who then start to press Cabinet Ministers.' Richard Norton-Taylor, *Guardian*, 27 June 1985.

a completely new system, such as Poseidon, it was conveniently unnecessary to bring the matter into the open. The commitment was made definite by a Cabinet decision in September 1975. In April 1976 the government sanctioned the conversion of a nuclear-power plant at Chapel Cross to a tritium-production plant to ensure that Britain would have sufficient fissile material for a new generation of warheads and would not have to rely on the uncertainties of purchase from the United States. As John Simpson points out, in these decisions the Labour government was making a drastic reversal of its previous policy not to develop new weapons, and disguising it by allowing it to be understood that nothing more than maintenance of Polaris was involved.[21] However, there was some internal controversy later among Cabinet Ministers. In particular, dissent came from David Owen, the Foreign Secretary, who believed that other Soviet cities could be threatened with destruction more cheaply—with cruise missiles, for instance—and that the Moscow Criterion should be abandoned. But so much money had by that time been spent on the project that these objections were overridden on financial grounds. The cost had meanwhile increased enormously, from an estimated £175m in 1972 to £598m in 1976, and was to rise to £1000m in 1980 (£530m by 1972 prices). None of this ever appeared in the annual Defence Estimates of the Labour government, presumably in order to keep the embarrassing topic off the political agenda during the lifetime of the government.

Not only the renewal of the British deterrent force, but also the moral questioning which it had previously provoked were off the agenda throughout the period covered in this chapter. Apart from the publication of works which had been a long time in gestation, there were no contributions to the moral debate in Britain from 1965 until late in 1979. This is surely a very remarkable hiatus in the most prolonged and public moral controversy of the century. Some debate continued in the United States, centred around the relative moral status of MAD and counter-force targeting doctrines: a choice that British planners could not consider because of their fixed belief in the importance of being free to eliminate Moscow.

<hr>

[21] John Simpson, *The Independent Nuclear State* (London: Macmillan, 1983; 2nd edn. 1986), 175, 199.

Conclusions

Polaris and *Détente* made it possible to tidy away the strategic and moral objections to Britain's nuclear status for a long time. The impression was successfuly conveyed to most people that 'the bomb will never be used'. It was a welcome relief. What moral opposition remained was confined to a dwindling band of the anti-nuclear faithful. The invention of Flexible Response to replace Massive Retaliation also contributed to defusing the controversy which had been inflamed by the Dulles–Sandys doctrine of all-out incineration at the first stage. The inherent contradictions of FR did not, for various reasons, become the subject of public anxiety until much later. Since no significant innovations in Britain's nuclear programme were made during this period, governments did not need to defend it, except by reiterating established positions, notably the argument that any change of nuclear status would involve a huge increase of expenditure and probably conscription as well. Continued economic crises made sure that economy—rather than prestige or strategy—remained as the chief rationale for continued reliance on nuclear weapons.

8

CRISIS OVER MODERNIZATION, 1977–1987

The New Insecurity

If we are to look for the reasons for the dramatic renewal of public conflict over nuclear weapons at the end of the 1970s, we would need to distinguish immediate causes from long-term changes in the political–strategic environment. Immediate causes were the storm over the neutron bomb in 1977–8 and the 1979 NATO decision to deploy cruise and *Pershing* II missiles in Europe. Along with these developments in hardware came one of the periodic American renewals of interest in the possibilities of 'limited nuclear war', sometimes expressed with devastating disregard for European feelings. However, at the root of these policy decisions were long-term changes, some of which have already been mentioned, and which may now be summarized:

- alarm and fear in the West over the Soviet buildup and achievement of parity in nuclear systems, with apparent superiority in some areas, such as ICBMs;
- new technical developments coming along in the pipeline, especially increased missile accuracy, cruise technology, and enhanced radiation weapons;
- the loss of confidence in Mutual Assured Destruction (MAD) and re-emphasis of counter-force doctrines and ideas of limited nuclear war; [1]
- paradoxically, the arms-control process itself, in that the SALT agreements between the US and the USSR, settled over the heads of the European members of NATO, appeared to them to be institutionalizing a local imbalance in favour of the

---

[1] See Desmond Ball, 'Can Nuclear War Be Controlled?', *Adelphi Papers*, no. 96 (Autumn 1981), 2: 'Whereas in the 1960s . . . the concept of deterrence was starkly contrasted with that of defence, both are now seen as integral parts of a continuum; the capacity for nuclear-war fighting is now regarded as an essential ingredient of a successful deterrent.'

Warsaw Pact, and, at the same time, to be weakening the American guarantee to defend Western Europe with its strategic nuclear weapons;

• the rise in the United States of powerful lobbies hostile to the aims of *Détente* and arms control as previously understood.

In Britain, these developments had their repercussions and happened to coincide with the domestic battle over the renewal of the strategic deterrent force, which brought up once more the old question of Britain's independent nuclear status.

Long-Range Theatre Nuclear Weapons

In December 1979 a meeting of NATO Ministers decided to deploy on European soil a force of Long-Range Theatre Nuclear Weapons, since renamed the Intermediate-range Nuclear Force (INF): 464 Ground-Launched Cruise Missiles (GLCM) and 108 *Pershing* II ballistic missiles. The deployment went along with a parallel offer of arms control talks for this grade of weapon. The latter was a highly unusual feature for a force deployment of this kind and arose from the political sensitivity in Europe to weapons of this type. The leading actors in these events were the United States and West Germany. British officials and ministers participated in the discussions leading to the decision, wholeheartedly accepted the outcome, accepted 160 GLCMs for deployment in Britain, and were forced to launch a massive public relations exercise as a result of the political uproar caused by the decision. European governments completely miscalculated the public impact of the highly visible mobile ground-launched missiles and the ability of the apparently burnt-out anti-nuclear movements to oppose them. The arrival of cruise missiles in Britain became a symbol of its dependence on United States strategic plans, of the willingness of the latter to wage nuclear war in Europe, and of Britain's vulnerability to pre-emptive attack.

The decision must be seen, not as a totally new development in the East–West arms race, but as the latest episode in the strained nuclear relationship between the United States and its European allies, which has been discussed briefly in earlier chapters. Whereas the Europeans have tended to advocate a strategy of absolute deterrence through the threat of immediate all-out nuclear war, the United States has tried to avoid the appalling choice between all-out war or defeat by providing a range of options, including the use of 'theater' nuclear weapons. As a consequence, the American stance often appears to be indistinguishable from a readiness to fight a 'limited' nuclear war, i.e. one that is confined to the European 'theater'. The difference of outlook again came to a crisis in 1977, owing to the long-term changes in the political–strategic environment mentioned above.

The issue was first brought into the open by the West German Chancellor Helmut Schmidt, in a lecture to the International Institute for Strategic Studies in London in October 1977. It discussed several different aspects of security, only one of which was the necessity for a military balance in Europe. But that was the one which everyone afterwards chose to emphasize.[2] He certainly called for Flexible Response to be strengthened by redressing the balance of forces in Europe which had been upset by the SALT process. But although it came very close to it, it was not a direct call for tactical nuclear-weapons improvement. The main demand of the speech appears to be for an equalization of conventional arms. However, when the final decision was made in 1979, the priorities were somewhat different. Whereas for the Chancellor arms control had priority as the only policy with a real future, for the NATO planners in 1979 it was the nuclear deployment which had priority—as a test of NATO's resolve and of America's leadership. This was deemed to be necessary in order to regain credibility lost when President Carter had to cancel the neutron-weapon deployments in the face of massive European popular protest in 1978— afterwards attributed to a successful Soviet propaganda offensive. In the view of some informed commentators, the real purpose of the 'dual-track' arms control proposal was purely political—to disarm public protest and make it easier for the host governments to accept the missiles.[3]

But there were several factors influencing this shift of priorities. Among them was the momentum of the new technologies, especially that of advanced cruise missiles, which had great attractions for European military planners. They were relatively cheap, promised to be highly accurate, capable of avoiding air

[2] The text of Chancellor Schmidt's 1977 Alastair Buchan Memorial Lecture is reproduced in *Survival*, IISS (Jan.–Feb. 1978), 2–10.

[3] For instance, Simon Lunn, who prepared a comprehensive report for the US Congress on the matter: 'It was to gain public acceptance for modernization— people should be very clear about that', *New Statesman* (1 May 1981), 3.

defences when used in substantial numbers, and could be fired from a variety of different platforms, on land , sea, or in the air. The British government seriously considered them as a replacement for the ageing Polaris force. They promised to be very cost-effective weapons, useful for all sorts of tasks, both nuclear and conventional. In some sense the cruise missile was like the neutron weapon—a new weapon 'looking for a role'. There were powerful pressures at work on both sides of the Atlantic urging its large-scale deployment in the European 'theater'.

Moreover, there were anxieties among European NATO members that, in the SALT negotiations, the United States might bargain away freedom to deploy cruise missiles in Europe. The Soviet Union had already pressed for restrictions on cruise missiles, and some United States officials favoured restricting their range as a bargaining concession.[4] There was also the threat of a non-circumvention clause which would restrict the United States' right to transfer technical information about nuclear weapons to other countries. British ministers were particularly worried by these developments, as might be expected considering the traditional heavy dependence on American technology. Moreover, there were those in the United States opposed to the SALT negotiations who, as a tactic for destroying the credibility of the Treaty, were ready to persuade the European allies that SALT II was undermining their security.[5]

The third major factor was anxieties about the Soviet medium-range ballistic missile modernization programme—the SS-20s. These replaced old, cumbersome and less accurate medium-range missiles aimed at European targets. However, according to Simon Lunn, 'NATO's modernization requirements were not initially related to the number of SS–20s deployed, but were a function of the requirements of Flexible Response.'[6] But, as a rationale for the NATO modernization, the SS–20 threat was pushed to the forefront after the December 1979 decision. It was easier to gain public support by stressing the menace of the new Soviet missiles

    [4] Simon Lunn, *The Modernization of NATO's Long-Range Theater Nuclear Forces*, Report prepared for the Sub-committee on Europe and the Middle East of the House Committee on Foreign Affairs. 96th Congress, 2nd session (Washington, DC: US Government Printing Office, 1981), 17.
    [5] Simon Lunn, 'Cruise Missiles and the Prospect for Arms Control', *ADIU Report*, 3/5 (Sept.–Oct. 1981), 2–5.
    [6] Ibid. 3

than to try to explain the difficult and alarming concepts of linkage, escalation dominance and the like, which were part of Flexible Response.[7] Already, by 1978, the annual *Statement on Defence* was stating that the main purpose of NATO's theatre nuclear weapons was to 'deter the use of similar weapons by the Soviet Union', instead of the traditional purpose of compensating for the Warsaw Pact predominance in conventional weapons, although this remained implicit in the continuing attachment to first-use.[8]

The political purpose of the modernization programme within NATO was fairly clear. However, the strategic rationale of the new weapons was not so clear, and various purposes have been offered by the different parties involved. This is how it is described in a US Congress document:

Should deterrence fail, the US and its NATO Allies would possess effective new capabilities to engage military targets located well behind the forward edge of the battle area. These targets include: fixed IRBM/MRBM sites; naval bases; nuclear and chemical storage sites; air-bases; command, control and communication centres; headquarters complexes; fixed surface-to-air missile sites; munitions and petroleum storage areas and transfer facilities; ground forces installations; choke points; troop concentrations; and bridges. Their military significance derives from the potential contributions of those targets to the support of sustained military operations by the Warsaw Pact. [9]

This is a pretty comprehensive counter-force role for cruise and *Pershing* II missiles. Also in the document quoted above are some indications that the missiles have a first-use function. Among a list of ways in which they will enhance existing capabilities it is stated that they perform the function of currently deployed Quick Reaction Alert (QRA) aircraft. These include the F-111s stationed at Lakenheath and Upper Heyford. They are permanently equipped with nuclear bombs and ready at all times to take off at very short notice.[10] Their destruction would be of the highest priority for the

[7] Ibid.

[8] Cmnd. 7099, *Statements on the Defence Estimates: 1978*, 119. See also *Cruise Missiles, The Important Questions and Answers* (London: MOD, 1981).

[9] 'Long Range Theater Nuclear Missile Systems and the Sea-Launched Cruise Missile', *Fiscal Year 1982 Arms Control Impact Statements*, 96th Congress, 1st Session Joint Committee Print (Washington, DC: Government Printing Office, Feb. 1981), repr. in *Nuclear War In Europe: Documents* (Washington, DC: Center for Defense Information, 1981), 38.

[10] Cf. Simon W. Duke, *US Defence Bases in the United Kingdom* (London: Macmillan, 1987), 178.

Warsaw Pact in the opening stages of any war, which would create pressure for first- and early-use. That the GLCMs at Greenham Common were seen to be in the same category of weapon was confirmed by official statements made about their dispersal during times of tension so that they might not become easy targets for Soviet counter-force attacks. 'Use them or lose them' is the dilemma which would face NATO commanders in the event of hostilities. Of all medium range weapons, *Pershing* II missiles close to the border with East Germany are most vulnerable in this respect.

As may be expected, British government explanations of the purpose of cruise missiles in this country were less forthcoming about targets. As a Ministry of Defence brochure distributed in the Greenham Common area put it, the purpose of the missiles was to fill a 'gap in our defences', which might be exploited by the Soviet Union.[11] How the absence of a particular type of offensive missile can constitute a gap in defence is never adequately explained in the official literature. To put the most reasonable construction on it, it may mean that, in the event of a large-scale conventional force invasion by the Warsaw Pact, the Western Alliance might only be able to reply with the type of weapons which would escalate the conflict to strategic level straight away unless it had the kind of counter-force capability represented by the GLCMs and *Pershing* IIs. But against this, is the fact that NATO already has a large range of tactical nuclear bombs as well as SLBMs capable of a counter-force role against targets in the Soviet Union. Also, from the Soviet point of view, an attack with intermediate-range nuclear weapons would be indistinguishable from an attack with strategic weapons. However, it is more likely that the language of 'gaps' and 'shields' is no more than a useful rhetorical device, intended to convey to the general public the idea that without *these* missiles in place the Enemy could strike us down. In 1981 the Defence Secretary, Francis Pym, in announcing Greenham Common and Molesworth as the places where cruise missiles would be based, justifed the deployment thus:

If we do not protect ourselves adequately and if we do not have an adequate shield, freedom and democracy will not be continued into the future . . . If we are not adequately defended the whole world may be taken over by the Soviet Union . . .'[12]

---

[11] *Cruise Missiles* (Ministry of Defence, 1981).
[12] House of Commons Official Report, 17 June 1980, vol. 986, col. 1357.

The nearest the MOD came to describing a military use for the GLCMs was in the 1981 brochure, *Cruise Missiles*, in which they appeared as weapons of first-use:

... if we only had nuclear weapons like Polaris, and were in danger of defeat, we could be faced with two stark choices—surrender or all-out nuclear war. Having small medium-range nuclear weapons would give us another choice in those circumstances—allowing us to bring home to the Russians the appalling risks they would run if they pressed us further. *The aim of using them would be to persuade the Russian leadership—even at the eleventh hour—to draw back.* (Emphasis added.)

In any cruise-missile attack, many weapons would need to be used in order to be sure that some of them would be accurate enough to reach their designated targets, run the gauntlet of the promised interception by Swedish defence forces, and finally get through the Soviet defences, which would, by that time, be specially designed to stop them. There could be no question of single shots. Whether the Russian leadership would draw back, after such a blow, is a doubtful proposition, to say the least.

It would probably be answered that GLCMs and *Pershing* IIs were exclusively for *deterrent* purposes, intended to dissuade any military adventures by the Soviet Union before they began, by reminding them of the consequences, the possible use of the 'theater' missiles being more credible than that of 'strategic' weapons. If this was the case, there was some difference in perspective between the United States, which controls the weapons, and the British Government, which hosts them. In fact, it is the usual difference over the role of 'Euromissiles' which has existed since the early 1950s: what the British government saw in terms of total deterrence, with only a nuclear exchange as the alternative, the United States administration saw in terms of limited nuclear war-fighting. In a report from the North Atlantic Special Committee on nuclear weapons in Europe, made to the US Senate in 1981, it was argued that American officials 'believe that Long-Range Theater Nuclear Forces constitute war-fighting capabilities rather than political signalling assets as many Europeans tend to perceive them'.[13]

[13] *Interim Report on Nuclear Weapons in Europe*: prepared by the North Atlantic Assembly's Special Committee on Nuclear Weapons in Europe, to the Committee on Foreign Relations, Senate, 97th Congress: 1st Session, Dec. 1981, p. 14, cited by Duke, *US Defence Bases*, p. 180. The Committee included two British MPs: Julian Critchley (Con.) and John Cartwright (SDP).

Replacing Polaris

Despite the Labour government's unwillingness to provoke public discussion on the eventual modernization of the strategic deterrent force, by 1978 the issue was being forced on its attention by others who were afraid that a decision would be made by default, and that there would be a period in the 1990s when Britain would be without any credible independent deterrent. By that time the Polaris submarines would be too unreliable and too noisy to avoid Soviet anti-submarine warfare with any confidence.[14] It was said that if there was to be any replacement system it would have to be chosen early in the 1980s. But the government did not agree with this and did not want to make it an election issue for 1978–9. However, the traditional small, secret committee of ministers was formed to look into the matter, and they set up two expert study-groups to work on alternatives. According to Lawrence Freedman, the committee noted that

A future force . . might not follow the 'Moscow Criterion' followed by the Chevaline programme but make do with an ability to attack some nine major cities other than the capital.[15]

Meanwhile a Parliamentary Expenditure Committee collected evidence from interested parties on the replacement question without coming to a conclusion, because the general election of May 1979 cut short its work. In the evidence given to the Committee, only that of Robin Cook the Labour MP, and Dan Smith took morality as the basis for their joint argument against any replacement. A memorandum from the IISS explicitly set moral considerations aside as being merely a matter of speculation about the effects on world opinion of the nuclear option. Other witnesses did not bring up such matters at all and the dominant criteria were cost and independence.[16] Between the likely options of choosing another SLBM force, a sea-based cruise missile force or simply

[14] See especially the influential study by Ian Smart for the RIIA: *The Future of The British Nuclear Deterrent: Technical Economic and Strategic Issues* (London: RIIA, 1977).
[15] Lawrence Freedman, *Britain and Nuclear Weapons* (London: Macmillan, 1980), 60.
[16] See 'The Future of the United Kingdom's Nuclear Weapons Policy', *Sixth Report from the Expenditure Committee*, Session 1978–9, No. 348 (London: HMSO), 64.

letting the improved Polaris expire, no decision was made by the Labour government before the electorate removed it from office.

In May 1979 the incoming Conservative government made it clear that there would be a replacement for Polaris. The only question was: which system? On 15 July 1980, the Secretary for Defence Francis Pym announced the decision to purchase Trident I SLBMs from the United States at a cost of about £5 billion, as almost everyone by that time expected. The decision was made by the usual small Cabinet committee and the rest of the government were simply informed.[17] In his statement, Pym used quasi-moral language to justify the decision—something which perhaps better fitted the out-in-the-open, crusading style of the new Tory regime than the pragmatic 'cost-effectiveness' language of the Wilsonite Labour politicians:

. . . it is necessary for us to have this capability, because if we were to lower our guard, if our shield were to be in any way inadequate, we should be committing *a major failure of responsibility* for the protection of the citizens of this country and those of our friends . . . We must contribute as much as we can to relieving the distress of humanity. It would however, be *a serious crime* if we were to allow our defences to fall to too low a level. [18]

The assumption was that only Trident would be an adequate 'shield' against Soviet military might. It may be a mixed metaphor, but it served to convey the impression that only the most powerful and up-to-date weapon that money could buy would give adequate security against an enemy that is watching for our every weakness in order to strike.

The more considered, official rationale for the Trident decision was set out the same year in another MOD publication.[19] The main rationale for continuing, i.e. replacing, the British independent deterrent is said to be that of providing a 'second centre', influencing the calculations of some future Soviet leadership which 'might believe that it could impose its will on Europe by military force without becoming involved in strategic nuclear war with the United States'. This indicates a triggering function for the British force, something the document appears to confirm when discussing

[17] Report by Julia Langdon, *Guardian*, 6 Oct. 1980.
[18] House of Commons Official Report, 15 July 1980, vol. 988, cols. 1245, 1248 (emphasis added).
[19] *The Future United Kingdom Strategic Nuclear Deterrent Force*, Defence Open Government Document 80/23, 1980.

the desired capability of the force. It should be able to cause the 'type and scale of damage the Soviet leaders might think likely to leave them critically handicapped afterwards in continuing confrontation with a relatively unscathed United States'. There is no mention of the fact that the British strategic force cannot be operated without the assistance of American satellite targeting data, which could be withheld if there was a difference of policy in a crisis.[20] The suggestion is then made that the Soviet Union might find a much larger degree of nuclear destruction tolerable than NATO countries. What evidence there is for thinking that Russians have less regard for human life is not clear. The requirement is therefore said to be the ability to ensure a substantial number of strikes against *key aspects of Soviet state power*—a formula which had long been the official way of giving no direct information about targeting the British deterrent. In view of the preceding debates, it is not difficult to read 'major Soviet cities, especially Moscow' in this carefully tailored Whitehall phrase.[21] It may be that by this time, the actually intended targets within those cities were more precisely pinpointed installations of government and military power, but, if so, there is no indication of this. And there is no way in which Polaris, or its successor, could destroy such targets without destroying many millions of non-combatant civilians at the same time.

Two factors were crucial in choosing Trident I: its long range, giving the submarines a greater area of ocean in which to wander and avoid Soviet ASW measures, and the fact that it is 'likely to remain in United States service for many years to come, during which all the economics of commonality will be available to us'. So Britain's dependence on United States' technological development remained decisive. It is worth asking what the United States stands to gain from a continuation of commonality. Freedman states that, among the strategic advantages was the continued availability of the Polaris/Poseidon base at Holy Loch, which otherwise might be in jeopardy.[22] The bases-for-weapons relationship appears to be alive and flourishing.

[20] A point made in the IISS memorandum to the Commons Expenditure Committtee, see the *Sixth Report*, p. 83.

[21] See the evidence of Mr Michael Quinlan of the Ministry of Defence to the Commons Defence Committee, 29 Oct. 1980, cited below, Chap. 9.

[22] Freedman, *Britain and Nuclear Weapons*, p. 67.

Complications followed very soon on this decision, when the new Reagan administration decided on an early switch to the advanced Trident II system with its D5 missiles, thus threatening to leave Britain high and dry with another unique weapon, more expensive to maintain than the one still in service with the US Navy. Even the Conservative government had to agree that the striking power of Trident II is far more than Britain would ever require. The D5 missile is one of a new generation of highly accurate MIRVed missiles capable of destroying hardened targets, such as ground based missiles in their silos. Whereas the present Polaris force is able to destroy either 16 or 32 targets, depending on how many boats are available, and with no great accuracy, a British Trident D5 force will be able to destroy up to either 448 or 672 with a Circular Error Probable of some 300ft. This is clearly a capability of a type far different from what has hitherto been described as meeting Britain's deterrent needs.

In 1982 another Defence Open Government Document was published to persuade the public of the need to buy the more advanced weapon, in spite of its superfluous power. The Ministry of Defence was clearly on the defensive in this document, chiefly against the accusation that Trident II had the characteristics of a first-strike weapon.[23] Despite the disclaimers, it should be recognized that the Trident D5 system is a product of recent American counter-force doctrines; that it carries with it the notion that it is possible to prevail in a strategic nuclear exchange; that Britain's Trident force will be targeted and controlled by the Joint Strategic Nuclear Targeting Committee at Omaha as an integral part of NATO's flexible response strategy;[24] and that it is likely to be seen by those against whom it is targeted as part of an increasingly aggressive British nuclear stance.

By the end of the 1970s then, Britain's multiple dependence on the United States for continuing as a nuclear power had forced it further and further into the embrace of American counter-force strategies. Both cruise missiles and Trident are symptomatic of this. The GLCMs at Greenham Common and Molesworth were to be part of NATO's Flexible Response forces, intended to hit precise

[23] *The United Kingdom Trident Programme*, Defence Open Government Document 82/1, 1982.
[24] See Malcolm Chalmers, *Trident: Britain's Independent Arms Race* (London: CND Publications, 1984), 30; and Andrew Pierre, *Nuclear Politics* (London and New York: OUP, 1972), 316.

targets of military value in the Soviet Union and to provide linkage with American strategic systems. As such they were probably employable only as weapons of first-use. They must also be seen— along with the QRA force of F-111s—as part of the United States forward defence in the European theatre and were thus associated with the nuclear war-fighting doctrines which have always been part of American military plans, and which have received added recognition in recent years in the ascendancy of the idea of prevailing in a nuclear war against the Soviet Union. Trident II is part of an American strategic system, tailored to hit precise, multiple, hardened targets from anywhere in the oceans, in the course of a strategic counter-force strike against the Soviet Union. It is ill-suited for the ultimate deterrent of British popular imagination and government propaganda. Its independence is largely symbolic and its separate use by Britain is purely notional. But whether it is used in a counter-force war or in an act of final retaliation, many millions of Soviet citizens who live in the areas of the 'key aspects of Soviet State power' would be destroyed by it.

Britain has also continued to develop its own array of tactical nuclear weapons and delivery systems. These include the 220 Tornado strike aircraft which have recently replaced the much smaller number of Vulcan and Buccaneer tactical bombers. They are nuclear-capable and able to deliver bombs of up to 500 Kt yield over a combat radius of 800 miles.[25] They are equipped for low-level penetration of hostile airspace. This very expensive programme (equal in cost to the Trident programme) represents a large increase in the RAF's medium-range tactical nuclear capability.

The INF Agreement

The first Western offer for negotiating away the missiles to be deployed in the INF modernization programme—the so-called 'zero-option' put forward by President Reagan in 1981—proposed a mutual abolition of medium-range missiles. This would include the GLCM and *Pershing* II deployments and all Soviet SS-20s, even those deployed east of the Urals, which were said to be targeted on China, although they were equally capable of reaching Europe. This would render Europe free of all ground-launched medium-range nuclear weapons, i.e. roughly speaking, those which could reach deep into the enemy's territory. Most independent comment-

[25] Paul Rogers, *Guide to Nuclear Weapons, 1984–85* (University of Bradford School of Peace Studies, 1985), 75.

ators saw this as a bluff made on the calculation that the Soviet leaders would never agree to anything so unequal. The latter considered that their superiority in ground-launched missiles was necessary compensation for the many other nuclear weapons deployed by NATO members, including those of the American Poseidon fleet and the British and French nuclear armoury directly threatening Soviet territory. They insisted that the latter should be included in any calculation of the balance of nuclear weapons in Europe. Britain and France categorically refused to consider their weapons as part of any Soviet–American deal and the demand was eventually dropped. After several years of abortive negotiations the new Soviet leader Mr Gorbachev proposed in July 1987 the 'double zero' plan, which accepted that the Soviet Union would destroy its greater numbers of INF missiles and its shorter-range weapons (300+ miles) if the US did the same, on the understanding that it was the first stage towards a more comprehensive agreement for a 50 per cent reduction of long-range weapons. This had the advantage of greatly simplifying the verification process, which could ignore complex questions about ranges. The agreement would thereby deal with all nuclear missiles with a range of from 300 to 3000 miles. This included seven types of Soviet missile, including the short-range SS-23s and SS-12s deployed in East Germany and Czechoslovakia. On the Western side, the relevant missiles were the all GLCMs and *Pershing* IIs deployed after the 1979 decision. The only missiles in the relevant short-range category—which excluded battlefield weapons with less than 300 miles range—were the *Pershing* I missiles in West German possession and under dual control. These were included in a separate agreement after some German government resistance to their removal.

There are 2,000 missiles covered by the agreement signed on 10 December 1987—about 4 per cent of those in existence. According to the agreement, the US has to destroy 859 missiles with one warhead each, and the Soviet Union 1,752, including 405 SS-20s with three warheads each.[26] All this has been accompanied by a

---

[26] Among other surprises, the treaty has revealed that the Soviet Union deployed fewer SS-20s than US intelligence believed they had identified—405 against 441—and that the British government had kept the arrival of cruise missiles at Molesworth secret and had given false figures about those at Greenham Common: instead of 24 launchers and 96 missiles, there are 29 launchers and 101 missiles (see *Guardian*, 10 Dec. 1987). But this still leaves the Soviet Union with many more short- to medium-range missiles than the West.

hitherto unheard-of Soviet readiness for on-site verification at very short notice, which has removed the major traditional obstacle to East–West disarmament. Since this part of the agreement must have involved close co-operation between the US negotiating team and the European governments, it demonstrates the extent to which the United States administration was able to carry the other Western governments with it, even when the whole thing represents a major source of uncertainty for them in the future. The British government has chosen to give the agreement an enthusiastic welcome, asserting that it proves the rightness of the original INF deploy-   · ment, while at the same time talking openly of compensatory measures to shore up Flexible Response.

The year 1987 ended with both the British government and the Peace Movement claiming that the INF deal confirmed the rightness of their actions since 1979. Credit must be given to the anti-nuclear movements in the West for creating and maintaining public awareness of all aspects of the nuclear arms race during the 1980s. In Britain, the bizarre journeys into the English countryside of cruise missile convoys and their American operatives, protected by the local police, have been rendered a constant source of official embarrassment by the attentions of the Greenham Common women's peace-camp and Cruisewatch. However, there are prob-ably only two things which have the power to convert popular fear and dislike of nuclear weapons into real disarmament agreements: a major nuclear accident or a world-wide economic crash triggered by a breakdown in the American and Soviet economies. The Soviet Union and much of Europe experienced something like the first in Chernobyl in April 1986, and the beginnings of the second are now upon us. Another facilitating factor in the INF agreement was, of course, the pressure always felt by an outgoing American president to achieve a major peace-initiative and thus to go down in history as a world statesman and a man of peace, whatever the tough stance which brought him to power in the first place.

But the consequences of the agreement are of greater interest than the steps which led up to it. Europe is by no means de-nuclearized by the agreement, since free-fall and stand-off weapons carried by bombers are not included. Nor are battlefield nuclear weapons or weapons deployed at sea. However, the elimination of a whole category of extremely powerful weapons designed to destroy essential targets in the Soviet Union in the event of invasion, and to engage the United States in the nuclear defence of Western Europe, exposes all the old anxieties about Soviet local superiority and American commitment. If NATO members thought of the zero-option as a bluff then it has been called in an unexpected way. It has exposed any pretence that it was mainly the SS–20s which necessitated the INF deployment, and it has made plain the real reasons: linkage with US strategic systems and the consistent refusal of the European members of NATO to try to meet Warsaw Pact in terms of conventional forces.

The INF agreement had the immediate result of causing a widespread rethink about European defence. On the one hand, a report from the Western European Union, an inter-parliamentary organization committed to strengthening the European component of the NATO alliance, demonstrated that the Warsaw Pact predominance in conventional forces is not the overwhelming military advantage that it is routinely made out to be.[27] It is in any case far short of the 3 to 1 advantage thought to be necessary for a successful land offensive. Moreover, NATO has a large advantage in naval forces, with a monopoly of aircraft carriers and a clear superiority in ocean-going forces. There is a rough equality in aircraft, but NATO is thought to be generally superior in technology. And most of the large surplus of Warsaw Pact tanks are old machines outclassed by modern NATO models.

On the other hand, almost before the ink was dry in Washington, European leaders started to talk about compensatory arrangements that would have to be made. Mrs Thatcher was heard to say publicly that, although the treaty banned ground-launched cruise missiles, air-launched missiles were a different matter.[28] In the usual manner, this was explained as a necessary 'modernization', which the Government had a duty to undertake. In February 1988 she welcomed American suggestions of increases of up to 60 aircraft in its F-111 forces at Lakenheath and Upper Heyford. They would be capable of carrying air-launched cruise missiles then being developed in America which would be capable of striking targets well inside the Soviet Union.[29] The intention was to plug the gaps in

[27] Report by John Palmer, *Guardian*, 25 Nov. 1987
[28] ITV interview, Thurs. 10 Dec. 1987.
[29] Report by John Witherow, *Sunday Times*, 14 Feb. 1988, and Dan Plesch, *NATO's New Nuclear Weapons* (London and Washington: The British–American Security Information Council, Jan. 1988).

Flexible Response left by the INF Agreement. Such developments should, of course, be expected if the arguments used to justify the INF deployment in the past are still believed in. However, there appeared to be differences of outlook on the consequences of the INF agreement in Europe itself. While the West German government continued to press for further reductions of nuclear forces on both sides—to include battlefield weapons and nuclear artillery, which would devastate Germany if used—British ministers opposed what they saw as the slippery slope towards Western denuclearization and vulnerability to Soviet pressure. At the end of February 1988 it was reported that Mrs Thatcher had, over the heads of Parliament and the Ministry of Defence, ordered the development of a new generation of air-launched missiles for the RAF's Tornado bombers.[30] At the NATO summit which followed, she strongly opposed any further de-nuclearization by NATO. However, the outcome included no clear commitment to the British demand for modernization of NATOs tactical nuclear forces. West German opposition to it sprang largely from domestic politics—the government of Chancellor Kohl would not be able to persuade its electorate that a new round of nuclear rearmament in Europe was the best way to follow the first real East–West disarmament aggreement ever achieved.

The British government has sought to justify its demand for compensatory measures by referring to an agreement made by NATO defence ministers in October 1983 at Montebello in Canada concerning the modernization of existing battlefield and short-range nuclear weapons. At that time, the NATO ministers announced the staged withdrawal of 1400 ageing short-range nuclear warheads from Western Europe before 1988. Prior to the INF agreement this had been presented as a major act of unilateral disarmament by NATO. Before the 1987 general election, the Conservative government repeatedly claimed in Parliament that no decisions about replacements had been made. Revelations made in the aftermath of the INF agreement showed this to have been a deliberate deception and management of public opinion. In fact the Montebello decision laid the groundwork for a modernization programme encompassing much of the US short-range nuclear arsenal in Europe, starting with nuclear artillery, which allowed numbers to be reduced without lessening military power and

[30] David Fairhall, *Guardian*, 29 Feb. 1988.

enhancing range and efficiency. The British government consistently denied that such a modernization was in progress until, early in 1987, the facts became available in the United States by virtue of the Freedom of Information Act. It was then revealed that British representatives had endorsed the plan in detail from the outset. Many of the 2,000 or so new weapons (with ranges between 300 and 500 km, designed to strike WP forces before they cross the border) are being issued to British forces in Europe. They could include air-launched cruise missiles. [31]

Besides these compensatory measures, a far-reaching realignment of forces appears to be in progress. This is largely a matter of further moves towards European self-sufficiency in defence matters. By January 1988, the economic difficulties of the United States, which have already resulted in major cut-backs in the rearmament programmes initiated by President Reagan, were producing Congressional demands for further American force withdrawals from Europe as well as calls for Europeans to contribute much more towards their own defence. Besides the previously unheard-of willingness of Britain and France to co-operate on nuclear matters, there has also been a French offer to participate in the direct defence of German territory.

The New Nuclear Debate

The moral debate was revived first in the United States in the early 1970s as a result of the breakup of the consensus over MAD.[32] Part of the disenchantment with MAD in United States strategic studies circles was morally-based. An influential paper by Fred C. Iklé,[33] declared that doctrines like MAD, which plan the mass killing of civilians, are unnecessary and are only possible because the strategic planners' 'sensitivity to the distinction between combatants and civilians—long cultivated through civilizing centuries—had become dulled by the strategic bombing of World War II'. This type of critique, from within the arms-control fraternity, coincided

[31] See Ian Mather, *Observer*, 30 Oct. 1983, and 22 Mar. 1987; and Paul Brown, *Guardian*, 23 Mar. 1987; Plesch, *NATO's New Nuclear Weapons*.

[32] See articles of J. Bryan Hehir and Robert A. Gessert in James Finn (ed.), *The New Nuclear Debate* (New York: Council on Religion and International Affairs, 1976).

[33] Fred Charles Iklé, 'Can Nuclear Deterrence Last Out the Century?', *Foreign Affairs* (Jan. 1973), 267–85.

with new missile accuracy due to MIRVing. So the interest in limited nuclear war came round again with its usual moral component, designed to show how the new technology enables moral choices to be made. In 1973, Secretary for Defence James Schlesinger came to office already committed to this approach. In the following year he declared a policy of selective options which would develop the capacity for small, accurate nuclear strikes in a possible counter-force war. However, at the end of the day, MAD was still in place, as Schlesinger himself made clear in 1974. The threat to destroy cities at a particular stage of nuclear exchange, and a capacity for final retaliation remained central to American strategic doctrine. However, the re-emergence of a doctrine of limited nuclear options reopened the moral dilemma between city-targeting, which is so irrational that it is thought to be the best promise of preventing war altogether, and counter-force targeting, which might just be rational enough to let it happen. As a consequence, the focus of US moralists was the possibility of legitimate nuclear *use* rather than the dubious intentions involved in deterrence. The just-war school mentioned in Chapter 1 of this book continued to advocate the development of small, accurate nuclear weapons for use in just and limited wars.[34] However, the church leaderships on the whole declared themselves opposed to nuclear use in any form because of the very great risk of uncontrolled escalation and destruction of innocent non-combatants.[35] But the qualified acceptance of deterrence which accompanied this position was unable to deny the risk of nuclear use which is always entailed by deterrence. The position is consequently still impaled on the dilemma of intentions: how could one have the intention to deter with weapons of mass destruction without at the same time having the conditional intention of using them—something which has been declared as inevitably immoral?[36]

In Britain, the moral debate, which had been smouldering since

[34] Cf. James Turner Johnson, *Can Modern War be Just?* (New Haven, Conn.: Yale University Press, 1984), and William O'Brien, *The Conduct of Just and Limited War* (New York: Newman Press, 1981).

[35] e.g., the United States Catholic Bishops' Conference in *The Challenge of Peace: God's Promise and Our Response* (London: CTS/SPCK, 1983).

[36] For an excellent analysis of the American Catholic bishops' position, see Richard McCormick, 'Nuclear Deterrence and the Problem of Intention: A Review of the Positions', in Philip J. Murnion (ed.), *Catholics and Nuclear War: A Commentary on the Challenge of Peace* (London: Geoffrey Chapman, 1983), 168–82.

the neutron-bomb issue, suddenly burst into flame in 1980 with the cruise-missile announcement and the Trident debate. This time, far from pretending that it was a purely strategic or economic matter, as governments had tended to do in the past, the Conservative government used moral language from the beginning. The decisions were justified as being the ineluctable results of the first obligation of government: defence of the realm. [37] The moral rhetoric became more and more apparent as they tried to meet the arguments of the burgeoning anti-nuclear movement in the early 1980s. The official case centred on the argument that nuclear weapons are—since they 'cannot be disinvented'[38]—the only available means of preventing war, and that it would be criminal neglect for Britain not to deploy them. Their purpose was 'not to use them'. It was seldom acknowledged that another goal—defeat of a Soviet attack—might force a choice and that use of the weapons would then have priority over non-use. As in the 1950s when the power of the hydrogen bomb to destroy the world first dawned on public consciousness, there were large numbers of people who considered that nothing could justify such a choice.

Because of the lack of official interest in anything but all-out deterrence, using the threat of nuclear holocaust to prevent any war, the moral debate in Britain has remained preoccupied with the topic of deterrent intentions. Limited-war use of nuclear weapons has never been presented as an option. The theory frequently met with in apologists for nuclear deterrence from the 1950s onwards is that we are in a quite different moral situation now, while the weapons are being merely possessed and our future responses are unknown, from the one we will be in later if deterrence fails and decisions about using the weapons have to be made. It has been argued that there is no question of a real intention to use the weapons until the conditions are satisfied—and by keeping the enemy guessing by having sufficient hardware to cause unacceptable damage, we can prevent such conditions ever coming about.

---

[37] See John Nott, Secretary of State for Defence, Introduction to *Statement on the Defence Estimates, 1981*, p 1.

[38] It is seldom recognized by those who use this as a clinching argument for deterrence that many other terrible things cannot be disinvented either: extermination camps and bacteriological weapons, to name but two. Nuclear weapons are deployed because they are thought to have potential political and military uses, not because 'they cannot be disinvented'.

Therefore deterrence does not entail an actual immoral intention.[39] In the latest phase of the debate, renewed attempts have been made to drive a moral wedge between the intention to deter with nuclear weapons and the conditional intention to use them if the worst comes to the worst. Thus the moral theologian Gerard Hughes argues that:

There is no logical relationship between the intention to use the deterrent force in circumstances where only having that intention will in fact ensure that it need never be used, and the intention to use the deterrent in circumstances where it has already failed. In that eventuality, a crucial set of beliefs which may have led to the formation of the original intention will have been, unfortunately, shown to be false. The agent is no longer committed in logic to take any particular view of the new situation with which he would then be faced. [40]

This argument betrays a belief that intentions are some kind of *mental event*, which permits us to claim that the real intention behind possession is to prevent war, and that a threat of future use is merely instrumental to this overall good intention. But it has been rightly pointed out that the prevention of war is not an intention at all.[41] It is a highly desirable state of affairs which those who practise deterrence hope to maintain by means of the real intention to use the weapons if certain circumstances arise. Those who control a country's nuclear forces can only intend what human beings have the sufficient means to do. They do have the sufficient means to wage nuclear war, but not to prevent it, since that depends on other factors, some of them unforeseen and uncontrollable, which may intervene to frustrate their best desires. Their only real intention, far from being simply a mental event, is the real and conditional one embodied in the hardware and pre-planned

---

[39] See e.g. Arthur Hockaday, 'In Defence of Deterrence', in Geoffrey Goodwin (ed.), *Ethics and Nuclear Deterrence* (London: Croom Helm, 1982), 68–93. Hockaday, who was at the time of writing Second Permanent Under-Secretary of State at the Ministry of Defence, admits that there may be an element of evil in this situation but that it is an acceptable price to pay in preventing war and checking Soviet nuclear blackmail. A similar argument that nuclear deterrence is the 'lesser evil' has been put forward by the Catholic bishops of France and by Cardinal Hume of Westminster in *The Times*, 17 Nov. 1983.

[40] Gerard Hughes, 'The Intention to Deter', in Francis Bridger (ed.), *The Cross and the Bomb* (London: Mowbray, 1983), 33.

[41] Cf. Barrie Paskins, 'Deep Cuts are Morally Imperative', in G. Goodwin (ed.), *Ethics and Nuclear Deterrence*, p. 99.

procedures, including the formation of dutiful human agents, which constitutes deterrence practice. Intentions are not, properly speaking, reducible to mental events. They are rooted in the things we do and the material preparations we make for future contingencies. As such they are open to moral criticism like all means adopted to achieve desirable goals.

A further consequence of a better understanding of intentions is that it will not permit us to make the easy distinction that is often made between intentions and capabilities, whether these are the Soviet Union's or NATO's. Real Soviet intentions are those which are embodied in their weapons and war plans, just as they are in the West. This may give a more alarming view of the Soviet threat than many Peace Movement critics would like to admit, even though it is not the same as the simple worst-case deduction that the Soviet Union would immediately use its weapons against us if we did not have a sufficient response.

Conclusions

The ethical slumber of the *Détente* period was broken by forces engendered by deterrence practice itself. For various reasons to do with the internal dynamics of weapons development and procurement, and the assymetry of the strategic relationship between the two power blocs, deterrence was shown not to be a stable state which could continue indefinitely in the same way, preventing war and providing reassurance to the public. It was inevitably subject to periodic modernizations which would always involve improvements and a heightening of the arms competition between East and West. The introduction of MIRVing, of accurate 'theater' missiles, and of SDI are the most notable examples of this de-stabilizing process. Arms control appears to be incapable of preventing it. Modernization continues, even after the INF agreement, with the introduction of an entire new generation of tactical nuclear weapons into Europe, notably air-launched cruise missiles. It is, of course perfectly logical that if—as Mrs Thatcher says—nuclear weapons are indispensable they will need to be up-dated periodically. However, the de-stabilizing effects of the qualitative changes that are thus introduced are ignored. Bland reassurances from official sources about the indefinite stability of deterrence have been unable to prevent fears of pre-emptive strikes and 'limited' nuclear war in the European 'theater'. The public statements and nuclear force modernizations of both superpowers have shown their leaders to be subject to the same fears. Moreover, they have both made it clear that they believe nuclear deterrence to rest on immoral threats to retaliate against cities full of people. They both seek to make cities immune from such attack, but by different means: President Reagan by Strategic Defence in space, and Secretary Gorbachev by the total abolition of nuclear weapons. The British government believes in neither of these solutions and holds out no alternative to city-threatening deterrence.

Many of the critics of deterrence have taken these developments on board, with the consequence that the debate is less academic in tone than the previous one. It has become clear to them that the manifest instability of deterrence in the long term has further weakened the argument for a moral separation between the intention to deter and the intention to use. There is nothing which can guarantee that the weapons now targeted on cities will never be used. However, the British government and the Ministry of Defence persist in trying to conduct the argument about nuclear weapons on the simplified, abstract level of deterrence, with its supposed 40-year record of preventing war (in Europe), as if nothing essentially has changed. Comforting images of defensive shields against Soviet adventurism are put forward to deal with the complex and alarming possibilities of nuclear war in the future. No questions are admitted about the de-stabilizing properties of theatre nuclear weapons and counter-force targeting, although Britain herself has inevitably been drawn into both by the processes of modernization. Despite the INF treaty, which promises the first-ever nuclear disarmament, new ways of upgrading existing nuclear forces are continually being sought. Meanwhile Britain continues, for one reason or another, to target civilian populations in the Soviet Union with its independent nuclear force, now to have its destructive potential hugely exanded by the acquisition of Trident.

None of these changes have weakened NATO's attachment to its Flexible Response strategy, to the ethical implications of which we can now turn.

PART III

THINKING IT OUT

9

THE ETHICS OF FLEXIBLE RESPONSE

Moral arguments for deterrence often get their force from keeping to a certain level of abstraction from reality. At this level, simplified certainties and fears can be manipulated so as to reinforce the impression that deterrence is indispensable without ever discussing the contradictions and dangers of the actual weapons and strategies that are in place—which constitute the practice, rather than the theory of deterrence. Since 1967 the actual strategy which the British government has defended under the general category of deterrence is Flexible Response, the origins and development of which have been sketched in preceding chapters. We must now examine these efforts at explanation, especially in so far as they set out to justify FR as a moral imperative.

Preventing War

In the 1981 *Statement on the Defence Estimates* there appeared a somewhat unusual feature: a brief essay defending the UK–NATO nuclear policy against criticism from the Peace Movement, especially against the charge that it was a strategy for fighting wars with nuclear weapons.[1] It was later revealed that the author of the essay was a Ministry of Defence civil servant, Mr Michael Quinlan, Deputy Under-Secretary of State (Policy and Programmes). Quinlan is anything but a faceless bureaucrat, and has been an eloquent defender of nuclear deterrence on moral grounds. Unusually for an active civil servant, he has frequently spoken on the topic in public, especially before church groups and bishops. There is considerable continuity between the essay in the *Statement* and the moral arguments which are made more explicit in his other utterances.[2]

[1] 'Nuclear Weapons and Preventing War', in Cmnd. 8212–1, *Statement on the Defence Estimates: 1981*, p. 13.
[2] Michael Quinlan, 'Preventing War', in *Tablet*, 18 July 1981, 688, reprinted along with another essay, 'Nuclear Weapons: A View of the Moral Problem' in Francis Bridger (ed.), *The Cross and the Bomb* (London and Oxford: Mowbray, 1983), 137–54; 'Can the Possession of Nuclear Weapons be Morally Justifiable?', *Modern Churchman*, 27/2 (1985), 22–7; 'Nuclear Weapons: The Basic Issues', *Ampleforth Journal* (Autumn 1986), 61–70; 'The Ethics of Nuclear Deterrence: A Critical Comment on the Pastoral Letter of the US Catholic Bishops', *Theological Studies*, 48 (1987), 3–24.

They provide moral backing for government policies, using the just-war categories of discrimination and proportionality. They consequently invite criticism on the same grounds.

What is defended in the essay is the European conception of FR as it has developed since the mid-1960s: the strategy of total deterrence by making it clear beforehand that the West would always have options other than surrender, even if this means the use of nuclear weapons up to strategic level. In a world in which a determined totalitarian aggressor will always have access to nuclear weapons, the aim is to prevent war altogether by blocking-off all pathways to victory in the aggressor's mind. It is for this reason that there has to be a credible use for nuclear weapons. Deterrence is said to operate 'precisely through capability for actual use'.[3] But this does not amount to a war-fighting strategy, even though it looks so much like it that the critics have understandably been misled by appearances. In fact, 'NATO does not believe that nuclear wars can be won *in anything like the traditional sense*.'[4] No one could win such a thing because, 'the side temporarily coming off worst would always have a powerful alternative to defeat—the alternative of raising the stakes, of escalation'.

If nuclear wars cannot be won in a traditional sense, yet NATO still considers it worthwhile to deploy a wide range of nuclear weapons with elaborate plans for their use in battle, one is entitled to ask in what sense they could be won. It is no answer to say that the strategy aims to deter any aggression whatsoever, since the effectiveness of the deterrence depends on there being a *credible* strategy for use. In fact, what is at the heart of Quinlan's interpretation of FR is not a battle in which deterrent weapons become defensive weapons, but a series of nuclear strikes of increasing violence, which are designed to signal the resolve to proceed to yet higher levels of nuclear attack if the enemy does not stop the action. The hope is that, when met with a nuclear response from NATO forces, the enemy will 'prefer to back off rather than take the risks of going on'. A halt to progressive escalation must, of course, be a real probability, otherwise the strategy will lose the credibility that it hopes to gain by its apparent war-fighting potential. But the responsibility for such a halt is to be thrust on to the shoulders of the aggressor, not of NATO itself. If the aggressor

[3] Quinlan, 'Preventing War', p. 688.
[4] Ibid. (emphasis added).

does not halt the process at an early stage he 'risks bringing down thousands of nuclear weapons on his homeland'. Needless to say, a credible conventional defence is not part of this view of FR, since it would signal a desire to postpone indefinitely the use of nuclear weapons—and the threat of early use is essential if all war is to be prevented. If the aggressor thought that NATO would try to rely on conventional weapons he might try his conventional strength—still 'massively preponderant'. As Quinlan puts it, 'Action about nuclear weapons which left, or seemed to leave the field free for non-nuclear war could be calamitous.'[5]

A readiness to use nuclear weapons first is also essential: there are reasons why it must be declared that *any* conventional attack on the West would risk starting a process which may lead to a full nuclear response from NATO. In Quinlan's account the reason is that of simple deterrence: the would-be aggressor is supposed to foresee every possible move of the defender up to the use of strategic nuclear weapons against his homeland, and realize that even the slightest aggressive 'adventure' would not be worthwhile because of what it could lead to. Everything depends upon his being rational in his own interest. The model of rationality which is offered to make sense of the whole strategy is that of the chess-master: on NATO's side, blocking off every pathway to checkmate, on the Soviet side, realizing that every pathway is blocked-off.[6]

As a first step in criticism, it must be said that it is impossible to take this description of FR at face value, for a number of reasons. Although these reasons are not in themselves moral ones, they have important bearing on any moral assessment of the strategy. First, the description is excessively abstract, and is therefore likely to be highly misleading. The abstraction shows itself especially in a model of combat already encountered in official statements: that of an 'aggressor' (the Warsaw Pact), facing a 'defender' (NATO). The rationality of the model depends largely on maintaining this moral assymetry—it provides its theoretical stability. However, it could be said that this model conflicts with one of the cardinal rules of deterrence theory itself: that deterrence is about *perceptions*.

[5] Ibid. 689.
[6] The Defence Statement essay was afterwards re-issued in pamphlet form against the reassuring background design of a chess game. In the *Tablet* essay, Quinlan used another homely image of one-to-one contest in order to depict NATO's nuclear 'resistance' if it should come to a fight—that of resisting the school bully.

Whatever NATO's declarations of intent, it does not require much imagination—though perhaps more than can be permitted at NATO headquarters—to realize that its nuclear posture must appear highly aggressive from the receiving end. If this is the case, the kind of combat which the strategy is intended to deter is not likely to be the one that would happen in practice. The trigger for hostilities between East and West may be something quite different from a planned Warsaw Pact attack across the border. It may be something that neither side anticipates or wants. In this case, the chess model of deterrence is likely to be dangerously misleading to those who operate it.

Nuclear war in Europe could come about through a sudden international crisis acting as a catalyst in a situation of long-term strategic instability.[7] The latter is largely a function of the direction taken by qualitative innovations in the nuclear arms race. In the past 20 years, MIRVing has been the most serious of these, since it raises the possibility of a first strike being made by a superpower with the use of only a fraction of its arsenal. Although there are formidable obstacles to this at present, the behaviour of both superpower leaderships in the 1980s has demonstrated their fear of such an action becoming a possibility to the other side as the technical problems come within sight of solution. The United States, for instance, has for many years been engaged in a search for an invulnerable ICBM system, and work done by both sides on strategic defence in space is partly a response to this danger. This situation is therefore considered as increasingly unstable, since in time of crisis each side may consider launching its missiles rather than risk their destruction.[8] There could, for instance be pressure to use them before they are neutralized at the height of a superpower confrontation, perhaps begun in the Middle East or the Gulf. Moreover, MIRVing has resulted in a vast surplus of warheads, for which a multitude of counter-force targets have been found.[9] From

---

[7] See Daniel Frei and Christian Catrina, *Risks of Unintentional Nuclear War* (London: Croom Helm, 1983), 5–22.

[8] Ibid. 36.

[9] Some idea of the proliferation of targets is given by Desmond Ball: 'Simply by virtue of associated industrial and military targets, all of the 200 largest Soviet cities and 80% of the 866 Soviet cities with populations above 25,000 are included in US war plans. Many of these cities would receive more than 10 warheads. Approximately 60 warheads would be detonated within the Moscow city limits.' 'Can Nuclear War Be Controlled?', *Adelphi Papers*, 169 (Autumn 1981), 30.

the receiving end, there is little or nothing to distinguish thorough counter-force plans from the attempt to achieve first-strike capability: something often pointed out by Soviet leaders.

One could still say that, in terms of perfectly rational behaviour, no side could possibly see any advantage for themselves in striking first with nuclear weapons. But this too is an abstraction from reality. It is a fallacy to move from 'it is not rational' to 'it cannot happen'. Irrational behaviour of the most fateful kind cannot be ruled out in an international military crisis. Such a crisis could arise either from a sudden, quite unexpected incident—like the shooting down of KAL 007—or by both superpowers being sucked into a confrontation in a war between clients, as almost occurred during the Yom Kippur war of 1973. Crisis stress, misperceptions of enemy intentions (leading to situations of 'called bluff' in which neither side can afford to back down without serious loss of credibility), failures of intelligence and communications in which vital messages go astray, inflexibility due to standard operating procedures: these may all reinforce each other to induce non-rational behaviour in the participants. All these factors are known to have operated in crises since World War II. In Europe such crises would happen within a strategic environment characterized by extremely short warning times, great pressure to use rather than lose vital weapons systems, and with no perceptible difference between the effects of counter-force and counter-city nuclear strikes.

As a second step in criticizing the model of Flexible Response that has been offered, it must be pointed out that discussion cannot be restricted to a single interpretation, as the history and political purpose of the strategy have demonstrated. FR is meant as a deliberately ambiguous formula aimed at satisfying a number of disparate requirements within the NATO alliance, some of them mutually contradictory. Chief among them are, on the one hand, the need to provide a comprehensible escalatory process leading up to the use of American strategic nuclear weapons and, on the other hand, the need to retain control. In attempting to satisfy these needs, it postulates a sequence of perceptions and responses, especially in the 'aggressor', which may be very remote from reality. Nothing that is known about Soviet military doctrine leads us to suppose that, when NATO uses nuclear weapons for the first time, there might be a pause during which the Soviet leaders would

consider the wisdom of backing off before they get into any further
trouble. What is promised is a massive bombardment of Western
resources with all the weapons at the Soviet Union's disposal. Even
in theory, every escalatory move represents a threatened loss of
control over events, as it provokes further blows from the enemy,
who does not want to come off worst, any more than NATO does.
Actual loss of control is likely to come much sooner in practice, as
we shall see.

The tension between the needs for escalation and control are seen
in the different understandings of FR that exist between the MOD
interpretation set out above and that made by the American
military commanders who would be responsible for operating it in
a conflict. Whereas for most Europeans in NATO, FR is a strategy
for making sure that an East–West conflict goes nuclear as soon as
possible, for the Americans it is a strategy for delaying nuclear use,
but after that, if the worst comes to the worst, for fighting with
nuclear weapons.

A most significant illustration of this difference occurred in 1983,
when General Bernard Rogers, the Supreme Allied Commander in
Europe, expressed acute anxiety about the lack of credible
conventional defence and the risks of premature escalation. He
stated that the Alliance is so deficient in conventional weaponry
that:

We're the ones, under current conditions, that are going to have to initiate
the first use of theater nuclear weapons. I don't like that. The option to
that, though, if attacked conventionally, is capitulation. [10]

He went on to say some things of the greatest relevance to the
rational and moral status of the strategy:

We have mortgaged our defence to the nuclear response . . . Under today's
conditions . . . I'd have to request fairly soon the release of theater
(intermediate-range) nuclear weapons . . . I'm not talking about weeks, I'm
talking about days . . . a few days . . . I do not believe that you can fight
long with nuclear weapons without escalating to a strategic exchange.
Here, again, I think it would be a matter of days—only a matter of days
before there would be that escalation.

In a more lengthy explanation of his anxieties in *Foreign Affairs*, at
about the same time, General Rogers wrote:

[10] Interview in the *Los Angeles Times*, 12 July 1983, 4.

Instead of possessing a variety of capabilities which would truly translate into flexibility of response, NATO is left in a posture that in reality can only support a strategy more accurately labelled a 'delayed tripwire' . . . . Against large-scale conventional aggression, even with adequate warning and timely political decisions, our posture might at best be sufficient to allow NATO only the time and security necessary to deliberate and escalate to the use of nuclear weapons. We must not delude ourselves— NATO's continuing failure to fulfill its conventional needs means that we now must depend upon the use of theater nuclear weapons to accomplish our missions of deterrence *and* defence.[11]

He then went on to argue for a 4 per cent increase in conventional defence spending by NATO members—something which conflicts with the European concept of deterrence, since it indicates that American forces might be planning for an extended war in Europe without committing its nuclear weapons.[12]

According to Paul Bracken, the current NATO force structure and command system, which causes General Rogers so much anxiety, accurately reflects European understandings of FR, rather than American ones.[13] As Lawrence Freedman has put it:

For Europeans, once the peace/war threshold has been passed the consequences will be catastrophic, so that their interest lies in removing the firebreaks so that there is a clear risk of inexorable escalation attached to the start of any war.[14]

---

[11] 'The Atlantic Alliance: Prescriptions for a Difficult Decade', *Foreign Affairs*, 60/5 (Summer 1982), 1145–57. General Rogers has not been the only senior figure to criticize the European members of NATO for their lack of commitment to a conventional defence which is well within their power.

[12] In case the mistaken impression is given that General Rogers is some kind of nuclear disarmer, it should be added that he has made a good many other pronouncements about NATO strategy which are not at all welcome to those who are. In 1983 he advocated a 'deep-strike' strategy which would radically alter the posture of NATO conventional and battlefield nuclear forces from defensive to offensive. (See his article in *Guardian*, 26 Sept. 1983.) Upon his retirement as Supreme Allied Commander in 1987 he made it clear that NATO should continue to depend on a wide range of nuclear weapons, that the battlefield modernization programme should be pursued, that 100 or so cruise and *Pershing* missiles should be retained until the East–West conventional balance is redressed, and that sea-launched cruise missiles should partially replace the INF forces lost by international agreement. (See David Fairhall, *Guardian*, 1 May 1987.)

[13] Paul Bracken, *The Command and Control of Nuclear Forces* (New Haven, Conn. and London: Yale University Press, 1983), 164.

[14] Lawrence Freedman, 'The No-First-Use Debate and the Theory of Thresholds', in Blackaby, Goldblat, and Lodgaard (eds.), *No-First-Use* (London: SIPRI, Taylor and Francis, 1984), 71.

The difference of outlook on the function of tactical nuclear weapons is real, and not merely the accidental product of economic problems.

The Question of Limits

If the strategic rationality of FR in the form presented by Michael Quinlan is highly questionable, even more so is its morality. In the context of strategic plans, to ask whether something is rational is to ask *whether* it will achieve the desired end. To ask whether something is moral is to ask certain questions about *what* is being done in order to achieve it. It is a question of the intrinsic value of the means. In both cases it is always relevant to ask General Rogers' question: what is likely to happen if deterrence breaks down and the weapons have to be used in defence? Since the future is strictly-speaking unforeseeable, our present arrangements are always hostage to unforeseen events which may take us by surprise and, using the very thoroughness of our preparations against us, compel us to put into practice plans which were formulated to prevent something else happening.

With regard to morality however, the question about what will happen needs a further refinement: it is necessary to ask what we would find ourselves *doing* if deterrence broke down, rather than simply what would *happen*. Moral analysis cannot be indifferent to the agency of events.[15] FR cannot be considered to be a morally coherent or acceptable response to the dangers we are in unless there is a strong possibility of our setting deliberate limits to the type and extent of the destruction we would *do* if deterrence were to fail and the weapons have to be used in defence. At the extreme, there is no sense in which a threat to inflict unlimited destruction could be considered to be morally intelligible, for it would be a threat to destroy the human world itself, without which no morals, security, strategy, or anything else has any meaning. The uppermost limits of acceptable destruction in war may be endlessly debated, but anyone with their moral imagination intact would accept that the destruction within a few days, by nuclear weapons, of several

---

[15] This is not the place to argue for this important thesis of moral theory. 'Eventism', which holds that not the agency, but only the event itself and its consequences are relevant to moral judgement is well disposed of by John Finnis in *Fundamentals of Ethics* (OUP, 1983), 113–20.

million people and their environment, would fall outside any meaningful limits. Yet all the studies since the 1950s of the likely effects of tactical nuclear use in Europe have shown that destruction on such a scale is the most likely outcome.[16]

The question we must address to the defender of FR, such as Quinlan, is whether it is going to be possible to *impose* any morally recognizable limits on the use of NATO forces if deterrence fails.

The arguments of David Fisher in *Morality and the Bomb* appear to answer this by describing a limited-war deterrence. [17] Fisher is employed by the Ministry of Defence and acknowledges a debt to the thinking of Quinlan. Fisher's case for deterrence is no doubt a personal rather than an official one. But it is an effort—fostered by his employers—to strengthen the moral credentials of NATO's deterrence in the face of the severe criticisms it has been getting in the last few years. Despite the fact that Fisher's approved form of deterrence shows some theoretical departures from current NATO practice, it is still this practice—from first-use to strategically invulnerable SLBMs—that he is defending.

What makes Fisher's case recognizable as a moral argument is that he is prepared to apply the notion of limits to deterrent intentions. Like Quinlan, he is certain—as one would expect with someone in his position—that deterrence is extremely stable and likely to remain so indefinitely. The chances of breakdown are called 'infinitesimal'. But he is not willing to rest his moral case on a consequentialist calculation of this sort. Stable or not, it is still necessary to square nuclear preparations with just-war morality, in case the preparations lead to actual use. Nuclear weapons are, for Fisher, criticizable mainly on grounds of proportionality, and there are very few goals indeed which would justify their use in combat. He believes that the NATO Alliance would have to be in extreme peril to justify the use of such destructive weapons. Deliberate counter-city use is certainly ruled out, and so also is any wholesale

---

[16] See Robert S. McNamara, 'The Military Role of Nuclear Weapons: Perceptions and Misperceptions' in *Survival* (Nov.–Dec. 1983), pp. 261–71. Cf. the UN document, *General and Complete Disarmament: A Comprehensive Study on Nuclear Weapons*, Report of the Secretary-General, Fall 1980 (United Nations, 1981).

[17] David Fisher, *Morality and the Bomb* (London: Croom Helm, 1985). The arguments in the book were first expounded in a series of seminars with Anthony Kenny. Kenny's contrary arguments can be found in *The Logic of Deterrence* (London: Firethorn Press, 1985).

use of strategic nuclear weapons against military targets: in either case the scale of destruction of civilian life would be out of all proportion to any legitimate military goal. 'No moral casuistry can sanction the inception of Armageddon.'[18] So Fisher finds that there is 'an immense moral presumption' against the use of nuclear weapons.

But if the use of the weapons holds such great moral dangers, how can the threat to use them be legitimate? It is not difficult for Fisher to show that, if someone regards certain acts as impermissible in *all* circumstances, then they must be ruled out as options. Therefore, 'if deterrence is to be morally justified, it would appear that the advocate of deterrence must be prepared to concede that their use might be morally justified in *at least some circumstances*.'[19] Thus it becomes possible morally to justify the deterrent threat 'provided any manifestly impermissible use has been eschewed'. This, according to Fisher, is enough to lay a very heavy moral responsibility on the shoulders of the political leaders, an obligation of 'deep and anguished moral thought long before the crisis point was reached in which a use of nuclear weapons might be morally justified'.[20] As for the conditional intentions of the Polaris commander—the one who receives the orders:

He would need to be satisfied that the targeting and other plans related to use adequately reflected the moral constraints and, in particular, eschewed any manifestly ethical impermissible use. [21]

Whether any of these preparatory and precautionary reflections are likely is something we will come to later. Fisher does not even discuss the matter.

These apparently rigorous demands need to be filled out with further determinations of just war limits. Although Fisher believes that an evil of Nazi proportions would justify the use of nuclear weapons—the *circumstances* would be right—he does not believe that any *manner* of using them would be right: 'any very large-scale use even against military targets, still more cities, would be morally forbidden.'[22] Here then, is some kind of limit, though a vague one.

[18] Fisher, *Morality and the Bomb*, p. 59.
[19] Ibid. 82. Cf. Quinlan, 'Can the Possession of Nuclear Weapons be Morally Justifiable?', p. 26.
[20] Ibid. 85.
[21] Ibid. 86.
[22] Ibid. 87. So also Quinlan, see n. 2, p. 137.

The question now is, what kind of deterrent practice would measure up to both the needs and limits of a morally acceptable deterrence? In the first place, writes Fisher, the widespread assumption that only MAD-type deterrent threats are sufficient for stability is not sustainable. It is not necessary to threaten the adversary with more harm than he can do to us, but only with enough damage to outweigh any conceivable gain of his aggression. This is the fundamental truth of deterrence, and it points to *counter-combatant targeting* as the preferred form. It could cause sufficient damage to enemy forces, it would be credible, it would not be provocative by threatening to make counter-force strikes, and it would not make nuclear war any more fightable than hitherto. On the face of it this is a form of deterrence by denial rather than by threats against hostage populations and could be morally acceptable.

But could it be done within the proper moral limits? Would not the damage done to civilian life even with such targeting restrictions still be out of all proportion to the military goals? Whether this is so, we are told, depends not only on the scale of the damage but also on the imminence and magnitude of the evil to be overcome. There is always something relative about proportionality. It cannot be assumed, says Fisher, that the use of nuclear weapons by NATO in resisting aggression would be disproportionate, *even if the casualty level were to run into millions*. What prompts him to say this is the historical example of resistance to Hitler, which claimed many millions of lives. We could one day be faced with a 'nuclear-armed Hitler bent on world domination and genocide'. To resist such an evil and to prevent the suffering of innocents it would draw in its wake, 'quite significant damage levels might be deemed proportionate'.[23]

But what of the dangers of escalation beyond these limits? It is quite rightly stated that only a *deliberately limited escalation* would be morally acceptable, and also that deterrence need not depend for its effectiveness on the threat of non-limited escalation, deliberate or otherwise. The risk of inadvertent, non-limited escalation is said to be small. But nowhere is reference made to the large volume of expert testimony which leads to the opposite conclusion.[24] Instead

---

[23] Ibid. 94.
[24] A selection of such testimony: (1) McGeorge Bundy, George F. Kennan, Robert S. McNamara, and G. Smith, 'Nuclear Weapons and the Atlantic Alliance',

we are presented with a picture of decisions being coolly weighed on both sides well before each critical stage of the nuclear conflict by men in full possession of their reason and the necessary information about what is happening and why.

One of the things which makes it easier for Fisher to suppose that reason and restraint will prevail is his uncritical acceptance of what we may call the 'Ministry of Defence model' of conflict, which we have already met in the writing of Michael Quinlan and many times in official statements made throughout the past thirty years and more. NATO is purely defensive, so there is 'no rational ground for the Soviet Union to fear' any attack from the West.[25] The Soviet Union however, with its 'massive conventional superiority' could attack the West and probably would do so, were it not for NATO's nuclear weapons. Moreover, in any conflict the West's vital interests would be more engaged than those of the Soviet Union, since the West would be defending its very homeland and way of life. The Soviet Union, with less to lose and being in pursuit of the prize rather than defending its homeland, would therefore see reason as soon as NATO started to use nuclear weapons, and would withdraw. Therefore, deterrence does not depend for its effectiveness on the risk of non-limited escalation, even though this risk is still present, and helps to reinforce deterrence.

One can only say that this kind of argument owes more to ritual incantation of those who guard sacred truths than to reason or any realistic appreciation of the nature of the confrontation in

Foreign Affairs, 60 (Spring 1982), 757: 'It is time to recognize that no one has ever succeeded in advancing any persuasive reasons to believe that any use of nuclear weapons, even on the smallest scale, could reliably be expected to remain limited.' (2) Gen. A. S. Collins, Jr. (former Deputy Commander-in-Chief of the US Army in Europe), 'Theater Nuclear Warfare: The Battlefield', in J. F. Reichart and S. R. Sturn (eds.), American Defense Policy, 5th edn. (Baltimore: Johns Hopkins University Press, 1982) p. 359: 'From my experience in combat there is no way that nuclear escalation can be controlled because of the lack of information, the pressure of time and the deadly results that are taking place on both sides of the battle line.' (3) Harold Brown (when US Defense Secretary) in the Department of Defense Annual Report, FY 1980, p. 67, 'In adopting and implementing this policy we have no more illusions than our predecessors that a nuclear war could be closely and surgically controlled . . . I am not at all persuaded that what started as a demonstration, or even a tightly controlled use of the strategic forces for larger purposes, could be kept from escalating to a full-scale thermonuclear exchange.' See also (4) S. Zuckerman, 'Judgement and Control in Modern Warfare, Foreign Affairs, 40 2 (1962), 196–212; and (5) Sidney D. Drell and Frank von Hippel, 'Limited Nuclear War', Scientific American, 235/5 (Nov. 1976), 27–37.

[25] Fisher, Morality and the Bomb, p. 100.

Europe. No one who has read the recent literature on Soviet perceptions could possibly entertain such a simple abstract scheme.[26]

Fisher's conclusion is that:

It is not possible to establish in advance that there are no conceivable circumstances in which use, in some form, might be morally licit. And this minimal concession is all that is required for the version of deterrence that I have sought to defend. [27]

Despite the espousal of counter-combatant targeting, this version of deterrence is not markedly different from the one which NATO actually practises. When it comes to mentioning the policy implications of his theory, Fisher argues for the retention of first-use, a removal of early-use temptations by the elimination of short-range battlefield nuclear systems—which he claims NATO is already doing[28]—continuing priority to be given to submarine-launched systems, the elimination of multi-megaton weapons (of which NATO has very few), and the negotiation of deep cuts in nuclear arsenals in parallel with the Soviet Union. NATO needs to clean up its nuclear act somewhat, but no unilateral or radical changes are necessary. Clearly, the moral acceptability of FR relies, for Fisher, on that 'not possible to establish in advance', which gives the benefit of the doubt to NATO commanders in their future use of the immense nuclear power at their disposal. We need to ask whether this benefit of the doubt is sufficient moral basis for deterrence as it is normally understood.

Two Kinds of Deterrence

There are two very different views of what constitutes deterrence and two correspondingly different views about how it may be

---

[26] For instance, David Holloway, *The Soviet Union and the Arms Race* (London: Yale, 1983); Jonathan Steele, *World Power* (London: Michael Joseph, 1983); John Baylis and Gerald Segal (eds.), *Soviet Strategy* (London: Croom Helm, 1981); Michael MccGwire, 'Soviet Military Doctrine: Contingency Planning and the Reality of World War', *Survival* (May–June 1980), 107.

[27] Fisher, *Morality and the Bomb*, p. 104. Cf. Quinlan, 'Can the Possession of Nuclear Weapons be Morally Justifiable?', p. 26.

[28] In fact there is a major modernization of battlefield and short-range weapons taking place—see Chap. 8, p. 192.

justified morally. The first—deterrence$_1$—holds that deterrence is not peculiar to the nuclear era, and that it has always been a necessary and legitimate feature of defence and peace-keeping. It depends not on threatening hostage populations but on threatening any aggressor forces with such damage, or such obstacles to achieving their goal, that their attack would not succeed or not be worthwhile. It is otherwise called 'deterrence by denial'.[29]

The second view of deterrence—deterrence$_2$—is what people have normally meant by the word since the late 1940s. It is the result of the invention of weapons of mass destruction in the twentieth century, above all nuclear weapons. There is general—though not universal—acceptance of the idea that these are fundamentally different from all former weapons and may be called weapons in an odd sense only, since they cannot be used for fighting wars, at least in any sense previously understood.[30] They are used for threatening punishment by reciprocity against the civilian population of the enemy state. Deterrence$_2$ is otherwise called 'deterrence by retaliation'.

Some identify deterrence$_1$ with defence, since it envisages using the weapons in battle against other forces until they are beaten or fended off. This leads to defence being opposed to deterrence in its commonly accepted meaning, which is that of deterrence$_2$. However, as Buzan has pointed out, this is a narrow view which confuses the issue.[31] Logically, the concept of deterrence includes both denial and retaliation. There is a defence/denial deterrence and a retaliation deterrence. The end of both is to prevent unwanted actions before they occur. However, they differ fundamentally as to means. Consequently, the way is open for a means/end analysis in ethical as well as strategic terms for both types of deterrence.

[29] Cf. Barry Buzan, *An Introduction to Strategic Studies* (London: Macmillan/ IISS, 1987), 136–8. There are other ways of dividing deterrence besides the one described here. For instance, it is common to distinguish between passive and active, or extended deterrence, where the former is defined as deterrence of a direct offensive assault on one's own nation, and the latter as deterrence of military aggression against allies and other powers. See Phil Williams, 'Deterrence', in John Baylis *et al.*, *Contemporary Strategy: Theories and Policies* (London: Croom Helm, 1975), 76.

[30] The bombs of World War II present a marginal case, since they could have been used in other ways than mass destruction of civilians. However, the marginal case is of the greatest importance since it led directly to the use of atomic weapons and the establishment of deterrence$_2$ after the war.

[31] Buzan, *Strategic Studies*, p. 135.

Deterrence$_1$ may be wholly within the framework of just-war doctrine and the humanitarian laws of war. This entails self-imposed limits on what one may threaten to do to the enemy if he attacks, and it assumes that the use of the weapons one deploys *can* be limited in these ways. For instance, disproportionate collateral damage should be avoided by limits on weapon design as well as on targeting. In other words, it assumes not merely that this 'can' is a theoretical possibility only, but that it is also *what the force is designed for*—even though any force may be used in illegitimate ways in the midst of battle. Deterrence$_1$, then, would determine what kind of weapons are possessed and how they should be controlled. It would rule out (1) weapons which are targeted on cities or which could only be used so as to cause indiscriminate destruction, and (2) weapons systems which, if used, would easily escape central political control and result in the deaths of millions. According to that way of thinking, there could be no sound reason for keeping weapons of mass destruction. Even if the enemy were to use them against us it would not be permissible to retaliate in kind.

The attempt to justify deterrence$_2$ within the framework of just-war doctrines comes up against formidable obstacles, since the doctrine rules out the use of weapons of mass destruction, even in reprisal.[32] Even if we say that the purpose of the weapons is to prevent war, our best intentions are still hostage to future contingencies which might bring about conditions in which we have no alternative but to use the weapons we have prepared. And it is not possible to argue that nuclear deterrence is at any level founded on a bluff.[33]

It is conceivable that political leaders may be bluffing, although it is very unlikely, and contrary to their public declarations of intent. It is also possible that they have not yet made up their minds what they would do if the awful decision were to be thrust upon them, hoping that it never will be. But it is not possible that the many other people in the chain of command—commanders of Polaris submarines, pilots of nuclear bombers, operators of missile keys, as

[32] See Chaps. 1 and 3. Cf. the *1949 Geneva Convention IV Relative to the Protection of Civilian Persons in Time of War*, Article 33, and the *1977 Protocol I* additional to it, Article 51.6, in Adam Roberts and Richard Guelff, *Documents on the Laws of War* (OUP, 1982).

[33] The following paragraphs on the bluff argument constitute an altered version of the author's argument in *Nuclear Deterrence, Right or Wrong?* (Abbots Langley: Catholic Information Service, 1981), 61–2.

well as all the other operational personnel—can be bluffing. They are under orders. They have to be in instant readiness to use the weapons when they are told to do so. They must be chosen and trained for their willingness to do this.

These observations also provide us with an argument for showing that possession of nuclear weapons cannot be regarded as morally neutral. It is not simple, physical, pre-moral possession we are dealing with: it is *preparation*. Nuclear weapons are always the hard core at the centre of a fully established, working structure of readiness to use when the conditions arise and the order is given. Various targeting programmes and procedures are ready at hand to be activated at a few minutes notice. If this were not true they would be quite useless as a deterrent. At no other time in history has the possession of weapons during peacetime entailed such complex preparation and commitment to use on command. This structure incorporates thousands of men and women trained in maintenance and firing routines who are ready at very short notice to do exactly as they are told and have been trained to do. Their intentions are well established. It is absurd to expect any of them, on receiving their order to operate the weapons to ask difficult questions about the licitness of this or that target which has been selected. From what we know of firing procedures they are, in any case, unlikely to know anything about which of the various targeting programmes have been selected. Only a few strategic planners and commanders know that. The fact remains that these people—on whom we rely for our deterrence of the enemy—have every intention of sending the missiles, if and when the order is given, without asking questions about morality.

Therefore it is not possible that bluff could be a national policy, if those who are bluffing depend on the non-bluffing intentions of those who are ready to fire the weapons when they are told. It must be acknowledged that the conditional intention to use the weapons is essential to possession for deterrent purposes. The distinction required by some defenders of deterrence morality—that which is said to exist between *intention to use* and *intention to deter*—cannot be maintained in practice.

Hence, justification for deterrence$_2$ is usually sought along consequentialist lines.[34] It involves consequentialist calculation in

[34] Consequentialism is a general theory of ethics which holds that the value of an action or a policy is to be assessed entirely in terms of its consequences. Therefore

two ways. First, it proposes that we will refrain from using the weapon of mass destruction for prudential rather than for strictly moral reasons: that is, we will refrain because the enemy might use it against us if we were to use it against them. Second, we will nevertheless keep the weapon in readiness as a warning to the enemy not to use it against us. So the object both of keeping it and of not using it is to prevent its use against us. This reasoning is quite different from the just-war reasoning which forbids the use of weapons of mass destruction because they are directly contrary to justice. In that case, we would refrain from using the weapons because it would kill large numbers of innocent people and cause disproportionate destruction to the human environment, and so would contradict the very nature of warfare as a human activity bound by political, legal, and moral restraints.

But even on consequentialist assumptions, it would not be right to retaliate once we have been struck massively with strategic nuclear weapons. It could do no good, but simply add massively to the sum of human misery. Pure vengeance cannot be a rational motive in consequentialist ethics. But retribution can have the consequentialist function of deterrent example—to persuade the criminal and others that the crime is not worth committing. And it is in something like this form that consequentialist thinking enters into the justification of Flexible Response.

Flexible Response is the outcome of a long development of military thinking in the European context which seeks to combine the two types of deterrence. Before the nuclear era, deterrence$_1$ (denial/defence) was not always sufficient to prevent wars even when defence forces were adequate, since wars tended to be started by people who were confident of surprise, early victory, and the avoidance of crippling losses to themselves—nearly always mistakenly. Nor did deterrence$_2$ (retaliation) work before 1945, for reasons discussed in Chapter 2. The West's acquisition of atomic bombs in 1945 seemed to ensure deterrence$_2$, but once the Soviet Union got them, it left Western forces with nothing short of Armageddon to threaten against local aggression. There have always been those who saw this as the weakest point of Western deterrence: it seemed to leave a 'window of opportunity' for a

there are no intrinsically evil acts. Consequentialist arguments for and against nuclear deterrence are discussed by Finnis, Boyle and Grisez in *Nuclear Deterrence, Morality and Realism* (OUP, 1987).

Soviet leadership willing to take risks in Europe. Those who took this view—notably the US military command of NATO—have always considered that a strong element of denial should be part of deterrence in the European 'theater'.[35] It was considered to be an essential part of extended deterrence. In principle there is no reason why this role should not have been played by conventional weapons. However, as we have seen in previous chapters, the European members of NATO put political obstacles in the way of such a development, and considered the tactical nuclear weapons— which the United States army was only too willing to supply—as the solution to the problem. When they appeared in the 1950s, tactical nuclear weapons seemed to be a way of elevating the risk to aggressors to a very high level at an early stage in the conflict. They played this role in early theories of graduated deterrence (see Chapter 5). Meanwhile the Americans tended to think in terms of limited nuclear war. The Eisenhower administration thought they could be as effective and moral as bullets, and NATO commanders have continued to plan for their use in battles. In addition, since the late 1950s, just-war moralists in the United States have repeatedly called for the adaptation of nuclear weapons, through reduction of yields and increased accuracy, to the requirements of just and limited war.[36] Tactical and battlefield weapons appeared to be the most promising line of development towards this goal—the latest favourite being the neutron bomb, mainly for use against Soviet tank forces.

But for European strategists, who have tried to avoid the notion of limited nuclear war, Flexible Response appears to have the advantage of combining the benefits of deterrence$_1$ and deterrence$_2$. On the one hand, tactical nuclear weapons are still so destructive that not going to war at all will always seem to be the most rational option. On the other hand, they appear to offer a chance of precise targeting and controlled destruction which could perhaps be kept

[35] Cf. Buzan, *Strategic Studies*, pp. 152 f.

[36] See Thomas E. Murray, *Nuclear Policy in War and Peace* (Cleveland and New York: World Publishing Co., 1960); John Courtney Murray, 'Remarks on the Moral Problem of War', *Theological Studies*, 20 (March 1959), 40–61; Paul Ramsey, *War and the Christian Conscience* (Durham, NC: Duke University Press, 1961), and *The Just War* (New York: Charles Scribner's Sons, 1968); William O'Brien, *Nuclear War, Deterrence and Morality* (New York: Newman Press, 1967), and *The Conduct of Just and Limited War* (New York: Newman Press, 1981); James Turner Johnson, *Can Modern War Be Just?* (London and New Haven, Conn.: Yale University Press, 1984).

within limits and thus enhance credibility by giving the appearance of realistic use. Defenders of the ethical status of FR such as we have considered want to bring this quest for limits into relation with just-war criteria. They wish to see the gap closed between: (1) the destruction that is severe enough to prevent war itself, and (2) the destruction that is restrained enough to conform to just-war limits. The experience of the war against Hitler has suggested to them that the level of destruction may need to be—and may legitimately be—set very high. They claim that this level is high enough to include the use of at least some nuclear weapons against military targets, despite the very great collateral damage to civilians that is bound to occur. This would also include the possible use of some strategic weapons, even those which Britain targets on Moscow—although no sound argument has ever been produced which shows how this would be allowed by just-war thinking. But even here, the tendency is to argue that the use of such weapons against 'key aspects of Soviet State Power' could be proportionate to the evil which is to be prevented—a Soviet victory (it would be too late to prevent a Soviet attack).

But this attempt to explain FR in terms of just-war limits must be challenged both in its theory and in its practice. *Theoretically*, the notion of restraint which is part of FR owes nothing to just-war thinking despite both Quinlan's and Fisher's use of just-war categories. The restraint is not for the purpose of imposing moral and legal limits on destruction, but for the purpose of enhancing deterrence by restoring credibility and demonstrating that there is much more to come if the enemy does not back off. In the successive declarations of limited options in American strategic policy, from McNamara in 1962 up to President Carter's PD 59 in 1980, the limited options were never a substitute for mutual assured destruction and counter-city war, but were always added to it, by way of intervening stages. The threat of final retaliation by surviving counter-city weapons in a second strike remains firmly in place. The simultaneous development of tactical nuclear weapons for all three services and the retention of counter-city targeting for the SLBM force has meant that Britain has followed essentially the same pattern.

The consequentialist thinking of deterrence$_2$ is thereby imported into the theory of escalation. The intention at each stage of nuclear use would be to secure a positive result—to cause the enemy to back off. This would be achieved not by ethically limited but effective counter-combatant targeting, but by upping the stakes: by demonstrating the power in reserve and the will to use it 'if necessary', right up to strategic level. Thus each level of nuclear use would be justified, not by the military damage it causes to the other side, but by the warning it gives to them not to proceed any further with their 'aggression' in case they receive even worse. Each level of destruction would be explicable by the *even worse destruction* it was designed to prevent. Very soon a level of destruction would be reached which would be justified neither by military logic nor by just-war intentions. In this way consequentialist reasoning could lead, by seemingly justifiable stages, to an outcome which is entirely irrational and unjustifiable even on consequentialist premises: the complete destruction of Europe, East and West. This could be achieved with a small fraction of the nuclear weapons currently deployed there. Consequentialist thinking is in principle open-ended towards very high levels of destruction, as the commonly-accepted justification of Hiroshima and Nagasaki demonstrate. The same reasoning—balancing up the consequences of acting now rather than later when it may be too late—provides the logic of pre-emptive strike.

The Limit of Limits

Whether or not Europe would be destroyed if FR were to be put into action is something which depends, not on theory, but on the *practice* of deterrence. It depends, not on *declaratory* policy, but on *action* policy.[37] A glimpse of NATO's action policy has been given us by General Rogers' revelations in 1983. But in addition to action policy, there are other realities of a less planned nature. Sophisticated ideas about self-imposed restraint—to say nothing of imposing restraint on the enemy—in the midst of nuclear exchanges are worthless if the physical and psychological realities are against it. That these realities necessarily exclude all possibility of restraint

---

[37] Desmond Ball explains this distinction in 'U.S. Strategic Forces: How Would They Be Used?', *International Security*, 7 (1982–3), 31–60. *Declaratory policy*, 'provides some official rationale for budgetary and other decisions, and the currency for most of the public debate about strategic policy, but it does not necessarily resemble at all closely how the United States would act in time of crisis or war'; *action policy* 'describes how the United States would actually use its strategic forces in the event of a nuclear exchange . . .'.

is, of course, not something which can be proved beyond all doubt, short of the actual experience of nuclear war, in the aftermath of which moral disputation will not be the first priority. However, a number of factors strongly suggest that meaningful restraints would not be observed—strongly enough, indeed, to provide the kind of moral certainty that is all we have a right to expect as a basis for action.

The problem of limits in nuclear conflict is radically different from the problem of limits in conventional war. Whereas the latter is always limited in the amount of destruction it can cause because of the limitations of the weapons themselves, nuclear warfare is potentially unlimited in this respect. It is well known that a small fraction of the superpowers' arsenals could destroy human society altogether. And if the 'nuclear winter' theory is to be accepted, it now appears that this is a much smaller fraction than was hitherto thought to be the case. There are no *intrinsic* limits to nuclear conflict and indeed, deterrent strategies, including FR, play upon this very fact in order to enforce inactivity on the potential 'aggressor'. Therefore, such limits as there need to be in order to make the strategy at all credible, would have to be rigorously imposed, and *at a very low level* with respect to the capabilities of the nuclear arsenals in existence.

Most speculation about how much destruction a country could 'absorb' in a nuclear war, even a 'limited' one in which only counter-force targeting was employed, have suffered from astonishing failures of imagination and judgement. It is common to speak only about the numbers of immediate casualties and to compare these with the numbers suffered during World War II, and then to assume that death tolls in the order of several millions is the kind of thing that countries can recover from in time, or even take into their calculations.[38] Such reasoning ignores the suddenness of the destruction, the terrible manner in which it would be inflicted, with blast, radiation, and fire, the complete failure of the life-sustaining environment, including medicine, the end of food production, the

---

[38] Fisher reasons in this way, *Morality and the Bomb*, p. 94. See also Colin Gray, 'Nuclear Strategy: A Case for a Theory of Victory' in Steven E. Miller (ed.), *Strategy and Nuclear Deterrence* (Princeton, N.J: Princeton University Press), 23–57. Also Home Office Publication, in *Domestic Nuclear Shelters Technical Guidance* (London: HMSO, 1981). For an excellent demolition of this way of thinking, see Kate Soper, 'Human Survival', in N. Blake and K. Pole (eds.), *Objections to Nuclear Defence* (London: RKP, 1984), 86–98.

delayed deaths of the survivors by radiation sickness and the very long-lasting, untreatable effects of radiation on health and repro-duction. Numbers of immediate deaths is the least of the factors which ought to be taken into account when trying to gain a true picture of the actual damage to the human world and its prospects of recovery.

If the limits to be observed so that survival is still possible are very low compared with nuclear capabilities, the limits which would be compatible with just-war criteria would be a good deal lower still. Many discussions of limited nuclear war simply mean by 'limited' some level of destruction which is less than what could be inflicted if all the weapons in the superpower arsenals were used. But this is not helpful to the ethical discussion. John Garnett has proposed four basic types of limit in warfare: limited geographical area, objectives, means, and targets.[39] Not all of these have equal relevance to the moral debate. It is clear, for instance that a nuclear war confined to the geographical area of Europe would be total so far as the inhabitants of that area—including Russia—were concerned. As for objectives, ethically-limited war would rule out certain intentions, such as the complete destruction of enemy society, or its elimination as a viable political–economic entity. In so far as policies of Mutual Assured Destruction aim at this in the event of war, they are far outside any moral framework, and those involved with them at any level should simply withdraw their co–operation. But what of the apparently limited objectives of military action within the exercise of FR, namely, forcefully to persuade the 'aggressor' to back off and cease hostilities before 'he' receives further punishment? If we pass over the common misuse of the domestic analogy, which tends to obscure the fact that the punishment will be received largely by innocent civilians, we could agree that it would be possible to have a truly limited objective, falling within the limits set by *jus in bello* criteria: if, for instance, it was proposed to bring it about by conventional weapons, which would form the means of deterrence by denial. But not if it were open-ended to unlimited escalation culminating in the destruction of population centres. FR is theoretically open to this, and the question now is whether it would be so in practice. So the prospect of limited or unlimited war as the result of the breakdown of

[39] John Garnett, 'Limited War', in John Baylis *et al.*, *Contemporary Strategy*, 114–31.

deterrence is primarily a matter of the remaining two types of limit: means and targeting. These have necessarily to be treated together, for with means as destructive as nuclear weapons, targeting limits cannot be judged simply on the basis of what is aimed at.

In 1983 the United States administration declared that it does not target populations as such.[40] This declaration may be seen, on the one hand, as a belated recognition of the importance of ethical criteria in targeting, brought about perhaps by pressure from church leaders; and on the other hand, as the result of the availability of accurate targeting and hard-kill capability for strategic missiles which has enabled an expansion of counter–force strategies. On the face of it, the just-war rule of discrimination now appears to be part of US targeting policy. However, there are good reasons for accepting the verdict of the Catholic bishops on it:

'. . . we cannot be satisfied that the assertion of an intention not to strike civilians directly or even the most honest effort to implement that intention by itself constitutes a 'moral policy' for the use of nuclear weapons. . . It would be a perverted political policy or moral casuistry which tried to justify using a weapon which 'indirectly' or 'unintentionally' killed a million innocent people because they happened to live near a 'militarily significant' target.[41]

Although the bishops went on to criticize American targeting policy in terms of proportionality, there are also good reasons for continuing to see it as a matter of discrimination. Discrimination is rightly understood, not merely as qualifying declared intentions, but as qualifying weapons themselves.[42] Current United States declaratory policy can only be considered as a moral advance by those who think that intentions are events in the head. Real

---

[40] See Secretary of Defense, Caspar Weinberger in *The Annual Report to Congress, Fiscal Year 1984* (Department of Defense, 1 Feb. 1983), 55. That statements made about this time on this subject were specifically aimed at heading off dissent from the religious leadership, is indicated by the letter sent to the Catholic Bishops' Conference on 15 Jan. 1983 by Mr William Clark, a national security adviser, and reproduced in the Bishops' Pastoral Letter on Peace, see *The Challenge of Peace* (London: CTS/SPCK, 1983), p. 51, n. 81.

[41] *The Challenge of Peace*, pp. 55, 56.

[42] See the 1977 Protocol to the Geneva Conventions of 1949, where the definition of indiscriminate attacks includes 'those which employ a method or means to combat the effects of which cannot be limited as required by this Protocol; and consequently, in each case, *of the nature to strike military objectives and civilians without distinction*'. See Roberts and Guelff, *Documents on the Laws of War* pp. 415–16 (emphasis added).

intentions are embodied in material preparations, or in the significant absence of them—as in the RAF's bombing plans prior to World War II (see Chapter 3). [43] If these are such as to make very little difference between the destruction of people that would be caused by a counter-city war on the one hand, or by a counter-force war on the other, they cannot be considered to be morally acceptable merely because of a change of wording, even when it is accompanied by greatly increased accuracy of the missiles.

The Control of Nuclear War

The question of whether morally meaningful limits can be imposed is really a question of whether nuclear war can be controlled. Two aspects of control are relevant: control over use and control over the effects of the weapons used.

On the strategic level, Desmond Ball has shown that the difference between a counter-city war and a counter-force war is insignificant on both counts. Despite the increased accuracy of long-range strategic weapons, there has been no corresponding decrease in yields, the reason being that the purpose of these developments has not been to avoid civilians 'as such' but to increase 'lethality'—the capacity to destroy hardened targets. And the majority of important Soviet military targets are already in or near population centres, since they are largely industrial in nature. Ball estimates that:

> . . . if the urban population were only 10 per cent sheltered, fatality from a US counter-ICBM attack would range from 6 million to 27.7 million . . . and a comprehensive counter-force attack could double these figures.

Moreover, these figures relate to immediate casualties and are almost certainly underestimates when other factors such as lack of medical care, destruction of food supplies and long-term cancers are taken into account. Most counter-force attacks would have to be ground-bursts, which would cause large amounts of fall-out on urban areas, depending on weather patterns at the time. [44] This introduces a large amount of uncertainty into the idea of

[43] For a critique of intentions as events in the head—though a rather difficult one for the non-philosopher—see G. E. M. Anscombe, *Intention* (Oxford: Basil Blackwell, 1957).

[44] The Chernobyl disaster has demonstrated how radioactive clouds can drift around in all directions for weeks, contaminating areas far away from their origins.

'controlled escalation', which Ball says 'belies the notion of a carefully executed attack calculated to inflict precise punishment in response to some specific act'. The result of these uncertainties is that:

much of the discrimination that has been programmed into US nuclear war plans in recent years is probably significant only to US target planners themselves' . . . Nuclear weapons are simply too powerful and have too many disparate effects, not all of which are predictable, and some of which may currently not even be appreciated, to be used in precise and discriminating fashion. Any nuclear attacks of military or strategic significance, beyond those intended merely to demonstrate political resolve, are likely to produce millions of casualties . . . [45]

These judgements also apply, *mutatis mutandis*, to the use of British strategic weapons, both in virtue of the NATO Flexible Response targeting and their 'independent' targeting. The official statement that they are targeted against 'key aspects of Soviet State power' does not amount to any real moral restraint. In October 1980, Michael Quinlan represented the Ministry of Defence at a Commons Defence Committee hearing on the modernization of Britain's strategic deterrent force. He described 'Soviet State power' as embracing a range of targets between 'hitting a large city and hitting a silo'.[46]

On being asked by Dr. John Gilbert MP whether the MOD believed it could hold Moscow at risk with any confidence, he replied that:

The essence of the Chevaline system is that it is an ABM-defeating system, and we judge it has been a considerable technical success in ensuring that the Soviet Union continues to be unable to get sanctuary for Moscow and surrounding areas.

When asked whether the Soviet Union knows if we can take out Moscow, he said he was sure they do. Asked what was meant by 'take out Moscow' he replied that it was not a phrase the MOD uses. He preferred to say, 'we have the ability to strike Moscow.' On being asked whether Polaris or Trident would enable them to take out the command and control system or merely to cause heavy

---

[45] Ball, 'Can Nuclear War Be Controlled?', p. 30.
[46] House of Commons Defence Committee, 29 Oct. 1980, *Strategic Nuclear Weapons Policy*, Fourth Report from the Defence Committee, H.C. No. 36 of 1980–1, 85.

civilian destruction, he declined to give an answer. It was not the policy of the British government plainly to state its targeting plans, but to allow the Russians to draw their own conclusion.[47]

Seven years later, the 1987 Defence White Paper was marginally more explicit about the purpose of NATO's nuclear weapons:

> In order effectively to deter a potential aggressor, it is important for him to calculate that he would run real risk in suffering unacceptable damage to his own territory or to *his own people* if he were to attack. Only nuclear weapons can threaten him with that risk.[48]

With regard to the lower levels of FR, it may appear that there is greater chance of meaningful limits being imposed on nuclear use. However, enough has already been said on this subject to show that there is a moral certainty that such limits could not be imposed. But it is still worth asking why this is so. The fundamental obstacle to the observance of morally relevant limits would be the inability to exercise sufficient *control* over the way the nuclear weapons are used so as sufficiently to limit their effects, either in the short-term or in the long-term (the problem of escalation). It is one thing to describe the function of the weapons, but another to say what is most likely to be done with them if they are used. There are two factors of great importance here: the decentralization of control in NATO and the very short flight times of missiles in the European 'theater', dictated by the close proximity of the Soviet Union. Added to these is the inherent vulnerability of command and control facilities, which are soft targets for nuclear attack.

Tactical nuclear weapons in Europe have been built into traditional military organizations which survive from World War II. In the early 1950s the weapons were simply added to existing armouries of all three services.[49] Control of weapons has been decentralized to national commands, all of which have dual-key arrangements with US forces—though there are some weapons including GLCMs, which are controlled by US forces alone, and Britain alone controls its independent tactical weapons issued to the

---

[47] Ibid. 106–7.

[48] Cm. 101, *Statement on the Defence Estimates: 1987*, 2 (emphasis added). It is worth noting the rhetoric of the 'domestic analogy' in this passage. The use of 'he' suggests one-to-one combat, so that 'his people' sounds like some personal value being threatened, whereas it includes a very large number of innocent individuals without powers of decision.

[49] Bracken, *The Command and Control of Nuclear Forces*, p. 137.

RAF and the Navy. In the event of hostilities, nuclear weapons would quickly be released for use by the dual US/national command. Any overall, European-wide control—which has to stretch from the North Cape to the Turkey/USSR border—would quickly be disrupted by an early use of nuclear weapons and the response from the other side. There is no confidence in NATO circles that the Soviet Union will recognize the signalling function of limited nuclear shots or that it will do anything but make an all-out nuclear attack on Western Europe, hoping to put out of action as much of NATO's nuclear forces as possible, once the nuclear threshold has been crossed by a NATO first-use.[50] NATO commanders themselves will need to order the use of nuclear weapons in hundreds if any significant military results are to be achieved with them.

The very short flight times of missiles will put much pressure on both sides to use them at an early stage in case they get destroyed on the ground. Soviet spokesmen have long said that the few minutes flight time of *Pershing* II ballistic missiles targeted on Russia from West Germany could only be dealt with by adopting launch-on-warning policies, although it is difficult to see such a suicidal threat as much more than a piece of crude political pressure.[51] However, the risk of early preventive attack on nuclear forces would—as in the case of the Quick Reaction Alert forces—dictate early use before they are lost. As Paul Bracken remarks, 'With ten minutes reaction time, there would be a strong bias in favor of decentralizing decision-making and the use of pre-planned procedures.'[52] As for control over the effects of using a large number of tactical nuclear weapons on the ground in a European battle, there is no good reason to alter judgements made repeatedly since the war games of the fifties and 1960s that the result would be totally devastating to many millions of people over a very wide area, and in ways far exceeding anything experienced in World War II. It would not, in fact, be a war in that sense at all but an unimaginable breakdown of human society and its environment with very long-lasting and deadly effects reaching far beyond the scene of battle.

[50] See McNamara, 'The Military Role of Nuclear Weapons', p. 264.
[51] Simon Lunn, *The Modernization of NATO's Long-Range Theater Nuclear Forces* (Washington, DC: US Government Printing Office, 1981), 52; and David Fairhall in *Guardian*, 30 Nov. 1982.
[52] Paul Bracken, *The Command and Control of Nuclear Forces*, p. 157.

Conclusions

The credibility of Flexible Response to those who stand behind it
is dependent on a particular model of East–West conflict which
sees the Warsaw Pact as the would-be aggressor and NATO as
always the reluctant, but resolute defender: a relationship which is
supposed to be clear to everyone, including the Soviet leaders.[53]
Various reasons, both historical and analytical, have been discussed
for believing that this model is a dangerous mistake, which reduces
the security of those countries who share it. This does not amount
to saying that the Soviet Union has never had any aggressive
intentions towards the West, or that it would not like to split the
Alliance and be politically dominant in Europe, or that its nuclear
weapons do not increasingly threaten West European populations,
or that the intentions of NATO are, contrary to claims, aggressive
rather than defensive. It means rather that the simplified aggressor/
defender model, which serves as a structural basis for deterrence—
not only rationally, but also morally—does nothing like justice to
the complexity of the situation or to the real dangers of it. If, as I
have maintained, intentions are not mental events and cannot be
assessed by exclusive reference to declaratory policies but are rather
embodied in the actual preparations which countries make to meet
certain contingencies, then it is not possible to make the simple
distinction that is sometimes made between capabilities and
intentions. On the one hand, we can take it as read that—for both
NATO and the Soviet Union—the avoidance of nuclear war has all
but the highest priority as a goal of action. (To have absolutely the
highest priority, there would not merely have to be a declaration of
no-first-use, or even no-use-whatever, but an actual dismantling of

[53] The Ministry of Defence continued to present this analysis up to the Defence
White Paper of 1985: 'NATO's strategy is reactive; it threatens no one; it has no
concept of pre-emption or of seizing the military initiative in a political crisis . . . The
message for the Warsaw Pact is simple and unambiguous: if you do not attack
NATO, you have nothing to fear.' Cmnd. 9430 *Statement on the Defence Estimates:
1985*, 12, 13. By 1987, the year of the INF Agreement, the attitude to the new Soviet
leadership has softened, and there is acknowledgement that 'There is nothing to
suggest that Soviet leaders have any desire for war in Europe. Indeed, rather the
reverse.' But this is attributed, not to a genuine desire for peace, but to the high risk
of military failure as a result of NATO's resolute defence posture. See Cm. 101
Statement on the Defence Estimates: 1987, 2. However, the recognition of
ambiguity in military postures involving nuclear strike forces—realistic as this is
when applied to the Soviet Union—does not extend to an examination of NATO
itself, which continues to be 'unambiguously defensive'.

nuclear arsenals so that a nuclear war could not be fought.) But after that, nothing can be said about the intentions of either side exept that, if war should come through some unforeseen military/ political crisis, they are resolved to use their nuclear weapons with the maximum military effectiveness. They will both find themselves using them in ways that are strongly predetermined by their present capabilities and action policies. To declare that the vast 'collateral damage' to civilian life which would inevitably follow, both immediately and as a result of radiation for a very long time afterwards, is unintentional, would be meaningless. NATO would find itself using large numbers of nuclear weapons within days. The threat and the readiness to do this is designed to deter the deliberate, far-sighted, 'chess-players' act of calculated aggression which weighs up all the advantages and disadvantages beforehand and comes to a rational decision—not the sudden, unwanted conflict into which both sides could be dragged against all their real interests by a combination of accident, over-reaction, pre-planned alert, short flight times, the need to get certain weapons off the ground before they are destroyed and to pre-empt the use of others, as well as the need to demonstrate resolve rather than take the humiliating course of backing off: all of which is part of the real world of deterrence practice.

Therefore it is not sufficient to maintain with the apologists of FR that 'because it is not possible to establish in advance that there are no conceivable circumstances in which use, in some form might be morally licit', that this form of deterrence is morally licit. On the contrary, both the theoretical commitment to the possibility of unlimited destruction (rather than backing off at any stage) and the high practical probability of it indicate that Flexible Response is ethically insupportable. An alternative system for defending Western Europe is required—one that is based on a more realistic view of the East–West relationship and a reappraisal of deterrence itself, to see whether an effective defence deterrence can be constructed without using weapons of mass destruction.[54]

---

[54] A good beginning is made by the Alternative Defence Commission in *Defence Without the Bomb* (London: Taylor and Francis, 1983), and *Without the Bomb* (London: Granada, 1985).

10

CONCLUSIONS

Britain has a three-fold commitment to nuclear weapons: as an independent nuclear power, as a participant in NATO Flexible Response strategy, and as host to American forward-defence bases. As a result of these commitments, in a forty-year period it has accumulated a large number of high-priority targets very close to major centres of population in a densely crowded island. And it has sustained a high level of readiness to use weapons of mass destruction at an early stage in a future war. During this period, Britain has moved steadily down the scale of economic and political power and is in a fundamentally different situation from that in which it imagined itself to be when the nuclear project was begun. As a result of its economic decline, Britain finds it increasingly difficult to maintain adequate non-nuclear components of its defence forces. About half its relatively small professional land-forces are deployed on the German frontier with the East, on the assumption that this is where Britain's defence begins. They are heavily reliant on the early use of tactical nuclear weapons. The development of a modern fleet for the Royal Navy capable of effective defence in the North Atlantic is severely hampered as the Trident submarine project takes a larger and larger share of the defence budget. Most of the home-based defence forces are employed in guarding military bases, including the American ones, rather than in defending the country and its people. In sum, it would be difficult for Britain to defend itself from direct attack without early recourse to counter-offensive nuclear strikes, which would probably invite its own complete destruction. It is also liable to be implicated in a war fought by the United States for its own purposes, without prior agreement. This could involve the use of American nuclear weapons from bases in Britain, provoking Soviet strikes which Britain would not survive.

The previous chapters have investigated the development of this state of affairs and the official rationales that have been put forward at each stage of the process. By way of an answer to the three questions posed in the Introduction, these rationales can now be summarized and briefly commented upon.

The Independent British Nuclear Force

It maintains Britain's status as a world power

During the early period, 1945–56, when Britain was becoming a nuclear power, this rationale was largely automatic and shared by almost everyone. It was considered that the up-to-date, decisive weapon was simply a necessary expression of Britain's true status in the world. A first-rate power has first-rate weapons. There were variants on this motif: nuclear weapons were the necessary back-up for foreign policy; they would enable Britain to hold its place in the councils of the world, usually expressed as councils of peace by Socialist leaders. It was important to make Britain's voice heard. Even after the permanent nature of Britain's reduced status became apparent to many, it was still supposed that being a nuclear power would be a way of restoring some of it. It was particularly stressed after the Suez disaster.

However, the hope that the bomb would maintain or restore Britain's lost prestige and influence has been illusory. Britain has had no significant share in the superpower debate, and has not been able to reverse its decline, which is a matter of economics rather than weapons. Having the bomb was not a ticket to the top table, except in the limited area of test ban treaties. But more serious than the failure of these hopes is the fact that investing in such powerful weapons encouraged illusions about Britain's real position in the world. One must ask whether the necessary task of rethinking Britain's real defence needs in its completely altered situation has not been avoided, while all the priority, research effort, and increasing amount of economic resources have been lavished on the symbols of power.

It enables us to stand up to the Americans.

Possessing the bomb was seen at a very early stage as the chief means of both getting close to and remaining independent of Britain's main ally. It was both the main symbol of the special relationship and the symbol of being something more than just a satellite with no independent policy. 'Not putting ourselves entirely into the hands of the Americans' was probably the primary concern of Attlee and Bevin. It remained a constantly repeated theme throughout the 1950s and was one of the reasons given by Harold Wilson for Labour's retention of Polaris in 1964. In the early days it was prompted by a number of factors: the American nuclear monopoly, and their withdrawal of co-operation in atomic matters; American diplomatic bullying, which was hard to swallow by officials of the once most powerful country; the danger to Britain of attacks on American bases in time of war. British-made and British-owned nuclear bombs were supposed to influence American policy in a number of ways: they would persuade them to share the secrets of atomic energy by showing them that Britain had something valuable to contribute; they would enable Britain to exert a moderating influence on the inexperienced Americans in the use of their new global power; they would cause the Americans to take Britain's interests seriously in both peace and war, especially where the use of nuclear weapons was contemplated. They were a vital symbol of British sovereignty when it looked as if it might be swamped by American power.

However, these hopes too were largely illusory, and have been fulfilled in only one respect: nuclear co-operation of a kind was eventually restored when Britain demonstrated its abilities to make its own weapons, though never to the extent that was hoped. The restored relationship enabled Britain to maintain a modern nuclear force at a relatively cheap price because of the advantages of 'commonality'. Even so, it is heavily dependent on American goodwill, supplies, and targeting data. But there was little of the expected influence on American policy, and Britain's position as chief European partner has been taken by West Germany, economically more powerful, strategically more central, but not a nuclear power in its own right. Moreover, the strategic crises of the Korean War, the Cuban missiles, and the Middle East War of 1973 demonstrated that Britain's fears are not likely to be taken into account. One must ask whether the partial success of the special nuclear relationship has not obscured Britain's real loss of influence, created the illusion of power where there was none, and diverted attention from the real defence needs.

It gives Britain a necessary counter-offensive capability against the Soviet Union.

This was the legacy of appeasement and war-time strategic

bombing. It was assumed that Britain's only effective response to a Soviet attack, using its superior conventional forces, would be an overwhelming World War II-type bombing strike, putting Soviet society out of action with atomic weapons. The Chiefs of Staff in particular envisaged a massive use of atomic bombs against Soviet industries and population in the first phase of war. Unable to make any significant contribution to Western defence in terms of manpower, Britain was expected to rely on its scientific lead and World War II experience to make an overwhelming counter-offensive. Contrary to the entire European tradition of moral and legal restraint in war, there would be no limitations of weapons or targeting.

When the Soviet Union became a nuclear power in advance of Britain, this early concept of deterrence became obsolete, and the rationale for Britain's independent nuclear force shifted to two functions: a contribution to NATO's deterrent force and, in moments of extreme national danger, a safeguard against pre-emptive attack on American bases. Britain's survival might depend on having its own targeting priorities. This was later to become the Second Centre doctrine, which remains the strategic rationale for the independent deterrent. It still gets its force from the suspicion that, in a crisis, American leaders will put their own interests first, and either withhold their strategic weapons from the defence of Europe, or provoke a Soviet strike on Britain.

It is impossible to say whether Britain's relatively small independent nuclear force is a real deterrent, that is, whether the Soviet Union would be prevented from trying to put American bases out of action by the threat of British Polaris warheads destroying Moscow. There is a certain logic in it, if Britain is to remain the site of such high-priority targets as the QRA force at Upper Heyford and Lakenheath, the Holy Loch submarine base, and the cruise missiles at Greenham Common and Molesworth until they are removed under an INF agreement. There is otherwise no conceivable reason why the Soviet Union should wish to destroy these rural spots. However, British plans for the massive bombardment of the sources of power in Russia have always suffered from the decisive objections that such acts of retaliation, once Britain has been destroyed with the expected 200 megatons,[1] would be entirely

---

[1] See *Domestic Nuclear Shelters Technical Guidance*, Home Office Guide (London: HMSO, 1981), 1.

irrational as well as totally immoral in any reasonable framework
of ethics.

*It allows for a much cheaper defence and the abolition of
conscription*

This rationale has served not only for Britain's independent nuclear
force, but also for NATO's reliance on nuclear weapons at all
levels. Economic justification for the British nuclear force was not
entirely new in 1957, since the economies to be made by the use of
such a powerful explosive had been in mind since the Maud Report
in 1941, and again with the Attlee government in 1945. However,
in 1957, with the Tory government's need for economic and
political recovery after Suez, it became a primary factor in domestic
politics. With the economic success of Polaris, it became the
standard argument to be used against critics of the independent
deterrent, even by Labour governments of later decades, who
depended on a continued economic recovery to realize their social
plans. It was routinely asserted that anything like an adequate
conventional defence force would be so expensive as to cripple the
British economy and post-war prosperity. Moreover, the apparent
demilitarization of society that was made possible by the ending of
National Service was also a powerful supporting argument for the
exchange of manpower for fire-power. It provided reassurance
among the general public that Britain was being adequately
defended in the face of the Soviet threat even at times when major
cuts were being made in force levels of all three services.

However, although Polaris itself cannot be said to have taken too
many resources away from other defence forces, it has promoted
the illusion that adequate conventional defences are not possible
and not even required. The oft-repeated objection that a purely
conventional defence would be economically crippling to Britain is
never explained in detail. What is required is a proper discussion of
the kind of conventional force that would be appropriate to
Britain's special situation in the changed circumstances that would
result from becoming a non-nuclear power. It will then be possible
to speak about the economic cost in realistic terms, and to ask
whether the country is willing to pay it.

Nato's Nuclear Strategy and Britain's Participation in it

It is necessary in order to counter the massive Soviet superiority in manpower and conventional arms

This was the first rationale for NATO's early abandonment of its conventional-force goals during the Cold War period and its option for American tactical nuclear weapons, which were being urged upon it for other reasons. The relative cheapness of nuclear explosions was a major consideration in the shift. As the Soviet Union acquired its own tactical nuclear weapons and the doctrine of Massive Retaliation became obsolete, the rationale altered somewhat. Soviet conventional superiority was still offered as the main explanation for NATO's heavy reliance on nuclear weapons, but there was the added argument about maintaining the nuclear balance in the European theatre, of keeping up the defensive shield, and of plugging gaps.

The assertion of Soviet conventional superiority has frequently been challenged, and its magnitude has undoubtedly been exaggerated from time to time in order to make NATO's nuclear reliance more acceptable.[2] It has not been possible to enter into the details of the controversies surrounding this topic. However, a number of eminent American defence experts have recently stated that NATO could, and for security reasons should, spend the money needed to bring its conventional forces up to a level sufficient to repel any Warsaw Pact aggression.[3]

In any case, the most recent episode in the drama of NATO's nuclear affairs has done much to weaken this traditional rationale. In the aftermath of the INF agreement, the efforts of the British

[2] A recent and authoritative estimate of the East–West Conventional Balance in Europe may be found in *The Military Balance 1986–1987* (IISS, 1986), 223–7. The results are too complex to present here, but in any case, give the lie to the regular propaganda about overwhelming superiority, especially in regard to numbers of ground forces, anti-tank weapons, reserve divisions, land-based bombers and most naval forces, where NATO strength is either close to, or exceeds, Warsaw Pact strength.

[3] For instance, McGeorge Bundy, George Kennan, Robert S. McNamara, Gerard Smith, 'Nuclear Weapons and the Atlantic Alliance', *Foreign Affairs*, 60 (Spring 1982), 753.

government to shore up Flexible Response be extensive modernizations have exposed an underlying commitment to nuclear
weapons which does not appear to depend any longer on the
condition of Soviet conventional superiority.[4]

It prevents war

Sufficient explanation of this claim and criticism of it have already
been made in Chapter 9. It was argued that the war being prevented
by Flexible Response is not the one likely to occur, and that the
strategy has an insurmountable problem of control once war has
broken out. However, the claim that NATO's deterrence also
prevents a catastrophic conventional war using modern weapons of
far greater destructive power than anything in World War II, and
that such a war would be very likely to occur in the absence of
nuclear weapons, is an argument that needs a careful answer.

In the first place, it must be recognized that there is no absolutely
safe deterrence, and that the weapons now in place would be used if
it were to break down. At present this means nuclear weapons, the
use of which would result in the destruction of very large numbers
of innocent people and the rendering of large areas uninhabitable
for a long time. There are ethical objections to this that are
considered here to be insurmountable. It is not certain that any use
of conventional weapons would have such a result, whatever the
brutality of the battlefield.

Secondly, the non-occurrence of another war in Europe may be
due to quite other factors. Since this book has not gone into the
matter of Soviet policies and intentions, this is not something that
can be argued here from evidence. But others have argued that the
picture of a Soviet Union poised to take over the countries of
Western Europe and add them to its socialist empire is quite out of
touch with reality. So long as the usual pathway of invasion from
the West is blocked, so long as the deadly nationalist quarrels of
Eastern Europe which have caused two world wars are suppressed,

---

[4] Paul Rogers reports an MOD memorandum entitled 'Nuclear Deterrence Post-
INF' submitted to the House of Commons Foreign Affairs Committee investigating
the political impact of the process of arms control and disarmament. Among other
revelations, it states that 'The role of TNF [theatre nuclear forces] is not to
compensate for any imbalance in conventional forces. The achievement of
conventional parity could have very positive consequences for the Alliance's strategy
of deterrence. But it would not, of itself, obviate the need for theatre nuclear forces.'
New Statesman, 24 June 1988, p. 18.

and so long as Germany is permanently prevented from developing a united, nuclear-armed state, then there is no plausible reason
why the Soviet Union—already over-extended, and traditionally
extremely cautious in its reactions—should ever wish to take on the
very different and even less manageable countries of the West. But
it would be difficult—perhaps impossible—to establish this with
absolute certainty, largely because of the ambivalent nature of
Soviet military preparations. Since 1945, Europe, East and West,
has been caught up in a power–security dilemma in which there
is an unresolvable confusion of capabilities and intentions. The
confusion has been made a great deal more intense by the
deployment of nuclear weapons in Europe, which always have an
offensive aspect, whatever is declared about their purpose. There is
undoubtedly a Soviet threat, which arises from the declared
intention of Soviet military leaders to use all the forces at their
disposal to carry hostilities forward into enemy territory in the
event of war, and from the deployment of their conventional and
nuclear forces to make sure this is possible. Soviet military doctrine
holds that war in Europe is not something the Soviet Union would
ever initiate, but that it would be ready to fight any war forced
upon it by Western powers.[5] Such a war could happen through
factors unwanted and unforeseen on both sides. This kind of threat
will not disappear because the West opposes it with tactical nuclear
weapons.

An answer to the threat of conventional war partly depends on
having a clear idea of the kind of conventional weapons that are
most suitable to Britain's defence needs, rather than allowing
worst-case fears to stifle all thought on the matter. There is no
prima-facie reason why a West European non-provocative, defensive conventional deterrence, which—unlike the present arrangement—would not lead to a holocaust within a few hours, should
not be as efficient in preventing a war by denying any invading
force the prospect of permanent gain. If to this were added back-up
plans for systematic civilian resistance in the event of invasion,

[5] See V. D. Sokolovsky, *Soviet Military Strategy*, 3rd edn. trans. Harriet F. Scott
(New York: Crane, Russak Co., 1975), and Michael MccGwire, 'Soviet Military
Doctrine: Contingency Planning and the Reality of World War', *Survival* (May–June
1980), 107–13. Nevertheless, the Soviet leadership does not accept the possibility of
limited nuclear war and has no illusions about there being any 'winners' in the
normal sense. Cf. Lt.-Gen. Milshtein in an interview for the *New York Herald
Tribune*, repr. in *Survival* (Nov.–Dec. 1980).

there would be a further strong instrument of denial available which would deter war. As many politicians and military men have stated over the last three decades, the path to war in Europe is more likely to come by mistake than by deliberate, calculated aggression. Non-provocative deterrence by denial would greatly lessen the chances of such a mistake being made, or of turning into a holocaust if it is.

It enables us to resist nuclear blackmail

This is also a standard rationale for the independent deterrent. It has been pushed to the forefront in recent years, as the plausibility of a direct Soviet aggression has been questioned. It is produced as a clinching argument to justify permanent nuclear readiness. It is said that, if NATO countries do not have access to nuclear weapons, the Soviet Union—or some other, more ruthless power which might arise in the future—would be able to get what it wants just by threatening to destroy cities one by one. This is a complex matter, and there are lengthy discussions of it.[6] It has to be admitted as a theoretical possibility. However, it should also be said that the realities of international political life are very much against the superpowers resorting to such a thing. The history of the past forty years shows that even in war, and even with the United States, which has shown itself far more ready to contemplate using nuclear weapons against non-nuclear opponents than the Soviet Union, there are prohibitive political and military obstacles in the way of it.[7] With the single exception of Japan at the very end of World War II, when it was already at the point of surrender, no non-nuclear country at war with a superpower has been attacked with nuclear weapons, even when it was winning. It would be an unprecedented political disaster for any country which attempted it. Moreover, it is necessary to ask why the general argument is not thought to apply to every country in the world, and what thinking had led Canada, Sweden, Switzerland and others to do without this seemingly indispensable guarantee of future safety. All rationale for

---

[6] e.g. Jeff McMahan, 'Nuclear Blackmail', in Nigel Blake and Kay Pole (eds.), *Dangers of Deterrence* (London: RKP, 1983).

[7] According to Desmond Ball, since 1945 there have been some 20 occasions during which responsible officials of the United States government formally considered the use of nuclear weapons. 'US Strategic Forces: How Would They Be Used?', *International Security*, 7 (1982–3), 41.

it would disappear with the removal of American nuclear bases from Britain.

Hosting American Nuclear Bases

British governments have not been very forthcoming in giving good reasons for the very large American military presence in this country. In fact, the full extent of it has usually been deliberately hidden from the general public by such devices as claiming there are only 12 bases, when if fact there are well over 100, and erecting road signs to 'RAF Upper Heyford', 'RAF Lakenheath' and the like, when there is nothing but a token RAF presence at these gigantic American military enclaves. However, from time to time there are general justifications, usually to the effect that the American presence is necessary in order to defend the free world against Soviet aggression. In the 1950s, Churchill and others stated that the American forces—especially the USAF with its atomic bombs— had prevented the Red Army from sweeping across Europe. This kind of statement was understandable in 1950, when there was a genuine fear among British statesmen of a Soviet invasion using Korea as a diversion, and when it was genuinely impossible to distinguish Soviet moves dictated by security fears from those motivated by expansionist designs.

However, despite the gradual realization that a Soviet invasion was not imminent, and that its central motivation was the security of its European border zone, the magnitude of the Soviet threat was more and more emphasized in order to provide a balancing justification for the West's possession and readiness to use the ultimate weapon, the hydrogen bomb. It was depicted as the only thing standing between us and slavery, which was considered to be a greater evil even than the destruction of the world with thermonuclear weapons. A generally accepted morality of con-sequences did the rest. In the *Détente* period, it was admitted that a direct Soviet aggression was one of the least likely pathways to war, and that a more likely one was a political crisis in Eastern Europe which might develop inadvertently into a military confrontation with the West.

A secondary, but important rationale for Britain's generous hospitality to American bases, but one which has not been spoken about openly, is the bases-for-weapons exchange. It has been a vital part of the nuclear relationship with the United States which has allowed Britain to stay in the nuclear club.

It should be recognized that the American presence serves American global interests in the first place, and that these interests may not correspond with British interests, either in time of peace or war. This has been so from 1948, when bases in Britain were needed by the American Air Force in order to get close enough to the Soviet Union, up to the present, when Britain serves a multitude of military, surveillance, and communications functions for American forces. Experience has shown that Britain's interests are unlikely to be considered very far when it is a question of the Americans using their bases for their own security concerns.

Neglected questions

The rationales examined above have all served as justifications for the possession of weapons, which the British government and service chiefs have never thought of in any other terms than as being weapons of mass destruction, notwithstanding recent attempts by Ministry of Defence authors to bring them within the ambit of just-war. Some of these rationales, such as the status argument and the threat of Soviet aggression, have been crucial in managing public opinion at times when major commitments to expanded and modernized nuclear forces were being made, as in the mid-1950s and 1980s. By the use of such rationales, the public have been persuaded to accept reliance on weapons which could not rationally be used for their defence. Much of the force of the argument has come from omitting to discuss certain crucial objections to them. It is time to consider briefly some of these omissions. They are in the nature of questions arising from what has been discovered about the conduct of Britain's nuclear affairs in preceding chapters.

First, the government treatment of Civil Defence in the face of nuclear war has been scandalously inadequate and misleading from the beginning, probably because of the adverse effects that any realistic airing of the subject might have on the public's willingness to accept the nuclear programme. This was especially true at the time the hydrogen bomb was being made and tested in the late 1950s. The deliberate playing down of the effects of nuclear war and the optimistic estimates of recovery chances have been features of Home Office publications in both main periods of controversy.[8] Home Office guides have tended to treat the matter on the model of the last war, and to concentrate on bomb damage and the resumption of services, rather than on the other effects of nuclear explosions and the total inadequacy of medical resources to cope with them. Maintenance of law and order, and the neutralizing of radical dissent, has been the main anxiety rather than protection of the people—something that has characterized official attitudes to home defence since the thirties. The fact that Civil Defence has been the province of the Home Office, preoccupied as it is with public order and policing rather than defence, may have aggravated the problem and contributed to the poor quality of the debate in Britain. It is worth asking why efforts to provide adequate home and civil defence were abandoned so easily by the nation as a whole.

Second, the failure to deal honestly or adequately with the medical and moral aspects of secondary radiation has been a feature of all stages of the debate. In the 1950s, when the extent of fall-out from H-bomb explosions was becoming known, government records show that the main anxiety among ministers was that the knowledge would have an adverse effect on public opinion and lessen the chances of the nuclear programme being accepted. The issue is a similar one in the 1980s. The reassurance which the government hopes nuclear deterrence will provide is in the balance with the fear of what nuclear war will do to people. Fall-out radiation transforms the entire moral framework of survival and resistance under attack. Memories of heroic perseverance under bombardment during World War II—on which the 'moral' appeal of a resolute deterrence to some extent depends—are entirely irrelevant to conduct during a future nuclear attack on Britain. There will be no place for heroic resistance in a nuclear war. The government's response to these facts is at one and the same time to play down the extent of radiation damage, to suggest unrealistic and futile recovery procedures, and to claim that such a great evil can only be prevented by resolutely going on to the next stage of nuclear deterrence—regardless of the destabilizing effects of the qualitative nuclear arms race.

A third important omission is any attempt to reconcile the

[8] George Crossley, 'Civil Defence', unpublished paper, Bradford University School of Peace Studies, 1983.

contradiction between the government's efforts in the area of International Laws of War, embodied in the progressive legislation at Geneva, and the known targeting policy of British nuclear weapons. To the 1977 Protocol prohibiting the use of indiscriminate weapons against civilians, the British government added a reservation to the effect that 'the new rules introduced by the Protocol are not intended to have any effect on and do not regulate or prohibit the use of nuclear weapons'. [9] In the event of war, British servicemen and women will be ordered to carry out attacks which are directly contrary to the ordinary military law respecting the immunity of defenceless civilians from direct or indiscriminate attack. This contradiction is known to cause anxiety to some, if not enough service personnel. It is not clear to them why nuclear weapons should be treated so differently. In the face of the known effects of even the most limited nuclear war, it is wholly inadequate to argue, as Ministry of Defence authors have done that 'we need not and cannot conclude in advance for every conceivable set of circumstances, that the evil effects of nuclear use would be plainly and inescapably excessive in relation to the objective sought'.[10] The consequentialist reasoning which is central to all attempts to justify Britain's independent deterrent and to the rationale of Flexible Response (see Chapter 9) is incompatible with the law-based concept of international relations. Its faults are multiple: it is open-ended to unlimited destruction, it could justify pre-emptive strikes, it fails to make the crucial moral distinction between what may 'happen' and what we may do, and it assumes we have a control over future events which we do not have. Despite the fact that they sincerely think of themselves as keeping the peace, British servicemen and women would, in the event of war, be required to commit war crimes in sending many of Britain's nuclear weapons to their targets.

A fourth important omission of the official arguments for continuing with nuclear deterrence is that they have nothing to say about where it is leading. It is without a future. Deterrence is spoken of as if it were a static state, needing only to be maintained by the appropriate modernizations, and as if it will last indefinitely.

[9] See Adam Roberts and Richard Guelff, *Documents on the Laws of War* (OUP, 1982), 462.

[10] Michael Quinlan, 'Can the Possession of Nuclear Weapons be Morally Justifiable?', *Modern Churchman*, xxvii. no. 2, 27.

But the history of the past decade related in Chapter 8 suggests that this is not the case and that insufficient attention has been paid to the disruptive tendencies of deterrence practice itself. The image generated for public consumption is often that of minimum deterrence, with a last resort weapon making aggression by an enemy too risky. However, deterrence as it has been developed in Europe is much more like maximum deterrence, with weapons being developed and supplied in large numbers for a host of different uses. Consequently, modernizations, such as MIRVing and cruise technology, have been destabilizing and have provoked fresh rounds of the nuclear arms race.[11] This is not something that is normally referred to when deterrence is described as stable. This is a significant omission, since the supposed stability of deterrence is made to bear the main moral weight in the usual consequentialist argument which is used in its support.

Fifthly, successive governments have not entered seriously into thinking about the alternatives to relying on nuclear weapons. An analysis of official rationales has suggested that preoccupations with status and influence, and the special relationship with the United States, have inhibited a realistic appreciation of Britain's defence needs and the best way to meet them in the long-term. In particular, there has been no serious consideration of ways of defending Britain which do not rely on mass destruction and the threat of general holocaust at an early stage. The constant tendency to dismiss all proposals for alternatives as if they amounted to having no defence at all is a serious obstacle to any rational debate on the topic. It ignores a number of important realities, including advances in defensive warfare and the kind of thinking that lies behind the security policies of industrialized, non-nuclear states, to say nothing of the moral realities. Equipping a non-nuclear Britain for defence by sea and air in collaboration with her European neighbours may well be much more strategically realistic and economically feasible than could be admitted while the nuclear obsession dominates. Moreover, the prospect of further de-nuclearization in Europe, following the INF agreement of 1987, opens up the possibility of a de-nuclearized Britain remaining in a European defence alliance, thus avoiding the confusions which beset the anti-nuclear section of Labour Party in the early 1960s.

[11] See Barry Buzan, *An Introduction to Strategic Studies* (London: Macmillan/ISSS, 1987), 196.

Unfortunately, the anti-nuclear critics have often helped the official silence on the matter of alternatives by failing to show how reassurance could be provided, either with an alternative defence or in the period of transition to it. It is arguable that, by concentrating on idealist and universalist goals to the neglect of practical and particularist ones, such as the real security needs of the United Kingdom in a changed economic and political environment, moral critics have failed to take account of the people's real needs and so have endangered their own enterprise. [12] This is to say that the anti-nuclear cause is in urgent need of a positive theory of security. It is insufficient to be opposed to things that a government is doing without knowing how the supposed security needs of the public might otherwise be satisfied, or what a real account of security needs might be. This need not—almost certainly cannot—amount to a detailed set of propositions for a defence policy, which in Britain is the job of a political party in combination with the military. However, some notion of how security at the individual level relates to security at the state level is a requirement of any proper security policy. This needs to take into account, not only the defence–offence dilemma which all states with powerful weapons are caught up in, but also the security perceptions of the public, manipulated by government as these may be. A theory of security applied to Britain needs to explain in detail why, for instance, there has been (1) a fairly constant and large majority opinion against American-owned cruise missiles; (2) an equally constant and large majority in favour of retaining a British 'independent' nuclear force; but (3) a majority disapproval of an 'improvement' in the shape of Trident. [13] The security perceptions of the British public are complex and need to be disentangled before any work can be done on trying to influence them in a better direction, or finding an alternative defence system which will satisfy them without violating basic moral values. Before people can be expected to turn moral conclusions into policies, they need to be shown a way out of the predicament they believe themselves to be in. We have seen how British governments since the early 1950s have refused to distinguish between moral and immoral weapons and targets, partly

[12] Cf. Peter Johnson, *Neutrality, A Policy for Britain* (London: Temple Smith, 1985).
[13] See, e.g. the results of opinion polls before and after the 1983 general election, reported in *Guardian*, 24 Jan. and 22 Oct. 1983.

because British strategy is not adaptable to the distinction, and partly because of a distaste for anything which might weaken deterrence. They are not interested in the distinction, for reasons not altogether different from the RAF's lack of interest in the distinction between precision and civilian bombing that we encountered in Chapter 3. The recent attempts of Ministry of Defence officials to enter the arena with just-war arguments is untypical and ill-suited to Britain's actual practice. Britain remains committed to acts of final retaliation against densely populated cities. This refusal to allow moral distinctions into practical policy has had its counterpart in the limitations of the debate among British moralists. Unlike American moralists, they have not attempted to use just-war doctrine in a practical way to demand changes in weaponry and targeting. Britain's strategic situation and lack of interest in limited war has discouraged this. Another reason for the lack of constructive just-war thinking in Britain has been that the Americans are perceived to be in charge of events, and it is their policies that will determine how another war will be fought. Britain's weapons are primarily symbolic, unusable for anything except Armageddon, and so there is no scope for speculation about possible moral uses for them. This reticence is not altogether a bad thing, since the efforts of American moralists to promote just and limited nuclear war have ended in failure, owing to the radical unadaptability of nuclear weapons to any such thing, and to the failure of the American administration to change anything but declaratory policy.[14] However, it has also encouraged an abstractness about the moral debate, an over-theoretical treatment of deterrent morality and a belief in government circles that moral issues are irrelevant to the real world of politics and practice. This was specially true during the period of Britain's decisive commitment to nuclear deterrence, 1955 to 1964. It encouraged the divergence between history and ethical principles that was noted in the introduction. But there are now signs that the lessons have been

[14] The latest American just-war moralist to advocate the development of tactical nuclear weapons—in this case the neutron bomb and the cruise missile—is James Turner Johnson, *Can Modern War Be Just?* (New Haven, Conn.: Yale University Press, 1984). On the whole, strategic analysts such as Paul Bracken and Desmond Ball, working from a knowledge of weapons and plans, are better guides to the moral realities than the professional moralists like Johnson, who are working from theory and who do not seem to have a realistic idea of what would happen if nuclear weapons were to be used in Europe.

learned in that serious attempts to rethink Britain's real defence requirements and to provide a better reassurance than that provided by nuclear weapons is being made by some of those who reject present policies on moral grounds.[15]

It would be false to claim that morality and expediency necessarily point in the same direction, and this book does not put foward such a claim. Pacifist writing in the 1930s fell into this pitfall when it attempted to give added weight to the moral case for pacifism with the claim that it is also the best method of preventing war. I am not supporting the claim that nuclear deterrence is morally wrong with the logically unconnected claim that it will not work anyway. Nor am I supporting the claim that conventional defence is morally preferable to nuclear defence with the unconnected claim that it is more likely to work, in Britain's case at least. It does not, of course, follow that because a deterrence policy is fundamentally flawed from a moral point of view it is not going to work. Nor does it follow that a defence policy which excludes immoral means is thereby a better guarantee that we will not be attacked.

However, in the case of nuclear deterrence, it belongs to the very centre of moral concern that deterrence is always open to the possibility of unforeseen events bringing a country to the point of using the weapons which it has deployed in order to deter the enemy. The fact that destabilizing trends and unforeseen political and military events can undermine *any* deterrence policy and lead to the use of the weapons, means that moral vigilance is always required before it comes to the point of using them. This includes in the first place an examination of what the weapons would do to others if they were used against them, and secondly, what consequences would follow for us if we used them. So my argument has not been that 'it will not work anyway', but that it is immoral to deploy weapons which can only be used indiscriminately, the nature of our contingent and unpredictable historical existence being what it is. Moral arguments have to take place at this level of contingency: they are about things which are true 'for the most part', as Aristotle says, and not about the logically necessary or the ideally true.[16] Many of those who support nuclear deterrence seem

---

[15] See, The Alternative Defence Commission, *Defence Without the Bomb*, (London: Taylor and Francis, 1983) and *The Politics of Alternative Defence* (London: Paladin, 1987).   [16] *Nicomachean Ethics* I, 1094b. 20.

to argue on the logical level only and to want to keep things on that level. Morality is thus consigned to a sphere of its own, conveniently unconnected with policy-making. But it is necessary to get the moral realities straight before serious thought can be given to any alternative pathways to security.

As to the argument that nuclear deterrence is more perilous to Britain than a conventional deterrence, because, for instance, it makes Britain the number one target for Soviet nuclear strikes, it should be admitted straight away that this consideration is not central to the moral argument, which primarily concerns the use of nuclear weapons against others, rather than their use against us. However, it cannot be left out of the moral debate altogether, for two reasons. First, the fear of nuclear attack has played a crucial part in the development of the debate in Britain since the early 1950s. It has been one of the main factors in the fluctuations of the anti-nuclear movement. There is nothing like fear for making people more morally aware. This does not have to be seen in a cynical light, since the consciousness of what Soviet weapons might do to us has brought home to a wide range of people in Britain what our weapons might do to them. And without the realization of the world-wide, common peril of fall-out in the mid-1950s, there would have been no popular movement of protest. This was always partly moral, partly self-interested. The government's justified fear of broadcasting information on fall-out demonstrates this. Second, it does belong directly to the morality of a particular defence policy to ask what consequences its activation in wartime would have for the people it is supposed to be defending. It is a moral question, not merely a prudential one, although it is distinct from the moral question of the effects that the use of our weapons would have on others.

As to the possible superiority of conventional defence in Britain's case, I have not asserted this as proven, but simply raised the question, suggesting that emphasis on the symbols of power have distracted attention from the necessary task of rethinking Britain's real security situation and needs. At the same time it has had the practical effect of making it vastly more difficult for Britain to be defended in the event of an unwanted war. History strongly suggests that the preoccupation with nuclear fire-power—both American and British—has got in the way of thinking about this seriously and objectively.

BIBLIOGRAPHY

GOVERNMENT DOCUMENTS

A. *Documents released at the Public Records Office*
(in order of classification)

1. *Full Cabinet Meetings, memoranda, and minutes*

CAB 129/67, C (54). 149, Draft of Home Secretary's speech on Civil Defence, 13 April 1954.

CAB 129/69, C (54). 250, Report by the Committee on Defence Policy, 24 July 1954.

CAB 129/72, C (54). 389, Memorandum on Fall-out from the Minister of Defence, 9 December 1954.

CAB 129/74, C (55). 95, Distinction Between Large and Tactical Nuclear Weapons, 5 April 1955.

2. *Ad hoc Committees (Gen), memoranda, and minutes*

CAB 130/2, Gen 75, 1st meeting of Ministers on Atomic Energy, 10 August 1945.

CAB 130/2, Gen 75, 2nd meeting, Draft of letter from PM to President Truman, 7 September 1945.

CAB 130/2, Gen 75, 4th meeting, 11 October 1945.

CAB 130/2, Gen 75, 6th meeting, 18 October 1945.

CAB 130/2, Gen 75, 10th meeting, Report by Officials on United Kingdom Policy, 29 October 1945.

CAB 130/2, Gen 75, 12th meeting, PM's memorandum on forthcoming discussions with President Truman and the Canadian Prime Minister, 5 November 1945.

CAB 130/2, Gen 75, 13th meeting, Draft Instructions for United Kingdom delegation meeting in Washington, 10 November 1945.

CAB 130/2, Gen 75/8, Report from the Advisory Committee on Atomic Energy, 18 December 1945.

CAB 130/2, Gen 75/12, Definition of Weapons of Mass Destruction, 20 March 1946.

CAB 130/2, Gen 75/29, Advisory Committee on Atomic Energy, (46) 31, Draft Instructions to the UK Representatives on the United Nations Commission on Atomic Energy, 14 May 1946.

CAB 130/2, Gen 75/52 Professor Blackett's Memorandum on the Formulation of British Policy in regard to Atomic Energy, 8 February 1947.

CAB 130/16, Gen 163/1, Meeting to consider a request for directions from the Controller of Production (Atomic Energy), 8 January 1947.

CAB 130/100, Gen 458/1, Atomic Energy Estimates, 3 March 1954.

CAB 130/101, Gen 464, 1st meeting, Atomic Energy Development, 13 April, 1954.

CAB 130/101, Gen 465, 3rd meeting of the Atomic Energy Group, Proposed Moratorium on Experimental Hydrogen Bomb Explosions, 14 April 1954.

CAB 130/101, Gen 465, 4th meeting of the Atomic Energy Group, Nuclear Weapons Publicity, 5 May 1954.

3. *Cabinet Defence Committee, memoranda, and minutes*

CAB 131/14, Memorandum by the Chiefs of Staff on United Kingdom Defence Policy, 23 December 1954.

CAB 131/15, D.C. (55) 513 January 1955.

CAB 131/16, D.C. (55) 38, Future War Production Planning, 16 September 1955.

CAB 131/16, D.C. (55) 51, Shelter Policy. Annex: Report by a Group of Officials on 'The Defence Implications of Fall-out from a Hydrogen Bomb'. 11 November 1955.

4. *Chiefs of Staff Committee*

DEFE 4/70, COS (54) 53, United Kingdom Strategy, 10 May 1954.

DEFE 4/70, COS (54) 54, United Kingdom Strategy, 12 May 1954.

DEFE 4/97, COS (57) 64, Confidential Annex, 5 June 1957.

DEFE 5/76, COS (57) 134, Disarmament: United States Informal Memorandum to the Soviet Union Delegation, Memorandum by the Chiefs of Staff, 6 June 1957.

B. *Command Papers*

Cmd. 6743 *Statement Relating to Defence: 1946.*

Cmd. 7042 *Statement Relating to Defence: 1947.*

Cmd. 7327 *Statement Relating to Defence: 1948.*

Cmd. 7895 *Statement on Defence: 1950.*

Cmd. 8146 *Defence Programme: Statement made by the Prime Minister in the House of Commons on Monday, 29 January 1951.*

Cmd. 8475 *Statement on Defence: 1952.*

Cmd. 8768 *Statement on Defence: 1953.*

Cmd. 9075 *Statement on Defence: 1954.*

Cmd. 9391 *Statement on Defence: 1955.*

Cmd. 9691 *Statement on Defence: 1956.*

Cmnd. 124 *Defence: Outline of Future Policy: 1957.*

Cmnd. 363 *Report on Defence: Britain's Contribution to Peace and Security: 1958.*

Cmnd. 662 *Progress of the Five-Year Defence Plan: 1959.*

Cmnd. 952 *Report on Defence: 1960.*

Cmnd. 1288 *Report on Defence: 1961.*

Cmnd. 1639 *Statement on Defence: 1962*: The Next Five Years.

Cmnd. 1936 *Statement on Defence: 1963.*

Cmnd. 1995 *Polaris Sales Agreement.*

Cmnd. 2270 *Statement on Defence: 1964.*

Cmnd. 2592 *Statement on the Defence Estimates: 1965.*

Cmnd. 2901 *Statement on the Defence Estimates: 1966, Part I, The Defence Review.*

Cmnd. 3203 *Statement on the Defence Estimates: 1967.*

Cmnd. 3357 *Supplementary Statement on Defence Policy: 1967.*

Cmnd. 3540 *Statement on the Defence Estimates: 1968.*

Cmnd. 3701 *Supplementary Statement on Defence Policy: 1968.*

Cmnd. 3927 *Statement on the Defence Estimates: 1969.*

Cmnd. 4290 *Statement on the Defence Estimates: 1970.*

Cmnd. 4521 *Supplementary Statement on Defence Policy: 1970.*

Cmnd. 4592 *Statement on the Defence Estimates: 1971.*

Cmnd. 4891 *Statement on the Defence Estimates: 1972.*

Cmnd. 5231 *Statement on the Defence Estimates: 1973.*

Cmnd. 5976 *Statement on the Defence Estimates: 1975.*

Cmnd. 6432 *Statement on the Defence Estimates: 1976.*

Cmnd. 6735 *Statement on the Defence Estimates: 1977.*

Cmnd. 7099 *Statement on the Defence Estimates: 1978.*

Cmnd. 7474 *Statement on the Defence Estimates: 1979.*

Cmnd. 7826 *Statement on the Defence Estimates: 1980*: Defence in the *1980s.*

Cmnd. 8212 *Statement on the Defence Estimates: 1981.*

Cmnd. 8288 *The United Kingdom Defence Programme: The Way Forward* (July 1981).

Cmnd. 8529 *Statement on the Defence Estimates: 1982.*

Cmnd. 8951 *Statement on the Defence Estimates: 1983.*

Cmnd. 9227 *Statement on the Defence Estimates: 1984.*

Cmnd. 9430 *Statement on the Defence Estimates: 1985.*

Cmnd. 9763 *Statement on the Defence Estimates: 1986.*

Cm. 101 *Statement on the Defence Estimates: 1987.*

C. *Ministry of Defence Publications*

The Future United Kingdom Strategic Nuclear Deterrent Force, Defence Open Government Document 80/23, *1980.*

Cruise Missiles: The Important Questions and Answers, 1981.
Britain and NATO: Over Thirty Years of Collective Defence, 1981.
A Nuclear-Free Europe? Why it Wouldn't Work, 1981.
The United Kingdom Trident Programme. Defence Open Government Document 82/1, 1982.

D.   *Home Office Publications*

The Effects of Atomic Bombs at Hiroshima and Nagasaki: Report of the British Missions to Japan, Home Office and Air Ministry, HMSO, 1946.
Protect and Survive, HMSO, 1980.
Domestic Nuclear Shelters Technical Guidance, Home Office Guide, HMSO, 1981.

II.   HOUSE OF COMMONS

Sixth Report from the Expenditure Committee: 'The Future of the United Kingdom's Nuclear Weapons Policy', Session 1978–9, No. 348 (London: HMSO, 1979).
Fourth Report from the Defence Committee: 'Strategic Nuclear Weapons Policy', Session 1980–1, HC 36 (London: HMSO, 1981).
First Report from the Defence Committee: 'Strategic Nuclear Weapons Policy', Session 1981–2, HC 266 (London: HMSO, 1982).
House of Commons Official Report (Hansard), Debates, Oral and Written Answers, *ad loc.*

III.   BOOKS AND ARTICLES

Allen, A. F., and Bellany, I. (eds.), *The Future of the British Nuclear Deterrent*, Centre for the Study of Arms Control and International Security, University of Lancaster, 1982.
Alternative Defence Commission, *Defence Without the Bomb*, London: Taylor Francis, 1983.
—— *The Politics of Alternative Defence*, London: Paladin, 1987.
Anscombe, G. E. M., *Intention*, Oxford: Basil Blackwell, 1957.
—— 'Mr. Truman's Degree', 1957, repr. in G. E. M. Anscombe, *Collected Philosophical Papers*, iii. *Ethics, Religion and Politics*, Oxford: Basil Blackwell, 1981, 62–71.
—— 'War and Murder', in W. Stein (ed.), *Nuclear Weapons and Christian Conscience*, 1961 (2nd edn. 1981), 45 (repr. as above), 51–61.
Arkin, W. M., and Chappell, D., 'The Impact of Soviet Theatre Nuclear Force Improvements', *ADIU Report*, 5/4, July–Aug. 1983.
—— and Fieldhouse, R. W., 'Pershing and Cruise: No Room for Compromise', *ADIU Report*, 5/2, Mar.–Apr. 1983.

Bailey, Sydney, *Prohibitions and Restraints in War*, OUP, 1972.

Ball, Desmond, 'Can Nuclear War be Controlled?', *Adelphi Papers*, 196, Autumn 1981.

—— 'U.S. Strategic Forces: How Would They Be Used?', *International Security*, 7 (1982–3), 31–60.

—— 'Targeting for Strategic Deterrence', *Adelphi Papers*, 185, 1983.

Baylis, John (ed.), *British Defence Policy in a Changing World*, London: Croom Helm, 1977.

—— *Anglo-American Defence Relations, 1939–1984*, London: Macmillan, 1984.

—— Booth, Ken, Garnett, John, and Williams, Phil, *Contemporary Strategy: Theories and Policies*, London: Croom Helm, 1976.

—— and Segal, Gerald, *Soviet Strategy*, London: Croom Helm, 1981.

Best, Geoffrey, *Humanity in Warfare*, London: Methuen, 1980.

Bierzanek, Remigiusz, 'Reprisals as a Means of Enforcing the Laws of Warfare: The Old and the New Law', in Antonio Cassese (ed.), *The New Humanitarian Law of Armed Conflict*, Naples: Editoriale Scientifica, 1979.

Blackaby, Frank, Goldblat, Jozeph, and Lodgaard, Sverre, *No-First-Use*, London: SIPRI/Taylor and Francis, 1984.

Blackett, P. M. S., *Military and Political Consequences of Atomic Energy*, London: Turnstile Press, 1948.

—— *Studies of War*, London: Oliver and Boyd, 1962.

Blake, Nigel, and Pole, Kay (eds.), *Dangers of Deterrence; Philosophers on Nuclear Strategy*, London: RKP, 1983.

—— *Objections to Nuclear Defence; Philosophers on Deterrence*, London: RKP, 1984.

Bracken, Paul, *The Command and Control of Nuclear Forces*, New Haven, Conn. and London: Yale University Press, 1983.

Bridger, Francis, *The Cross and the Bomb: Christian Ethics and the Nuclear Debate*, London and Oxford: Mowbray, 1983.

British Council of Churches, *The Era of Atomic Power*, London: S.C.M. Press, May 1946.

British Medical Association, Board of Science and Education, *The Medical Effects of Nuclear War*, Chichester: John Wiley and Sons, 1983.

Brittain, Vera, *Testament of Experience*, London: Gollancz, 1957.

Brodie, Bernard, and Fawn, M., *From Crossbow to H-bomb*, Bloomington and London: Indiana University Press, 1973.

Brown, Anthony Cave, *Operation: World War III*, London: Arms and Armour Press, 1979.

Brown, Harold, 'The Objective of US Strategic Forces', *Survival*, Nov.–Dec. 1980, 267.

—— Department of Defense Annual Report, FY 1980, 67.

Builder, Carl H., and Graubard, Morlie, H., *The International Law of Armed Conflict: Implications for the Concept of Assured Destruction*, Santa Monica, Calif.: Rand, 1982.

Bull, Hedley, *The Anarchical Society*, London: Macmilian, 1977.

Bullock, Alan, *Ernest Bevin, Foreign Secretary 1945–1951*, London: Heinemann, 1983.

Bundy, McGeorge, 'America in the 1980s: Reframing our Relations with our Friends and Among our Allies', *Survival*, Jan.–Feb., 1982, 24.

—— Kennan, George F., McNamara, Robert S., Smith, Gerard, 'Nuclear Weapons and the Atlantic Alliance', *Foreign Affairs*, 60, Spring 1982, 753.

Butler, J. R. M., *Grand Strategy*, History of the Second World War: United Kingdom Military Series, ii. London: HMSO, 1957.

Buzan, Barry, *Peoples, States, and Fear*, Brighton: Wheatsheaf Books, 1983.

—— *An Introduction to Strategic Studies*, London: Macmillan/IISS, 1987.

Buzzard, Rear-Admiral Sir Anthony, Slessor, Marshal of the RAF Sir John and Lowenthal, Richard, 'The H-bomb: Massive Retaliation or Graduated Deterrence', *International Affairs*, 32/2, Apr. 1956.

Calvacoressi, Peter, and Wint, Guy, *Total War*, London: Penguin Books, 1972.

Campbell, Duncan, *The Unsinkable Aircraft Carrier*, London: Michael Joseph, 1984.

Ceadal, Martin, *Thinking of Peace and War*, OUP, 1987.

Centre for Defense Information, Washington, DC, and the Polemological Institute, Gröningen, *Nuclear War in Europe—Documents*, The First Conference on Nuclear War in Europe, April 22–4, 1981.

Chalmers, Malcolm, *Trident: Britain's Independent Arms Race*, London: CND Publications, 1984.

Church of England Board for Social Responsibility, *The Church and the Bomb*, London: Hodder and Stoughton and CIO Publishing, 1982.

Church of England, *The Church and the Bomb: The General Synod Debate*, London: CIO Publishing, 1983.

Churchill, Randolph S. (ed.), *The Sinews of Peace: Post-war Speeches by Winston S. Churchill*, London: Cassell, 1948.

Churchill, Winston S., *The Second World War*, i, *The Gathering Storm*, iii *The Grand Alliance*, and vi *Triumph and Tragedy*, London: Cassell, 1948, 1950, and 1954.

Clark, Ian, *Limited Nuclear War*, Oxford: Martin Robertson, 1982.

Clark, Ronald W., *The Birth of the Bomb*, London: Phoenix House, 1961.

Collins, A. S., Jr., 'Theater Nuclear Weapons: The Battlefield', in Reichart, J. F., and Sturn, S. R. (eds.), *American Defense Policy* (5th edn.), Baltimore: Johns Hopkins University Press, 1982, 359.

Crossley, George, 'Civil Defence', unpublished paper, Bradford University School of Peace Studies, 1983.

Dennis, Jack (ed.), *Nuclear Almanac*, Reading, Mass.: Addison-Wesley Publishing Company, 1984.

Divine, Robert A., *Blowing on the Wind*, New York: OUP, 1978.

Drell, Sidney D., and von Hippel, Frank, 'Limited Nuclear War', *Scientific American*, 235/5, Nov. 1976, 27–37.

Driver, Christopher, *The Disarmers*, London: Hodder and Stoughton, 1964.

Duke, Simon W., *US Defence Bases in the United Kingdom*, London: Macmillan, 1987.

Eden, Anthony (Earl of Avon), *Full Circle*, London: Cassell, 1960.

—— *Facing the Dictators*, London: Cassell, 1962.

Enthoven, Alain C., and Smith, K. Wayne, *How Much is Enough? Shaping the Defense Program 1961–1969*, New York: Harper and Row, 1971.

Eppstein, John, *The Catholic Tradition of the Law of Nations*, London: Burns, Oates & Washbourne, 1935.

Falk, Richard, Meyrowitz, Lee and Sanderson, Jack, *Nuclear Weapons and International Law*, World Studies Program, Occasional Paper No. 10, Center for International Studies: Princeton University Press, 1981.

Feis, Herbert, *The Atomic Bomb and the End of World War II*, Princeton NJ: Princeton University Press, 1966.

Finn, James (ed.), *Peace, the Churches and the Bomb*, New York: Council on Religion and International Affairs, 1965.

—— *The New Nuclear Debate*, New York: Council on Religion and International Affairs, 1976.

Finnis, John, *Fundamentals of Ethics*, OUP, 1983.

—— Boyle, Joseph M., Jr., and Grisez, Germain, *Nuclear Deterrence, Morality and Realism*, OUP, 1987.

Fisher, David, *Morality and the Bomb*, London: Croom Helm, 1985.

Ford, John C., 'The Morality of Obliteration Bombing', *Theological Studies*, 5, 1944, 281.

Frankland, Noble, *The Bombing Offensive Against Germany*, London: Faber & Faber, 1965.

Freedman, Lawrence, *Britain and Nuclear Weapons*, London: Macmillan, 1980.

—— 'The Evolution of Nuclear Strategy, London: Macmillan, 1981.

—— 'The No-First-Use Debate and the Theory of Thresholds', in Blackaby et al., *No-First-Use*, 1984.

Frei, Daniel, and Catrina, Christian, *Risks of Unintentional Nuclear War*, London: Croom Helm, 1983.

Gaddis, John Lewis, *Strategies of Containment*, New York; OUP, 1982.

Garnett, John, 'Limited War', in John Baylis *et al.*, *Contemporary Strategy, Theories and Policies*, London: Croom Helm, 1975, 114–31.

George, Margaret, *The Hollow Men; An Examination of British Foreign Policy Between the Years 1933 and 1939*, London: Leslie Frewin, 1967.

Gessert, Robert A., 'The Case for Selective Options', in Finn, J. (ed.), *The New Nuclear Debate*, 1976, 7.

Gilbert, Martin, *Britain and Germany Between the Wars*, London: Longman, 1964.

—— *The Roots of Appeasement*, London: Weidenfeld and Nicolson, 1966.

—— and Gott, Richard, *The Appeasers*, London: Weidenfeld and Nicolson, 1963.

Girard, René, *Violence and the Sacred*, London: Johns Hopkins University Press, 1977.

—— *Things Hidden since the Foundation of the World*, London: Athlone Press, 1987.

Goodwin, Geoffrey, *Ethics and Nuclear Deterrence*, London: Croom Helm, 1982.

Goold-Adams, Richard, *On Limiting Atomic War*, London: Royal Institute of International Affairs, 1956.

Gowing, Margaret, *Britain and Atomic Energy 1939–1945*, London: Macmillan, 1964.

—— *Independence and Deterrence*, London: Macmillan, 1974.

Gray, Colin, 'Nuclear Strategy: A Case for a Theory of Victory', in Miller, Steven E. (ed.), *Strategy and Nuclear Deterrence*, Princeton, NJ: Princeton University Press, 1984.

Griffiths, Richard, *Fellow Travellers of the Right*, OUP, 1983.

Groom, John, *British Thinking About Nuclear Weapons*, London: Frances Pinter, 1974.

Harbutt, Fraser J., *The Iron Curtain; Churchill, America, and the Origins of the Cold War*, OUP, 1987.

Harris, Robert, and Paxman, Jeremy, *A Higher Form of Killing*, London: Triad/Granada, 1983.

Hartigan R. S., 'Non-combatant Immunity; Reflections on its Origins and Present Status', *Review of Politics*, 29 Apr. 1967.

Hastings, Max, *Bomber Command*, London: Michael Joseph, 1979.

Hehir, J. Bryan, 'Political and Ethical Considerations', in Finn, J. (ed.), *The New Nuclear Debate*, 1976, 35.

Hockaday, Arthur, 'In Defence of Deterrence', in Goodwin, A. (ed.), *Ethics and Nuclear Deterrence*, London: Croom Helm, 1982, 68–93.

Holloway, David, *The Soviet Union and the Arms Race*, New Haven, and London: Yale University Press, 1983.

Howard, Michael, 'Temperamenta Belli: Can War Be Controlled?' in id., *Restraints on War*, OUP, 1979.

—— 'Reassurance and Deterrence: Western Defence in the 1980s', *Foreign Affairs*, Winter 1982/3, 309–24.

Hughes, Gerard, 'Is the Deterrent Really Immoral?, *The Month*, May 1980, 147.

—— 'The Intention to Deter', in Bridger, F. (ed.), *The Cross and the Bomb*, 1983, 25–34.

Hyde, H. Montgomery, *British Air Policy Between the Wars, 1918–1939*, London: Heinemann, 1976.

Iklé, Fred Charles, 'Can Nuclear Deterrence Last Out the Century?', *Foreign Affairs*, Jan. 1973, 267–85.

International Institute of Strategic Studies, *Strategic Survey, 1970* (issued 1971), and *Strategic Survey, 1971* (issued 1972).

—— *The Military Balance, 1986–1987* (issued 1987).

Johnson, James Turner, *Ideology, Reason and the Limitation of War*, Princeton, NJ: Princeton University Press, 1975.

—— *Just-War Tradition and the Restraint of War*, Princeton, NJ: Princeton University Press, 1981.

—— *Can Modern War be Just?*, New Haven, Conn. and London: Yale University Press, 1984.

Johnson, Peter, *Neutrality, A Policy for Britain*, London: Temple Smith, 1985.

Jones, Neville, *The Origins of Strategic Bombing*, London: William Kimber, 1973.

Jungk, Robert, *Brighter than a Thousand Suns*, London: Gollancz, 1958.

Kalshoven, Frits, *Belligerent Reprisals*, Leyden: A. W. Sijthoff, 1971.

Kenny, Anthony, 'Counterforce and Countervalue', *Clergy Review*, Dec. 1962, repr. in Stein, W. (ed.), *Nuclear Weapons and Christian Conscience*, 1981, 155.

—— 'Better Red than Dead', in Blake, N., and Pole, K. (eds.), *Objections to Nuclear Defence*, 1984, 12.

—— *The Logic of Deterrence*, London: Firethorn Press, 1985.

King-Hall, Stephen, *Defence in the Nuclear Age*, London: Gollancz, 1953.

Labour Party, *Report of the Fifty-Ninth Annual Conference of the Labour Party*, London: Transport House, 1960.

Liddell Hart, Basil H., *Deterrent or Defence*, London: Stevens, 1960.

—— *History of the Second World War*, London: Cassell, 1970.

Lunn, Simon, 'Cruise Missiles and the Prospect for Arms Control', *ADIU Report*, 3/5, Sept.–Oct., 1981, 2–5.

—— *The Modernization of NATO's Long-Range Theater Nuclear Forces*, Report prepared for the Subcommittee on Europe and the Middle East of the House Committee on Foreign Affairs, 96th Congress, 2nd Session, Washington DC: US Government Printing Office, 1981.

McCormick, Richard, 'Nuclear Deterrence and the Problem of Intention: A Review of the Positions', in Murnion, P. J. (ed.), *Catholics and Nuclear War*, 1983, 168–82.

MacCurdy, J. T., *The Structure of Morale*, CUP, 1943.

MacGwire, Michael, 'Soviet Military Doctrine, Contingency Planning and the Reality of World War', *Survival*, May–June 1980, 107.

—— 'The Dilemmas and Delusions of Deterrence', in Prins, G., *The Choice*, 1984, 75–87.

MacIntyre, Alasdair, *After Virtue: A Study in Moral Theory*, London: Duckworth, 1981.

McLaine, Ian, *Ministry of Morale*, London: George Allen and Unwin, 1979.

McKay, Alwyn, *The Making of the Atomic Age*, OUP, 1984.

McLean, Scilla (ed.), *How Nuclear Weapons Decisions Are Made*, London: Macmillan, 1986.

McMahon, Jeff, *British Nuclear Weapons: For and Against*, London: Junction Books, 1981.

Macmillan, Harold, *Winds of Change 1914–1939*, London: Macmillan, 1966.

—— *Riding the Storm, 1956–1959*, London: Macmillan, 1971.

—— *Pointing the Way, 1959–1961*, London: Macmillan, 1972.

—— *At the End of the Day*, London: Macmillan, 1973.

McNamara, Robert S., 'The Military Role of Nuclear Weapons: Perceptions and Misperceptions', *Foreign Affairs*, Fall 1983, repr. in *Survival*, Nov.–Dec. 1983, 261–71.

McReavy, L. L., 'The Morality of Atomic Bombing', *Catholic Times*, 17 May 1946.

—— 'The Debate on the Morality of Future War', *Clergy Review*, Feb. 1960, 77.

—— 'The Morality of the NATO Deterrent Policy', *Clergy Review*, Oct. 1960, 615, and ensuing correspondence, *Clergy Review*, Jan.–Mar. 1961.

—— 'The Morality of the Nuclear Destruction of a City', *The Clergy Review*, July 1962, 414.

—— *Peace and War*, Oxford: Catholic Social Guild, 1963.

Malone, Peter, *The British Nuclear Deterrent*, London: Croom Helm, 1984.

Markus, Robert A., 'Conscience and Deterrence', in Stein, W. (ed.), *Nuclear Weapons and Christian Conscience*, 1961; 2nd edn. 1981.

Mather, Ian, 'NATO's Double-talk on Nuclear Cutback', *Observer*, 30 Oct. 1983.

Middlebrook, Martin, *The Battle of Hamburg*, London: Penguin 1980.

Miller, Steven E., *Strategy and Nuclear Deterrence*, Princeton, NJ: Princeton University Press, 1984.

Montgomery, Field Marshal Lord, 'A Look Through a Window at World War III', *The Journal of the Royal United Services Institute*, 596 (Nov. 1954), 508.

Morgan, Janet (ed.), *The Backbench Diaries of Richard Crossman*, London: Hamish Hamilton and Jonathan Cape, 1981.

Murnion, Philip J., *Catholics and Nuclear War: A Commentary on the Challenge of Peace*, London: Geoffrey Chapman, 1983.

Murray, John Courtney, 'Remarks on the Moral Problem of War', *Theological Studies*, Mar. 1959, 40–61.

Murray, Thomas E., *Nuclear Policy in War and Peace*, Cleveland and New York: World Publishing Co., 1969.

Nott, John, 'Decisions to Modernize the United Kingdom's Nuclear Contribution to NATO Strengthen Deterrence', *NATO Review*, 29/2, Apr. 1981.

Nicholson, Harold, *Public Faces*, London, 1932, repr. by Penguin, 1944.

O'Brien, William, *Nuclear War, Deterrence and Morality*, New York: Newman Press, 1967.

—— *The Conduct of Just and Limited War*, New York: Newman Press, 1981.

Office of Technology Assessment, Congress of the United States, *The Effects of Nuclear War*, London: Croom Helm, 1980.

Paskins, Barrie, 'Deep Cuts are Morally Imperative', in Goodwin, G. (ed.), *Ethics and Nuclear Deterrence*, London: Croom Helm, 1982, 94–116.

—— and Dockrill, Michael, *The Ethics of War*, London: Duckworth, 1979.

Pierre, Andrew, *Nuclear Politics*, London and New York: OUP, 1972.

Plesch, Dan, *NATO's New Nuclear Weapons*, The British–American Security Information Council, Basic Report 88–1, London and Washington, 1988.

Prins, Gwyn, *The Choice: Nuclear Weapons Versus Security*, London: Chatto and Windus, 1984.

Pym, Francis, 'The Nuclear Element for British Defence Policy', *Journal of the Royal United Services Institute*, 126/2, June 1981.

Quester, George, *Deterrence Before Hiroshima*, New York: John Wiley and Sons, 1966.

Quinlan, Michael, 'Preventing War', *The Tablet*, 18 July 1981, 688, repr. in Bridger, F. (ed.), *The Cross and the Bomb*, London and Oxford: Mowbray, 1983.

—— 'Nuclear Weapons: A View of the Moral Problem', in Bridger, F. (ed.), *The Cross and the Bomb*, 1983 147.

—— 'Can the Possession of Nuclear Weapons be Morally Justifiable?', *Modern Churchman*, no.2 1985, 22–7.

—— 'Nuclear Weapons: The Basic Issues', *The Ampleforth Journal*, Autumn 1986, 61–70.

—— 'The Ethics of Nuclear Deterrence: A Critical Comment on the Pastoral Letter of the US Catholic Bishops', *Theological Studies*, 48 (1987), 3–24.

Ramsey, Paul, *War and the Christian Conscience*, Durham, NC: Duke University Press, 1961.

—— *The Just War*, New York: Charles Scribner's Sons, 1968.

Reichart, J. F., and Sturn, S. R. (eds.), *American Defense Policy* (5th edn.), Baltimore: Johns Hopkins University Press, 1982.

Roberts, Adam, 'A Critique of Nuclear Deterrence' in 'Defence and Consensus: The Domestic Aspects of Western Security', *Adelphi Papers*, 183, 1983.

—— and Guelff, Richard, *Documents on the Laws of War*, OUP, 1982.

Rogers, Bernard, 'The Atlantic Alliance: Prescriptions for a Difficult Decade', *Foreign Affairs*, Summer 1983, 60/5, 1145–57.

Rogers, Paul, *Guide to Nuclear Weapons 1984–85*, University of Bradford School of Peace Studies, 1985.

—— and Dando, Malcolm, *The Death of Deterrence*, London: CND Publications, 1984.

Ruston, Roger, *Nuclear Deterrence: Right or Wrong?*, Abbots Langley: Catholic Information Services, 1981.

—— 'Nuclear Deterrence and the Use of the Just War Doctrine', in Blake, N., and Pole, K. (eds.), *Objections to Nuclear Defence*, 1984, 41.

Schmidt, Helmut, 'The 1977 Alastair Buchan Memorial Lecture', *Survival*, Jan.–Feb. 1978, 1–10.

Schwartz, David M., *NATO's Nuclear Dilemmas*, Washington, DC: Brookings Institution, 1983.

Simpson, John, *The Independent Nuclear State*, London: Macmillan, 1983; 2nd edn. 1986.

Slessor, Marshal of the RAF Sir John, *The Central Blue*, London: Cassell, 1956.

Smart, Ian, *The Future of the British Nuclear Deterrent: Technical, Economic and Strategic Issues*, Royal Institute of International Affairs, London, 1977.

Smith, Dan, *The Defence of the Realm in the 1980s*, London: Croom Helm, 1980.

—— 'Soviet Military Power', *ADIU Report*, 4/1. Jan.–Feb. 1982.

Smith, Joan, *Clouds of Deceit: The Deadly Legacy of Britain's Bomb Tests*, London: Faber & Faber, 1985.

Smith, Malcolm, *British Air Strategy Between the Wars*, OUP, 1984.

Sokolovsky, V. D., *Soviet Military Strategy*, 3rd edn. trans. Harriet F. Scott, New York: Crane, Russak Co., 1975.

Soper, Kate, 'Human Survival', in Blake, N., and Pole, K. (eds.), *Objections to Nuclear Defence*, London: RKP, 1984, 86–98.

Steele, Jonathan, *World Power; Soviet Foreign Policy Under Brezhnev and Andropov*, London: Michael Joseph, 1983.

Stein, Walter, 'A Time for Decision', *Crux*, Easter–Pentecost, 2, 1948, 13.

—— (ed.), *Nuclear Weapons and Christian Conscience*, London: Merlin Press, 1961; 2nd edn. 1981.

—— 'Discerning the Real Situation', *Blackfriars*, July–Aug. 1964, 302.

—— 'Would you Press the Button?', in Finn, J. (ed.), *Peace, the Churches and the Bomb*, 1965, 20.

—— 'The Limits of the Nuclear War: Is a Just Deterrence Strategy Possible?', in Finn, J. (ed.), *Peace, the Churches and the Bomb*, 1965, 73.

—— 'Preventing War', *The Tablet*, 18 July 1981, 688.

—— 'The Case Against Deterrence', three articles in *The Tablet*, 20 Oct., 27 Oct., and 10 Nov. 1984.

Steinbruner, John, 'Launch Under Attack', *Scientific American*, 250/1 Jan. 1984, 22.

Taylor, A. J. P., *English History 1914–1945*, Harmondsworth: Penguin, 1979.

Thomson, James A., 'Planning for NATO's Nuclear Deterrent in the 1980s and 1990s', *Survival*, 25/3 May–June 1983, 98.

—— 'Nuclear Weapons in Europe', *Survival*, May–June 1982, 98–110.

The Times, *The Nuclear Dilemma*, London: Times Publishing Co., 1958.

Treverton, Gregory, 'Nuclear Weapons in Europe', *Adelphi Papers*, 168, 1981.

United Nations General Assembly, *General and Complete Disarmament: Comprehensive Study on Nuclear Weapons*. Report of the Secretary-General, 12 Sept. 1980.

United States Arms Control Agency, *Long-Range Theater Nuclear Missile Systems and the Sea-Launched Cruise Missiles*, Fiscal Year 1982, Arms Control Impact Statements, United States Congress, Feb. 1981.

United States Catholic Bishops' Conference, *The Challenge of Peace: God's Promise and Our Response*, London: CTS/SPCK, 1983.

Vann, Gerald, OP, *Morality and War*, London: Burnes, Oates & Washbourne, 1939.

Vitoria, Francisco, *De Iure Belli*, Classics of International Law, ed. James Brown Scott, Washington DC: Carnegie Inst., 1917.

—— *De Poteste Civili*, Classics of International Law, ed. James Brown Scott, Washington, DC: Carnegie Inst., 1917.

Walzer, Michael, *Just and Unjust Wars*, Harmondsworth: Penguin 1978.

Webster, Charles, and Frankland, Noble, *The Strategic Air Offensive Against Germany*, i–iii. London: HMSO, 1961.

Weinberger, Caspar, *The Annual Report to Congress Fiscal Year 1984*, US Department of Defense, 1983.

Wilkinson, Alan, *Dissent or Conform? War, Peace and the English Churches 1900–1945*, London: SCM Press, 1986.

Williams, Phil, 'Deterrence, Warfighting and American Nuclear Strategy', *ADIU Report*, 5/1, Jan.–Feb. 1983.

Williams, Philip M., *Hugh Gaitskell, A Political Biography*, London: Jonathan Cape, 1979.

Wilson, Andrew, 'Whitehall Rewrote Dresden Raid History', *Observer*, 10 Feb. 1985.

Wilson, Harold, *The Labour Government 1964–1970*, London: Penguin, 1974.

Yergin, Daniel, *Shattered Peace: The Origins of the Cold War and the National Security State*, London: André Deutsch, 1978.

Zaw, Susan Khin, 'Morality and Survival in the Nuclear Age', in Blake, N., and Pole, K. (eds.), *Objections to Nuclear Defence*, 1984, 115.

Zuckerman, Solly, 'Judgement and Control in Modern Warfare', *Foreign Affairs*, 40/2, 1962, 196–212.

—— *Nuclear Illusions and Reality*, London: Collins, 1982.

INDEX

Index compiled by Peva Keane